JOHN KILLEN was born in Belfast in 1954 and was educated at Queen's University Belfast. Since 1977 he has been a librarian at the Linen Hall Library, where he has organised exhibitions on a wide variety of themes, some of which have also been displayed in the National Library of Ireland. He has lectured on library and historical subjects in Britain and the USA and is a regular contributor to the *Linen Hall Review* and *Irish Booklore*. His publications include *John Bull's Famous Circus*, *The Irish Christmas Book*, *The Pure Drop: A Book of Irish Drinking* and *A History of the Linen Hall Library*.

The
FAMINE
DECADE

Contemporary Accounts
1841–1851

edited by
JOHN KILLEN

THE
BLACKSTAFF
PRESS

BELFAST

First published in 1995 by
The Blackstaff Press Limited
3 Galway Park, Dundonald, Belfast BT16 0AN, Northern Ireland
with the assistance of the
Cultural Traditions Programme which aims to encourage
acceptance and understanding of cultural diversity

Typeset by Paragon Typesetters, Queensferry, Clwyd

Printed in England by Biddles Limited

A CIP catalogue record for this book
is available from the British Library

ISBN 0-85640-560-4

to the memory of those
who perished
in the Famine

CONTENTS

1848

1849–1851

CENSUS OF 1851

POSTSCRIPT

INTRODUCTION

The time has not yet arrived at which any man can with confidence
say, that he fully appreciates the nature and the bearings of that great
event which will long be inseparably associated with the year just
departed. Yet we think that we may render some service to the
public by attempting thus early to review, with the calm temper
of a future generation, the history of the great Irish famine of 1847.
Unless we are much deceived, posterity will trace up to that famine
the commencement of a salutary revolution in the habits of a nation
long singularly unfortunate, and will acknowledge that on this, as
on many other occasions, Supreme Wisdom has educed permanent
good out of transient evil.

CHARLES E. TREVELYAN, ASSISTANT SECRETARY TO THE TREASURY, 1848

The census of 1841 was acknowledged to be the most
professionally conducted census of the peoples of the British
Isles until then undertaken. To enhance its effectiveness, the
Department of the Ordnance Survey provided a map of every barony
in Ireland, showing each barony's boundary and the extent of its parishes
and townlands; these maps also showed every house in the country. Based
on an enumeration of the people residing in Ireland on 6 June 1841,
the census computed that the population of Ireland amounted to
8,175,124 persons, of whom 4,019,576 were male and 4,155,548 were
female. This represented an increase in population on the previous census
of 1831 of 5.25 per cent. Ten years later the census of 1851 showed
a decline in population of some 19.85 per cent, brought about by the
effects of unprecedented failures of the potato crop in successive years
from 1845 until 1849 (ironically, excepting 1847, when the crop was
inadequate because of insufficient planting by a dispirited peasantry),
which resulted in famine. An enumeration of the people residing in
Ireland on 30 March 1851 computed the population of Ireland to be
6,552,385 persons, of whom 3,190,630 were male and 3,361,755 were
female. Applying a formula based on the birth and death rates in the
rest of the British Isles, and assuming that emigration and immigration
were equal, the census report reckoned that the population of Ireland
on 30 March 1851 should have been 9,018,789 instead of 6,552,385.
This indicated a loss of population in Ireland of 2,466,404 during the
famine decade.

Such figures, set out coldly in a government report, do not and cannot attempt to convey the stark reality of what happened in Ireland 150 years ago. That a fertile country, the sister nation to the richest and most powerful country in the world, bound to that country by an Act of Union some forty-five years old, should suffer distress, starvation and death seems incomprehensible today. That foodstuffs were exported from Ireland to feed British colonies in India and the sub-continent, while great numbers of people in Ireland starved, beggars belief. Yet the British and American governments, public and private committees, and private individuals expended vast sums of money on famine relief. In 1846 Prime Minister Sir Robert Peel repealed the Corn Laws to allow the immediate importation of corn into Ireland; the Society of Friends organised and administered relief in the form of food and clothing throughout the island; individual landlords (not the majority and not enough) granted their tenantry reductions in rent and in some cases exemption from payment of rent through the worst of the famine years; the world sympathised with the plight of the Irish peasant. But the net result of the catastrophe, and the attempts to provide relief to a stricken people, was a loss of population between 1841 and 1851 of almost two and a half million people, of whom almost half perished of starvation or fever and the remainder emigrated.

To try to understand how this could have happened and to come to terms with the horror endured, so recently in the life of Ireland, by our great-great-grandparents, we need to be aware of their lives, aspirations, ambitions and world-view. As the calamity of the famine unfolded, the reactions of the people of Ireland, the reactions of their religious, social and political leaders, and the reactions of the decision-makers must be understood. To this end, the extracts contained in the body of this work are taken from contemporary sources which would have been available to everyone affected by the tragedy of the famine decade. Travel books, gazetteers, periodicals, newspapers, agricultural pamphlets and reports, government reports, reports of relief agencies, sermons, novels and poetry – all then freely available – are used to give an insight into contemporary life and the seemingly inevitable progress of the famine in Ireland.

From very early in the nineteenth century it was recognised by all who gave attention to the matter that the reliance of the bulk of the population of Ireland on one food source – the potato – would necessarily give rise to occasions of shortage and distress if that food crop failed, as fail it did, most severely in 1822. William Cobbett, the English journalist and social reformer, called the potato 'the lazy root'

which sustained Irish poverty and wretchedness; others contended that 3
the potato was a just recompense to the poor and wretched Irish for
the confiscation of their lands by the Elizabethan and later settlements.
That the bulk of the Irish peasantry was poor and wretched there is no
doubt: a listing of the possessions of the inhabitants of the parish of
Tullaghobegley, barony of Kilmacrennan, County Donegal – four
thousand in number – reported that there was 'no wheel car . . . one
plough . . . two feather beds, eight chaff beds . . . no boots . . . no turnips,
no parsnips . . . no clover, or any other garden vegetables, but potatoes
and cabbage'. The dwellings of the peasantry were mean, dirty and
insanitary: even in County Down, in the prosperous north-east of Ireland,
a traveller in 1845 could come upon a

> hovel, the mud floor of which was . . . excavated several inches below
> the ground level without; and, as there was no sill, or raised threshold,
> there is no bar—I will not say to the water—but to the liquid filth that
> oozes to its lower reservoir within . . . All this, of course, is matter of
> choice, and so is the offal-heap,—situated in almost every instance, directly
> before the door, and draining its putrid mass into the hollow, under the
> peasant's table.

The writer was perversely wrong in suggesting that the above was
a matter of choice, for in reality the peasant had *no* choice but to live
in this way. In the aftermath of the Act of Union of 1801, those landlords
who wished to enjoy political and social preferment naturally gravitated
to London, where they paid for their lifestyle with the rents of their
lands in Ireland. Agents and middlemen were employed to collect the
rents and oversee their estates, resulting in neglect and exploitation of
the tenantry. Lord Devon, in his report on land tenure in Ireland (1845),
cited this fact: 'The number of proprietors of land in Ireland is small
when compared with its extent and the amount of its agricultural population. This circumstance . . . is one of the causes which has led to the want
of that personal attention to the condition of the tenantry which is at
once the duty and interest of landlords.' The relationship between
landlord and tenant, in its political and economic history and contemporary reality, lay at the crux of the peasants' attitude to life. Aware
that, in the dim and distant past, the land of Ireland had been confiscated
from their forefathers and distributed to foreigners, peasants had no
political or moral affinity with their landlords. Occupying land at the
whim of landlords, agents, or middlemen, certain that any improvement
they made to that land would be acknowledged by a demand for higher

rents and that failure to pay those higher rents would result in their eviction and the occupation of their farms by another desperate enough to pay what was asked, Irish peasants did not improve their land but resigned themselves to the reality of their existence, and determined to subsist only. J. Veneday, a writer on agricultural and social conditions in Ireland, explained the situation thus:

> The matter is . . . exceedingly simple, and most easy of explanation. The Irishman is shrewd, and he will not toil in the field, as the dumb beast does, without the prospect of receiving, at least, some little portion of the harvest . . . Thus it is that the Irish, on their scanty farms, will only do that which is absolutely necessary; that which will bring to themselves alone the immediate and profitable results . . . Neither the Irish landed proprietor, nor the Irish farmer confide or believe in the continuance of the existing relations between them. The consequence is, that both think solely of the present moment.

In June, July and August 1845 agricultural reports from all parts of Ireland promised abundant crops. The *Tyrone Constitution* of 16 July 1845 stated that there had not been such crops in that part of the north in the memory of the oldest inhabitant. Wheat, barley, oats and flax were all good, and potatoes were better in appearance than at any former period. Early in September 1845, news appeared in the Dublin papers of the failure of the potato crop in the United States, in Flanders and in France, but no fear was entertained even of a partial failure of the crop in Ireland. By the third week of September, however, the potato blight had struck Ireland with a vengeance, and, almost immediately, the word famine was upon everyone's lips. As the weeks passed, eminent agriculturists were asked to investigate the potato failure and suggest remedies. Robert Kane, John Lindley and Lyon Playfair of the Royal Dublin Society wrote to every newspaper in Ireland, giving 'advice concerning the potato crop to the farmers and peasantry of Ireland'. Their well-meaning advice, and that of others over the succeeding years, totally failed to affect the unfolding calamity. A Mansion House Committee was formed to examine the nature and extent of the failure of the potato crop: Sir Robert Peel assured the people that the situation was occupying the unremitting attention of Queen Victoria's confidential advisers; and the Poor Law Commissioners began to erect temporary fever hospitals in the west of Ireland.

The winter of 1845–6 saw hardship, deprivation and hunger in Ireland but little positive relief action from any source was instigated, although the general consensus was that action was needed immediately to

avert possible loss of life. April 1846 saw the introduction of Indian
corn into Cork to be distributed to the famished people, food riots in
Tipperary, and reports of hunger and distress on the outskirts of
Belfast. The deteriorating situation was discussed in the House of
Commons, where William Smith O'Brien MP, on 17 April, informed
the House that in Kilkenny, Clare, Cork and Waterford coroners'
courts had returned verdicts of death by starvation on many corpses.
Replying, Sir James Graham, the Home Secretary, cited the system of
workhouses in Ireland and the importation of Indian meal as evidence
of government action. He then spoke the words that would epitomise
government policy for the duration of the crisis – the rationale behind
which effectively undermined the efficacy of all government relief: 'If
the people of Ireland were starving in the midst of plenty, it was utterly
impossible for the government alone to meet such an emergency, unless
its efforts were assisted by the proprietors of the soil and the richer
portion of the community.' When Peel resigned and Lord John Russell
formed his ministry in July 1846, the basic premiss that Irish poverty
must be supported by Irish property would be his remit where relief
in Ireland was concerned, with Charles E. Trevelyan, appointed
Assistant Secretary to the Treasury, having overall responsibility for that
relief. Never before had such a challenge faced a British government,
a government which did not have the official machinery, or, more
importantly, the intellectual and political will to do other than follow
this policy. Universal public relief to an entire nation was outside
contemporary understanding – relief of distress on an ad hoc basis,
and at the most economic price, was the most that could be
contemplated.

On 15 August 1846 the recently appointed Relief Commissioners
disbanded according to the stipulations of the act that had called them
into existence. The distress arising from the previous year's failure of
the potato crop had been met, and a new crop had been planted for
the forthcoming winter. By mid–September 1846 that crop was known
to have been lost to the potato blight, and the cry, 'Give us food or
we perish', rang out throughout Ireland. Amendments to existing laws
were hurriedly passed to allow for outdoor relief to the labouring poor,
projects which were carried on as best they could be under prevailing
conditions. As winter fast approached the nature of the road-building
schemes originally undertaken changed to reproductive works, that is,
the draining and subsoiling of land with spades. But the continuing
effects of want and destitution were, in many cases, robbing the people

of their ability to work, even of their will to live. In December 1846 the *Cork Examiner* reported:

> Disease and death in every quarter—the once hardy population worn away to emaciated skeletons—fever, dropsy, diarrhoea, and famine rioting in every filthy hovel, and sweeping away whole families . . . seventy-five tenants ejected here, and a whole village in the last stage of destitution there . . . dead bodies of children flung into holes hastily scratched in the earth without shroud or coffin . . . every field becoming a grave, and the land a wilderness.

As 1847 opened, the newspapers, journals, parliamentary and private reports were filled with specific and general accounts of the horrors of the famine in Ireland. An inquest held in Sligo on 12 January upon the body of Thomas M'Manus, of Kilmactranny, heard this evidence from the doctor who had examined him:

> 'Examined the body of Thomas M'Manus; both the legs, as far as the buttocks, appeared to have been eaten off by a pig; [am] of opinion his death was caused by hunger and cold.' . . . Those who saw the body were of opinion, from the agonized expression of M'Manus's countenance, that he was *alive* when the pig attacked him.

More workhouses were built, and existing ones extended to accommodate the growing army of the destitute. At the same time a new Poor Law was passed which allowed for the reduction of the workforce on public works by 20 per cent to enable next year's wheat crop to be planted. This 20 per cent reduction of those in receipt of outdoor relief was a strictly logical and economic decision on the part of the Government: but its consequences were also strictly in adherance to the laws of logic – a further increase in the death toll.

Emigration now increasingly became the refuge of those strong enough, and with sufficient remaining capital, to avail themselves of it. Canada, the United States and Australia became the destination of thousands of Irish people, encouraged by government-sponsored societies for that very purpose. Even the widely reported losses at sea could not deter those frantic to flee the effects of the famine and the resulting pestilence.

On 15 May 1847, Daniel O'Connell, the Great Liberator, died at Genoa, en route to Rome. His political influence had been on the wane for many years, but he was still held in veneration by the majority of the people of Ireland. To have lost their acknowledged leader of over forty years in the midst of their suffering constituted a national disaster; but the increasing severity of famine conditions and the decreasing relief from government and other sources combined to produce a virtual apathy alongside the reality of the most appalling misery and starvation. The Reverend Henry Brennan, parish priest of Kilglass in County Roscommon, wrote to the editor of the *Freeman's Journal*, on 14 July 1847.

> Sir—There is not in Ireland any parish where fever and destitution prevail to so fearful an extent as here . . . By this time fever has made its way into almost every house . . . In very many instances the dead bodies are thrown in waste cabins and dykes and are devoured by dogs. In some parts the fields are bleached with the bones of the dead that were previously picked by dogs.

Throughout this harrowing time some wrong-headed clergy of the Protestant churches used the plight of the poor to canvass recruits to their religion. Although a vigorous and continuous trend existed from the late eighteenth century of missions to convert the Catholic population to Protestantism, it seems particularly offensive and objectionable at this time of destitution.

Despite repeated calls for continued assistance, the Government's relief machinery began to be wound down. Trevelyan outlined government thinking and policy in a letter to the editor of *The Times* on 7 October 1847, emphasising three points.

> First—That the new poor law will be enforced in Ireland to the utmost extent of the power of the government—that no assistance whatever will be given from national funds to those unions which, whether they have the will or not, undoubtedly have the *power* of maintaining their own poor . . .
>
> Secondly—That there are certain unions in the west of Ireland where the social system was so entirely based upon the potato . . . that it was impossible that the habits of the people could be so suddenly changed . . . as to allow of the crowded population which had grown up under the potato system supporting themselves without assistance in the second year after the failure.
>
> Thirdly—That the change from an idle, barbarous, isolated potato cultivation, to corn cultivation, which enforces industry, binds together employer and employed in mutually beneficial relations . . . is proceeding as fast as can reasonably be expected under the circumstances.

However well-reasoned this attempt to force the peasantry from a potato culture to the growing of corn and wheat was, the experiment was too novel to be understood or appreciated by the impoverished peasantry. Resistance to the change was widespread, even endemic. And still the people perished from want of food, and still evictions for non-payment of rent took place. In May 1848 in Roscommon, two hundred people were evicted from thirty-three acres of land owned by Mr M.R.W. Ormsby. The evictions took place after the ground had been tilled and the crops sown: the landlord seized the crops, levelled the houses and refused to accept full payment of rents when they were offered.

In July 1848 there was a recurrence of the potato blight and conditions in Ireland continued to worsen as winter approached. Relief aid was less forthcoming in the aftermath of the Young Irelanders' abortive attempt at rebellion, which ended with a brief skirmish with the police, but which undoubtedly stretched British patience and sympathy to the limit. The calamitous condition of the country was such, however, that in 1849 it was decided that a royal visit should be organised to rally morale and show royal sympathy to Queen Victoria's Irish subjects. Accordingly, in August, the Queen and her consort, Prince Albert, made a visit to Ireland which ended with a dance of the peasantry on the lawn at Carton, County Kildare. By that time, however, the potato crop had failed once more, and by December 1849 the familiar sight of ruined buildings and uncultivated land greeted the visitor to Ireland.

The logic of government remedies and the self-interest of landlords had produced the beginnings of a social and economic revolution in the tenure of land in Ireland. The correspondent of the *Illustrated London News*, on 15 December 1849, put it thus:

> Sixteen thousand and odd persons unhoused in the Union of Kilrush [County Clare] before the month of June [1849]; seventy-one thousand one hundred and thirty holdings done away in Ireland, and nearly as many houses destroyed, in 1848; two hundred and fifty-four thousand holdings of more than one acre and less than five acres, put an end to between 1841 and 1848; six-tenths, in fact, of the lowest class of tenantry driven from their now roofless or annihilated cabins and houses, makes up the general description of that desolation . . . The ruin is great and complete.

What was to come of this change? The Encumbered Estates Act saw the beginning of the transfer of land from financially embarrassed landlords to professional men with ready cash: in real terms the peasant benefited little, if at all. All he gained was a new master. A leader in the Dublin newspaper *The Nation*, on 5 January 1850, posed the question – 'What can Irishmen do?' The answer it gave was rhetorical and prophetic: 'In the year eighteen hundred and fifty the Irish people can if they will raise up and re-invigorate this Island. If it is still a social swamp in 1851, the fault will lie, not with Saxon or stranger, but primarily and in the chief degree with the people of Ireland.' The sentiment proved correct but the time scale was much too ambitious. The question of land tenure in Ireland was addressed over the next half-century but was not satisfactorily answered until the work of the Land Commission was completed in the middle of the twentieth century. The question of the government of Ireland was addressed continually over the next seventy years but was only drastically changed in 1921 with the Government of Ireland Act. The residue of that question is still being worked out. In the immediate aftermath of the famine decade, the Irish question became (and remains) an international issue. The *Illustrated London News* of 3 April 1852 stated:

> What has been called the 'Exodus of the Celtic races' continues. The return of spring has witnessed once more the flux of the emigrational tide towards the shores of the New World. The quays of Dublin, Cork, and Liverpool are crowded with Irish emigrants, departing to other lands, and carrying with them, in too many instances we are afraid, a feeling of bitter hatred to this country.

The people who remained in Ireland fared as best they could in the changing economic, social and political world in which they found themselves. The trauma of the famine decade struck a deep blow to the psyche of the Irish people then and in ensuing generations. Anger, hatred, fear and compassion have mixed with shame to produce a reluctance, possibly an inability, to address the enormity of that national tragedy. It is possible that only now in the last years of the century and of the millennium have the people of Ireland the self-confidence to seek to understand fully the causes, progress and consequences of the famine decade.

JOHN KILLEN
MAY 1995

1841–1844

CENSUS REPORT

1841

TO HIS EXCELLENCY THOMAS PHILIP EARL DE GREY,
LORD LIEUTENANT GENERAL AND GENERAL GOVERNOR OF IRELAND

MAY IT PLEASE YOUR EXCELLENCY,

We, the Commissioners appointed under the 3rd and 4th Vict., c. 100, for taking an account of the Population of Ireland for the Year 1841, have now the honor to present to your Excellency our Report, together with the Returns which have been prepared under our direction—prefacing the former with some account of the mode in which we proceeded to collect the required information.

Our first step was to procure from the Ordnance Survey Department a Map of every barony in Ireland, showing the boundaries and details of its several parishes and townlands, with classified lists of these sub-divisions. As the Survey had been completed, except in the counties of Cork, Kerry, and Limerick, we thus, for the first time, possessed the advantage of a set of maps which not only indicated correct boundaries, but exhibited every house upon the face of the country. For those three counties the maps were formed from less perfect documents, and ex-hibited, for the most part, no more than the boundaries.

It having been resolved that the Constabulary should be employed for the enumeration, we next distributed the maps and lists to the several Officers and Head Constables of the force, selected by the Inspector-General for each barony. They again divided these into districts of con-tiguous townlands, to each of which was assigned a Superintending Constable or Sub-Constable, or—in those districts where the constabulary were not sufficiently numerous—one of the coast-guard, or—where such assistance was not available—a Civilian selected by the Superintendent. We were thus enabled to mark on a general map the districts and stations of all the enumerators, and the whole force thus marshalled was in readiness before the arrival of the period fixed by the Act of Parliament for the enumeration.

In the mean time, having maturely considered the best mode of ascer-taining the various facts we had in view, we resolved to adopt the course of sending a form of Return to each family, to be filled by its head, as less intrusive than requiring it to be filled by the enumerator from *viva voce* inquiry. But we, of course, took means to check the returns so obtained, and required from the enumerator a certificate that they were true to the best of his belief. Another form was supplied to the enumerator, in which he was himself required to record the various particulars sought, as to houses and matters of a similar nature. The general distinction we followed was, that the statement of all facts which were of a personal nature, and only ascertainable by personal *inquiry* was, as far as possible, left to the head of the family, whilst that of all facts which could be ascertained by mere *observation* was demanded from the enumerator...

The Act required us to ascertain the Age, the Sex, the Occupation, and Place of Nativity of every person abiding in Ireland on the night of Sunday the 6th of June, with such other particulars as the Lord Lieutenant should direct... We also demanded a return of absent members, which, together with the measures adopted at the ports... we hoped would obviate the danger of error from the lateness of the season at which the Census was to be taken...

The columns under the head PERSONS contain the General Enumeration, and the first fact which presents itself for consideration in connexion with this subject is, the small amount of increase which has taken place in the total population of the country from 1831 to 1841, compared with what might have been expected from the increase shown by the returns of 1821 and 1831. The following table shows the comparative numbers in the different years:—

Sexes	1821	1831	1841	Increase per 100 between 1821 and 1831	Increase per 100 between 1831 and 1841
Males	3,341,926	3,794,880	4,019,576	13.55	5.92
Females	3,459,901	3,972,521	4,155,548	14.81	4.61
Total	6,801,827	7,767,401	8,175,124	14.19	5.25
Proportion of Females to 100 Males	103.5	104.7	103.4	•	•

From this it appears that whilst the addition to the population from 1821 to 1831 was about 14¼ per cent., the corresponding addition from 1831 to 1841 was but 5¼ per cent.

The accuracy of these per centages must, of course, depend upon the relative accuracy of the several Censuses of 1821, 1831, and 1841. We cannot take upon ourselves to pronounce with certainty, the extent to which any of these may vary from the truth. But we may remark, with respect to the Census of 1841, that the strict mode of inquiry which we followed, carried out as it was by a highly disciplined body of men, and executed on the same day in every part of the country, together with the system of verification we adopted, affords ground to hope that it is not far from the truth.

REPORT OF THE COMMISSIONERS APPOINTED TO TAKE THE
CENSUS OF IRELAND FOR THE YEAR 1841

DUBLIN, 1843

THE POTATO

MRS. S.C. HALL

There is little doubt that the first potatoes grown in the British empire were planted at Youghall—probably in 1586—by Sir Walter Raleigh, who was closely connected with the town, of which he was mayor in 1588 . . . It is uncertain when the potato became an article of general food in Ireland; and it is more than probable that, as in England, they had long been considered "conserves, toothsome and daintie," before they were in common use. Mr. Mc Skimin, the author of a valuable "History of Carrickfergus," is the possessor of a manuscript written between 1670 and 1679, in which potatoes are stated to have been sold so high as 1s. 8d. a bushel; and he states "very old people had informed him that in their district (the north of Ireland) few potatoes were formerly used after harvest, except a small quantity preserved as a treat for their Halloween supper, which were eaten with butter." But Mr. Crofton Croker has produced, in his "Popular Songs of Ireland," abundant proofs that, in the south, potatoes were ordinary food before the period to which Mr. Mc Skimin refers; and that previous to the Revolution of 1688 they were extensively cultivated and commonly eaten.

It is unnecessary to state that, for above a century and a half, the potato has been almost the only food of the peasantry of Ireland. They raise corn, indeed—wheat, barley, and oats, in abundance—but it is for export; and although the assertion may startle many, we have no hesitation in saying there are hundreds in the less civilized districts of the country who have never tasted bread. Whether the Irish have to bless or ban the name of Sir Walter Raleigh is a matter still in dispute—some siding with Cobbett in execrating "the lazy root," "the accursed root," as, if not the originator, the sustainer of Irish poverty and wretchedness; others contending that the introduction of the potato is an ample set-off against the wars and confiscations of Elizabeth, her counsellors, and her armies. It is universally admitted that a finer or hardier race of peasantry cannot be found in the world; and although it is considered that their strength fails them at a comparatively early age, it is impossible to deny the nutritive qualities of a food upon which so many millions have thriven and increased. But there can be as little doubt that the ease with which the means of existence are procured has been the cause of evil. A very limited portion of land, a few days of labour, and a small amount of manure, will create a stock upon which a family may exist for twelve months: too generally, indeed, the periods between exhausting the old stock and digging the new are seasons of great want, if not of absolute famine; but if the season is propitious the peasant digs day after day the produce of his plot of ground, and, before the winter sets in, places the residue in a pit to which he has access when his wants demand a supply. Nearly every soil will produce potatoes; they may be seen growing almost from a barren rock, on the side of a mountain, and in the bog where the foot would sink many inches in the soil. Every cottage has its garden—its acre or half acre of land, attached; and as the culture requires but a very small portion of the peasant's time and still less of his attention, his labour is to be disposed of, or his time may be squandered in idleness. He can live, at all events—if his crop do not fail; and he can pay his rent if his pig, fed like himself out of his garden, do not die. To decency of clothing, and to any of the luxuries that make life something more than mere animal existence, he is too often a stranger. Contentment may be the "parent of delight," but it is not the nurse of civilization; and he who has no wants beyond those of the appetites he shares in common with the "brutes that perish," is not likely to advance his social and moral condition. On the whole, it is perhaps to be lamented that the use of "Ireland's root" has been so universal in the country, and that the people have been so well contented with it that they have made no exertion to mix the potato with varied food.

But matters are, as we have stated, improving in Ireland; already, in a large proportion of the cabins, the potato has the accompaniment of meat and bread; the butcher and the baker are receiving the custom that was, not long since, given exclusively to the whiskey shops. We

refer, in a great degree, to our recollections, when we describe the lower
classes of the Irish as existing, almost universally, on the potato: we have
known many families who very rarely tasted flesh or fish, and whose
only luxury was "a grain of salt" with their daily meals; we do not speak
of families in poverty, but of those who laboured hard and continually—
the produce of whose labour barely sufficed to preserve them from utter want. Generally, however, they contrived to have a salt herring with
their dinners; this was placed in a bowl or dish, water was poured upon
it, and the potato, dipped into it, obtained a relish. We shall have other

occasions for describing the economy of the
Irish cottage; at present, we confine ourselves
to illustrate this branch of it. The peasant
usually has three meals—one at eight in the
morning; at noon; and at seven or eight in
the evening, when his work is done. The
potatoes are boiled in an iron pot—such as
that represented in the print—they are strained
in "the basket"—pictured also; from which
they are thrown upon the table, seldom
without a cloth, and around it the family sit

on stools and bosses (the boss is a low seat made of straw); the usual
drink is buttermilk, when it can be had: which drink goes round in a
small "piggin," a sort of miniature of the English pail. This, the three-
legged stool and the "borrane," are delineated in the annexed engrav-
ing. The borrane is formed of a scraped sheep-skin, drawn round a hoop;
and is used instead of a sieve for winnowing corn, filling sacks with grain,
holding wool when carded and ready for the spinning-wheel, or the
feathers—plucked three times in the year from an unfortunate gander
and his wives, and sometimes as a lordly dish—though of inexpensive
workmanship—to hold the potatoes which constitute the family fare.

IRELAND: ITS SCENERY, CHARACTER ETC., VOL. 1

LONDON, 1841

MAIN BUILDING OF THE NEW WORKHOUSES AT CASTLETOWN AND DINGLE.

THE WORKHOUSE

Among the diversity of persons likely to crave relief at the workhouse, many artisans and reduced traders may be included; to find useful employment for all such persons, according to their several capacities, may lead to the happiest consequences; industry will be greatly promoted; some of the younger inmates might evince a desire for instruction in any particular trade, the teacher and his pupil would be benefited, and the latter in time might be qualified to earn his livelihood abroad. If it be true, that "idleness is the mother of mischief," it naturally follows, that industry will be the parent to good habits. It is worthy of remark, what sources of industry are afforded by the simple culture of wheat. The preparing of the ground, and sowing the seed, is chiefly done by men; then comes the reaping, in which women take an active part; the saving of the crop, and making it up, next follows; afterwards, the threshing and winnowing succeeds—this process gives forth the grain and straw, the one convertible partly to the food of man, and partly for animals, and the other, rendered useful in a variety of ways, namely, bedding for the poor, and litter for cattle, not to mention the manufacture of hats, from only a few inches of the upper stalk. I have been told that the peasantry pay one shilling a piece for straw hats, not made by themselves, which if bought for all the inmates of the workhouse would amount to £40, and this, annually, would be no trifle. Let it then be considered the two fold advantage of manufacturing the article of hats by the females of the institution, namely, economy, and industry, well combined. It should not be forgotten, that the rearing of cows and other animals form an essential branch of farming, and that a considerable supply of butter may thus be obtained, without trenching on the comforts of the humbler classes. The raising of flax, and its ulterior uses, should not be overlooked. The lowest and most humid spots will grow osiers and willows, convertible to many purposes, besides giving employment to numbers. In short, the aggregate of benefits derivable from the system just detailed, ought, under favourable circumstances, to characterize the institution rather as a house of industry than a workhouse, and surely it will be conceded, that such would be a more appropriate term.

I have been assured upon authority that I consider good, that a farming concern of the description given, would afford means and convenience for preserving in store sufficient provision for two years' consumption. This circumstance gives birth to serious reflection. It is of too recent date to be forgotten, the instances of famine and scarcity that have periodically visited Ireland: meditate, for an instant, what might be the consequences, should such a calamity occur when the workhouses are thickly inhabited, and no more provision in store than is necessary for their own consumption; who can calculate the misery and confusion that would ensue from famished numbers flocking to the quarter where they knew the necessaries of life to abound, in a more or less degree? How could the governors of the asylum restrain such an onset? It is a common saying, that "hunger will break through a stone wall," may it not then be foreseen, that the same impulse will urge the starving wretches to penetrate or scale the confines of the place. Let these considerations, therefore, have their due weight with the ruling authorities, and prompt them to make their election—whether, to await the possible catastrophe—or anticipate its approach. In the former alternative, they cannot expect credit; whilst, in the other, they will be upheld by Scripture, after the example of Egypt during the famine in Canaan. If the precautionary measure should be adopted by all the institutions, and the already experienced calamity visit the land, who can calculate the relief it will be likely to impart to suffering fellow creatures? The several establishments acting in concert, will resemble, in some degree, branch banks, ready to pour in supplies, where the greatest run prevails; and when adversity has run its course, and the dearth subsided, how will the country rejoice, and bestow its praises and gratitude on those through whose instrumentality the career of famine has been arrested.

IMPORTANT SUGGESTIONS IN RELATION TO THE IRISH POOR LAW

DUBLIN, 1842

THE HARVEST

For the last eight years at least, there has not been such a favourable season for the farmer as that which we now enjoy, the havesting, consequently rapidly progresses; in fact, such is the demand for labour in certain districts that it appears one shilling and five pence a-day has been demanded and obtained by the reapers; a great bulk of grain having been ripe about the same time, causing each individual agriculturist to be anxious for having his own cut as early as possible.

There is no doubt but if the present glorious weather continues until the end of the month, the entire grain cut in the north will be safely off the ground. In this neighbourhood, and for many miles round, the greater part of the oats has already been carted, and it is only in some of the backward and more elevated spots, that the reaping of this crop has not been finished. Generally speaking, Oats, especially Poland, are rather light; the Potatoe, however, stooks well, but as far as has yet been ascertained, the produce will not be equal to that of last year; this may be attributed to many causes, perhaps the most probable is the very late and ungenial spring, together with the severe weather the young blades encountered during the latter end of May and early part of June.—The straw is excellent, and will make very superior fodder. Within the last eight days, Wheat reaping has considerably advanced, and the crop is decidedly the best of the season; there have been some complaints of blight among the growers, but this is very partial, as the most experienced farmers in the county never recollect a period when such fears were entertained of the safety of this crop in its early stage, and yet so little appearance of the epidemic to which more than any other it is even subject, observable in the after season. In quantity, Wheat will be abundant, and the quality such as to defy competition in that respect of any Continental produce. This affords additional proof that Wheat is a much hardier grain, at least in reference to superfluous moisture, than Barley or Oats. There are numerous tracts of country in which at the beginning of the season the rain water arose to the top of the ridges, and still sustained no injury. Apprehensions were entertained on Sunday that the weather was about to break up, and during that night and part of the next morning, there were some very severe showers, but such was the heat of the sun in a few hours afterwards, that scarcely a trace of the rain's effect was visible, nor did it in the least retard the labour of the husbandman. To the very late potatoes, particularly those which were replanted after the first seeding had been destroyed, the rain will be of great benefit. It is particularly gratifying to observe the great advancement made within the last few years in the cultivation of flax, and it reflects no small degree of credit on the Society here, to which the aroused feelings among the farming community relative to that species of husbandry must be attributed. In nearly every instance the staple commodity of our national produce has pulled well, the colour is good, and the state of the weather being so favourable upon the subsequent operations, the farmer need not fear its repaying all the care and attention necessary for its successful culture. Hay has been very heavy, and the after grass is excellent. Potatoes are very thin in the ground, and, generally speaking, will, it is to be feared, be much below the average in quantity. On the whole, however, the farmer's prospects are favourable, and much more cheering than they were last season.

BELFAST NEWS-LETTER, 22 SEPTEMBER 1843

THE PEASANTRY AND TENANTRY

J. VENEDAY

There are a great many *idlers* in Ireland. That is a fact which no one will attempt to deny. It is the greatest of all the misfortunes of Ireland; and it is one that consumes the very marrow of the country. Idleness, it may be affirmed, is the very flesh and blood of many Irishmen. They have actually learned how to be idle, and the habit is so easily acquired—there is so much of gentleness, and, we might add, of nobility, in the practise of it! . . .

And yet, with all this, it is a calumny to say of the Irish that they are *slothful*. They have, in truth, nothing to do, and they are of opinion . . . "when nought is to be done, there is no use in hurrying." For centuries they have had nothing to do, and so the *far niente* has become a habit. This is, beyond all others, the greatest misfortune of Ireland; because, whenever the Irishman has really got any thing to do, he is untiringly diligent—so diligent, that he far surpasses the Englishman himself . . . The noble-hearted Sadleir, indignant at the accusation of "idleness" against the Irish, says, "They cannot find employment, and therefore are they branded with the crime of idleness. It is false. In our harvest fields, on our farms, in the bowels of the earth, or on the highest buildings, wherever employment can be procured, no matter how dangerous or how difficult it may be, there the Irish are sure to be found . . .

The matter is, after all, exceedingly simple, and most easy of explanation. The Irishman is shrewd, and he will not toil in the field, as the dumb beast does, without the prospect of receiving, at least, some little portion of the harvest. He is the hardest worker for a day's hire, that can be found, but it is when the day's work brings a day's wages, even though they be ever so small. But when, on the other hand, he sees that all the profits of his toil go to another, and that other, perhaps, one that he hates, and has just reason for hating, then he sits himself quietly down, and—looks around him!

Thus it is that the Irish, on their scanty farms, will only do that which is absolutely necessary; that which will bring to themselves alone the immediate and profitable results. Systematically they "live from hand to mouth;" they believe that if they were to "put the land in better heart," if they were to beautify the appearance of their houses, to bring every thing into good order, the rent would be raised upon them, and made to keep pace with their improvements. What would they gain by that? A small landed proprietor . . . who was improving his land, asked one of his tenants to follow his example, and the latter answered— "what your honour says is perfectly right, and ought to be done; but then if these improvements were made, the time would be sure to come, when they would be a disadvantage to myself or my children."

Neither the Irish landed proprietor, nor the Irish farmer confide or believe in the continuance of the existing relations between them. The consequence is, that both think solely of the present moment. The greatest portion of the land belongs to the invading Anglo-Irish lords. These wish to extract the highest profit they can get for the moment. It is this struggle for the highest profit, which has led to the introduction of small farms, consisting of a hut, and a few acres, and for which the peasant, farmer, or occupier has to pay the highest possible rent. The most bitter hatred instantly arises between the occupier of the farm, and the landlord, either when the farmer refuses to improve his ground, or when the landlord ejects his tenant, upon the expectation of receiving a couple of pounds more in the year for the farm. The forty shilling freehold once added to the influence of the landlord; but the instant it ceased to do so, the poor were deprived of that small permanent fixture in the land . . .

The poor peasant is thus by law left without rights—the rich landlord on the other hand is, by law, made omnipotent. Is it then to be wondered at, that the peasant who has nought to hope for from the improvement of his house, and his farm should think only of providing for to day?

It is out of such relations between landlords and tenants, and the circumstances sure to accompany such, that we can trace out the causes, why the Irish peasantry are so often described, as trampling upon all law, and despising all legal forms of redress, madly, blindly, and wickedly devoting themselves to the attainment of revenge. But this is something like to what is said of their slothfulness. They are indolent; because they have not employment, and they are revengeful because they have no rights. In both cases, the result is not merely natural; but it is that only which could be expected from human beings.

IRELAND AND THE IRISH DURING THE REPEAL YEAR, 1844

DUBLIN, 1844

1845

THE REAL POTATO BLIGHT OF IRELAND.

(FROM A SKETCH TAKEN IN CONCILIATION HALL.)

LAND TENURE IN IRELAND

LORD DEVON

The number of proprietors of land in Ireland is small when compared with its extent and the amount of its agricultural population. This circumstance, while probably it is one of the causes which has led to the want of that personal attention to the condition of the tenantry, which is at once the duty and interest of landlords, renders also the impediments in the way of improvement, arising from the nature of the proprietors' tenure, a matter of more urgent public importance in Ireland than elsewhere.

It frequently happens that large estates in that country are held by the proprietors in strict limitation; and the pecuniary circumstances of the landed proprietors generally, arising in some cases out of family charges, and resulting in others from improvidence or carelessness possibly of former proprietors, disable many, even of the best disposed landlords, from improving their property, or encouraging improvement amongst their tenantry . . . Many of the evils incident to the occupation of land in Ireland may be attributed to this cause . . .

We must not omit to notice the system which prevails in a greater or less degree in every part of Ireland, of letting land for one or more crops, commonly known as the con-acre system . . .

Much has been said in condemnation of this system; but still, we are convinced that some practice of this nature is essential to the comfort, almost to the existence, of the Irish peasant. Under ordinary circumstances, the wages of his labour alone will not enable him to purchase food and other necessaries, and to pay even the most moderate rent. It becomes therefore necessary that he should resort to some other means for procuring subsistence, and these can only be found in the occupation of a piece of ground which shall furnish a crop of potatoes, for food. This he generally takes from some farmer in the neighbourhood, upon conditions which vary much according to the particular terms of agreement respecting the ploughing, the manure, the seed, &c.

Although the taker of con-acre ground may, in ordinary years, receive a good return for the rent which he assumes, yet, as the amount of such rent, although not unreasonable in respect of the farmer's expenditure upon the land, is always large with reference to the ordinary means of a labourer, a bad season, and a failure in the crops, leave the latter in a distressed condition, subject to a demand which he is wholly unable to meet...

In adverting to the condition of the different classes of occupiers in Ireland, we noticed, with deep regret, the state of the cottiers and labourers in most parts of the country, from the want of certain employment.

It would be impossible to describe adequately the privations which they and their families habitually and patiently endure.

It will be seen in the Evidence, that in many districts their only food is the potato, their only beverage water, that their cabins are seldom a protection against the weather, that a bed or a blanket is a rare luxury, and that nearly in all, their pig and manure heap constitute their only property.

When we consider this state of things, and the large proportion of the population which comes under the designation of agricultural labourers, we have to repeat that the patient endurance which they exhibit is deserving of high commendation, and entitles them to the best attention of Government and of Parliament.

REPORT FROM HER MAJESTY'S COMMISSIONERS OF INQUIRY INTO THE STATE OF THE LAW AND PRACTICE IN RESPECT OF THE OCCUPATION OF LAND IN IRELAND

DUBLIN, 1845

IRISH MENDICANTS.—BY ALFRED FRIPP.

THE PARISH OF TULLAGHOBEGLEY, BARONY OF KILMACRENNAN, COUNTY OF DONEGALL

LORD GEORGE HILL

"There is about 4000 persons in this parish, and all Catholics, and as poor as I shall describe, having among them no more than—

"One cart,
No wheel car,
No coach, or any other vehicle.
One plough,
Sixteen harrows,
Eight saddles,
Two pillions,
Eleven bridles,
Twenty shovels,
Thirty-two rakes,
Seven table-forks,
Ninety-three chairs,
Two hundred and forty-three stools,
Ten iron grapes,
No swine, hogs, or pigs,
Twenty-seven geese,
Three turkeys,
Two feather beds,
Eight chaff beds,
Two stables,
Six cow houses,
One national school,
No other school,
One priest,
No other resident gentleman,
No bonnet,
No clock,
Three watches,
Eight brass candlesticks,
No looking glasses above 3d. in price,
No boots, no spurs,
No fruit trees,
No turnips,
No parsnips,
No carrots,
No clover,
Or any other garden vegetables, but potatoes and cabbage, and not more than ten square feet of glass in windows in the whole, with the exception of the chapel, the school house, the priest's house, Mr. Dombrain's house, and the constabulary barrack."

FACTS FROM GWEEDORE: WITH USEFUL HINTS TO DONEGAL TOURISTS

DUBLIN, 1845

The genial and bounteous rain of Sunday has given another powerful stimulus to vegetation. Crops of all kinds exhibit a most cheering luxuriance. Wheat looks quite healthy and abundant. Oats have improved rapidly, and look right well. The seasonable rain of Sunday should inspire us with gratitude to a gracious Providence.—*Longford Journal*.

On Thursday night the weather in this part underwent a change from the great heat of the previous week, as there was a heavy fall of rain, which continued until Friday evening, and which on Sunday night was followed by storm. Finer growing weather there cannot be, the crops every where presenting the most cheering aspect.—*Galway Vindicator*.

We have had a good deal of rain this week, which will, no doubt, prove highly beneficial to the crops. At no time do we recollect having seen every description of crop in this district look better. The corn crops will be luxuriant, and the potatoes and turnips promise exceedingly well.—*Down Recorder*.

DUBLIN EVENING MAIL, 2 JUNE 1845

THE WEATHER—THE CROPS

From daily observations made at Athlone, it is ascertained that as much rain has fallen during the last fortnight as fell during four months previous, commencing at the first week of February,—*Athlone Sentinel*.

The weather has been rainy this week; nevertheless the crops, except in some cases, seem full of promise. The heavy showers which have fallen latterly, instead of being injurious, have proved of the greatest utility to the grass, oats, and wheat, which had been covered by the recent floods, as they have washed away the clay, which the water, after receding, had left behind; so that the damage sustained will not be at all so great as was anticipated. We have received this intelligence from a traveller who passed some parts of the country which had been inundated.—*Derry Sentinel*.

There have not been such crops in this part of the North in the memory of the oldest inhabitant. Wheat, barley, oats, and flax are all good—the hay will be a prime crop, and potatoes are better in appearance than at any former period.—*Tyrone Constitution*.

The heavy rains, to all appearance, have ceased, and we learn with much satisfaction from some that, notwithstanding all the threatened danger to the crops, there is every probability that it will pass over without doing damage generally to all—and that the injury, if any, will only be found in some few isolated spots. We have also in our possession letters from old experienced farmers, who say that the early wheat is now suffering most, and that the red rust has strongly marked it in many localities, particularly where it was near the shelter of plantations or woods, which prevented the wind passing through. Others say there is more harm done than any one is aware of, and that there is a melancholy miss in the potato crop. Our own impression is that the fears of the weather continuing unfavourable created considerable alarm, but that the damage will not amount to anything like that anticipated.—*Nenagh Guardian*.

DUBLIN EVENING MAIL, 16 JULY 1845

IRISH CABINS AND THEIR INMATES

But what shall I say of the *human habitations* in this (so called) most thriving and best-conditioned quarter of Ireland, the County of Down? If I had not seen every second face at a hovel door with a smile on it, and heard laughing and begging in the same voice everywhere, I should think here were human beings abandoned by their

32   Maker. Many of the dwellings I saw upon the road-side, looked to me like the abodes of extinguished hope,—forgotten instincts,—grovelling, despairing, almost idiotic wretchedness. I did not know there were such sights in the world. I did not know that men and women, upright, and made in God's image, could live in styes like swine, *with* swine,—sitting, lying down, cooking and eating in such filth as all brute animals, save the one "unclean," revolt from and avoid. The extraordinary fact of it, too, is that it seems almost altogether the result of choice. I scarce saw one hovel, the mud floor of which was not excavated several inches below the ground level without; and, as there was no sill, or raised threshold, there is no bar—I will not say to the water—but to the liquid filth that oozes to its lower reservoir within. A few miles from Drogheda, I pointed out to my companion, a woman sitting in a hovel, at work, with the muddy water up to her ancles, and an enormous hog scratching himself against her knee. These disgusting animals were everywhere walking in and out of the hovels at pleasure, jostling aside the half-naked children or wallowing in the wash, outside or in—the best conditioned and most privileged inmates, indeed, of every habitation. All this, of course, is matter of choice, and so is the offal-heap,—situated in almost every instance, directly before the door, and draining its putrid mass into the hollow, under the peasant's table. Yet mirth *does* live in these places—people *do* smile on you from these squalid abodes of wretchedness—the rose of health *does* shew itself upon the cheeks of children, whose cradle is a dung-heap, and whose play-fellows are hogs. And of the beings who live thus, courage, wit, and a quenchless love of liberty, are the undenied and universal characteristics. Truly, that mysterious law of nature, by which corruption paints the rose, and feeds the fragrant cup of the lily, is not without its similitude! Who shall say "What is clean?" when the back of the most loathsome of reptiles turns out on examination more beautiful than the butterfly? Who shall say what extremes may not meet, when amid the filth of an Irish hovel, spring, like flowers out of ordure, the graces of a prince in his palace?—*N.P. Willis.*

BELFAST PENNY JOURNAL, 19 JULY 1845

CORK, AUGUST 21.—Nothing could be more capricious than the changes during the last few days. Heat, cold, rain and sunshine succeed each other. Monday last was extremely wet—Tuesday was beautifully dry; yesterday was both wet and dry, and to-day again, is equally variable. The process of ripening must advance slowly. We have no facts to speak of beyond those already mentioned in previous notices, except that the gathering of the harvest has commenced in various places, and that no complaints from the interior of the country have as yet reached us.

ROSCREA, AUGUST 23.—During the last fortnight the weather has been very changeable, but the crops, we are happy to find, are not much injured. The harvest will, however, be later than was anticipated, and the wheat crop appears to have suffered more than any other grain.

NENAGH, AUGUST 23.—We have still to report unfavourably of the state of the weather. It is totally impossible that the crops can ripen in such an ungenial season. On the lands of a gentleman, within a mile of Nenagh, there is a splendid-looking field of Lamas wheat, of about twelve acres. The land steward was directed to go through the corn on Wednesday last; on passing right through the centre from end to end, he discovered a considerable quantity of the ears blighted and mildewed. The land steward says the picking out of every ear of such corn is imperative, otherwise the smut would destroy the appearance of any that was good. The new potatoes have suffered much from the heavy rains, any that have been dug out up to the present time were quite wet and unwholesome as food.

DUBLIN EVENING POST, 23 AUGUST 1845

POTATO PESTILENCE

In the part of THE EVENING POST dedicated to the interests of the Farming World, we have made rather an ample report of a matter of great importance, indeed—namely, the failure of the Potato Crop—very extensively in the United States, to a great extent in Flanders and France, and to an appreciable amount in England. We have heard something of the kind in our own country—especially along the coast—but we believe that no apprehension whatever is entertained even of a partial failure of the Potato Crop in Ireland.

Nevertheless, it is impossible that the subject can be otherwise in Ireland than one of the deepest interest, and it, therefore, became an imperative duty on our parts to collect all the information we could accumulate on the matter. The result will be found in the place we have indicated, and we should suppose that there is hardly one of our readers who will not peruse the different statements with interest.

There can be no question at all of the very remarkable failure in the United States, and with regard to Holland, Flanders and France, we have already abundant evidence of the wide-spread of what we cannot help calling a calamity.

We confess we do not altogether subscribe to the opinion of the American journals, that the species are superannuated, and though new creations succeed, of which there appears to be little doubt, we cannot entertain the theory, that the nutritive and hardy esculent to which we are all accustomed, has become suddenly worn out. That individuals may be superannuated, but that an animal or vegetable race becomes *effete* all at once by the prevalence of a general law, we cannot allow ourselves to believe.

In this case the Potato Cholera, as they call it, has become, as far as our information yet extends, almost universal. We hear of it in Normandy, and in the vicinity of Paris, in Canterbury, in Norfolk, in Liege and Namur, in the Old World—and in almost every one of the States of the Great Atlantic Republic, from Vermont and Rhode Island to Louisianna and Missouri.—This is most extraordinary—and, we repeat, that all the attempts of explanation that we have hitherto received, appear to us to be totally inadequate.

The Human, the Brute, and the Vegetable Creations, we know from experience, are subjected to periodical checks. Plague and Cholera are sufficient examples in the first case—the Distemper amongst Cattle in the second—and the great mortality of the Eel in the Boyue, and, perhaps, in other streams, if the matter was investigated in the third. With regard to the Vegetable World, it is well known to the Husbandman, that you must not continue, for more than two seasons or three, the same sort of crop on the same ground. It deteriorates—it becomes non-productive. But none of the reasons which supply an explanation to these phenomena, can account for the general and apparently simultaneous failure of the Potato in the United States, and in several parts of Europe.

It is to be observed, that the statement with regard to the failure of

the Crop of Potatoes in America, is confined to the year 1844. We do 35
not know how the Crop has turned out for the present year in the United
States; but, we know that it has failed, to a great extent, in Holland,
Belgium, and the North of France—probably in that part of Germany
conterminous to those countries—but, from these we had no communications recently on the subject.

It is altogether a very singular phenomenon; but, well acquainted as
we are with it, the History of the Potato is very remarkable. It is said
to have been introduced into these countries by RALEIGH; but, be this
as it may, it is not at present to be found indigenously in any part of
the Continent of America, from Cape Horn to the Coppermine River—
from the Table Land of Mexico to Cape Cod, in Massachusetts. What
has become of the parent plant—has it gone out?—has the race expired?
It is not the Yam, certainly, nor what is called the Sweet Potato. These
have been transplanted and tried, and failed altogether, or produced a
sickly and unwholesome resemblance of the parent stem. The Magna
Mater of all the Potatoes in the United States is Ireland, and not any
part of America—and there they used to flourish enormously. But, the
general failures of which we read, are producing serious apprehensions.
Yet, surely the United States have little real cause to fear. If the Potato
were entirely extirpated, the people would enjoy an ample sufficiency
of food. It is in the densely packed communities of Europe that the
failure would be alarming, and in no country more, or so much, than
in our own.

But, happily, there is no ground for any apprehensions of the kind
in Ireland. There may have been partial failures in some localities; but,
we believe that there was never a more abundant Potato Crop in Ireland
than there is at present, and none which it will be more likely to secure.

DUBLIN EVENING POST, 9 SEPTEMBER 1845

POTATO FAMINE

The failure of the potato crop in Ireland, which has for some
time been feared, is now confirmed by circumstantial accounts
from almost all parts of the country. A large portion of the crop
turns out to be quite useless for purposes of food. A dearth is inevitable;
and a famine is extremely probable.

A failure of the potato crop in Ireland is a calamity of the greatest magnitude. The Irish peasantry rely almost exclusively upon potatoes for their subsistence; and when the crop fails, they have nothing to fall back upon but grass, nettles, and seaweed. "Seven millions rejoice in potatoes," said a well-fed clergyman of Oxford; and when the potatoes fail, the said "seven millions" have no alternative but to "rejoice" in destitution and starvation.

The condition of a population dependent mainly on potatoes for their subsistence, must inevitably be wretched and miserable. They must always be verging on the borders of starvation. For potatoes cannot keep from year to year—they are not articles of import and export—they cannot be stored in granaries as corn is—they can scarcely be kept in a wholesome state until the next year's crop be ready—and if that crop be a failure, the result is *famine*, unless some other provision has been made to avert it—which, it is well known, the Irish peasantry never think of making. When the coarse and miserable diet of the Irish people fail, they have no remaining resource or alternative. The peasant must starve and pine until the next year's crop is ready—that is, if he should have the misfortune to survive so long.

Another evil of exclusive potato cultivation is, that it makes a people idle and grovelling. Potatoes are grown with the least possible effort of industry; the ground is turned over, the potatoes are dibbled in, and no more needs to be done until the crop is ready. The peasantry, who depend exclusively on their potato crop, and do not look beyond it, may go to sleep or to play, while the 'taties are growing; and when the crop is gathered up, they have got their winter's food, and may go to sleep or to play again for the rest of the year. This, unfortunately, is the state of matters in Ireland; the people are satisfied with their potatoes, and when their potatoes fail, they have famine. The Irish Agricultural Society might well style the potato "the upas tree of Ireland!"

It is to be feared that the continuance of our corn laws will, in course of time, reduce the English peasantry to the potato-dependent condition of the Irish. It is not to be concealed that, year by year, we are becoming more a potato-eating people. Our labouring classes are much more dependent on this root than they used to be; and the proprietors of the soil are doing what they can to increase the dependency. They screw up rents and prices of grain, and fancy they have cleared themselves from blame when they have dealt out allotments (at high rents too!) among their poor labourers, to grow their potatoes upon. Such is the only way of making the English people "independent of foreigners."

They are made dependent on potatoes. And what that is, let the state
of the Irish peasantry answer. "Whatever," says the *League*, "compels
a people to make the very utmost of their own soil that can be made
of it, with the view of keeping in life the *maximum* number of human
beings—drives them to the growing and eating of potatoes. The potato
is the last desperate and miserable solution of the miserable problem,
which a law like our corn law compels a people like the English people
to solve on pain of starvation."—*Leeds Times*.

THE VINDICATOR, BELFAST, 22 OCTOBER 1845

POTATO FAILURE IN INNISHOWEN

A HUMANE LANDLORD

TO THE EDITOR OF THE VINDICATOR

DEAR SIR.—Owing to the frightful ravages made throughout this
barony by the potato plague, Michael Loughrey, Esq, Binion
House, in this parish, sent his bailiff, on Monday last, through
all his tenantry, both in this parish and in Upper Moville, to state that
he will demand no rents at present; and that, should any of the tenants
be obliged to make sale of any part of their crop for other purposes,
he will give them the highest price in the market. Here is an example
worthy of imitation! Would to God that the landlords of Ireland would,
at the present time, walk in the footsteps and follow the praiseworthy
example of Mr. Loughrey. There are other landlords in this locality
sending round their bailiffs, not as messengers of peace and consolation,
but menacing, in the midst of approaching famine and distress, to distrain
and impound if the rent be not immediately paid.

It is not expected, from the rapid progress made by the potato rot
for the last three weeks in this neighbourhood, that the potatoes will
last longer than Christmas: and how are the poor (and they are all
comparatively poor here) to subsist during the remainder of the season,
if they are urged, by relentless landlords or agents, to dispose of their
grain to make up the rents?

The tenantry of Mr. Loughrey, on receiving this consoling
intelligence, assembled in crowds in the different villages, burning bon-
fires in thanksgiving, and pouring prayers and blessings on him, who,

in the hour of distress, afforded such balmy relief to their sorrowing hearts, softened their uneasy pillow, and converted their nights of restlessness and pain, to sleep, happiness, and contentment; whilst the vallies re-echoed with shouts of joy and cheers of gratitude and praise to their benevolent and humane landlord. This is not the only good trait in the character of this exemplary gentleman; he is also charitable, generous, and hospitable; he is as firm and staunch a patriot as Ireland can boast of, his purse is open to every call of his country or his religion, and he is a sincere Christian and practical Catholic.

I will, from time to time, trouble you with an account of how the poor in this barony are treated by some of the landlords and agents. Humanity, in many instances, is lost sight of, and cruelty and oppression the most barefaced practised with impunity. Well may the poor, persecuted Irishman curse the day he came under the misgovernment of English legislation.

AN OBSERVER
Clonmany, 22nd October 1845
THE VINDICATOR, 25 OCTOBER 1845

ADVICE CONCERNING THE POTATO CROP TO THE FARMERS AND PEASANTRY OF IRELAND

The dreadful disease which has attacked your potatoes is one, the effects of which you can only stop by strict attention to the advice of those interested in your welfare. Many plans have been proposed, and, after examining them all, we recommend the following as the best.

All competent persons are of opinion, that the first things to bear in mind are the following directions:—

1. Dig your potatoes in dry weather, if you can, and if you cannot, get them dry somehow as fast as you can.
2. Keep them dry and cool.
3. Keep the bad potatoes separate from the good.
4. Do not pit your potatoes as you have been accustomed to do in former years.

5. Recollect that if they get damp, nothing can make them keep; and do not consider them dry unless the mould which sticks to them is like dust.

6. Do not take them into your houses unless you want them for immediate use.

STORING.—When the potatoes are quite dry, and well sorted, proceed to store them thus:—Mark out on the ground a space six feet wide, and as long as you please. Dig a shallow trench two feet wide all round, and throw the mould upon the space; then level it and cover it with a floor of turf-sods, set on their edges. On this sift or spread very thinly, the dry mixtures, or any of the dry materials described below, and which you may call the *packing stuff*. Also get some dry slacked lime, and dust all the potatoes with it as well as you can. Then put one row of turf-sods laid flat, on the top of the floor, all round the sides, so as to form a broad edge, and within this, spread the dry potatoes, mixed well with the packing stuff, so as not to touch one another. When you have covered the floor in this manner, up to the top of the sods, lay another row of sods all round the first, so that half of each sod may rest on the bed of potatoes, and the other half on the first layer of sods: this will make another edge one sod deep, which must be filled up with dry potatoes, and dry packing stuff, as before. Then lay another edge of sods in the same way, fill it again and so go on till the heap is made. When the building of this pit is finished, it may be covered with sods at the top, and will be ready for thatching. If rightly made, it will look like the roof of a cottage cut into steps, as shown in this sketch, in which *a a a* are sods, and *c c* the ditch all round the heap; potatoes and packing stuff are the white and black spaces in the middle.

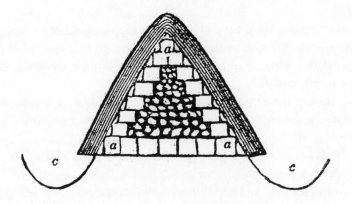

If you do not understand this ask your landlord or your clergyman to explain its meaning, and we are sure that they will give you every assistance; also recollect that the recommendation applies only to sound potatoes, after being well dried.

There will be of course a good deal of trouble in doing all that we have recommended, and perhaps you will not succeed very well at first; but we are confident that all true Irishmen will exert themselves, and never let it be said, that in Ireland the inhabitants wanted courage to meet difficulties against which other nations are successfully struggling.

ROBERT KANE
JOHN LINDLEY
LYON PLAYFAIR
Board Room, Royal Dublin Society,
3rd November, 1845.

DOWNPATRICK RECORDER, 8 NOVEMBER 1845

THE FAMINE

Experienced men have explained the ways and means useful to preserve some remnant of the People's food. Official Commissioners have given us, at least, reports; and humane individuals have stated the exact results of their own experience. Whatever could be done in this direction *is*, therefore, done, or being done.

But who will give us a guide—what Commission will report, on the POLITICAL RESULTS to us and our children (and hence to all coming time, till time is no more) of the pregnant and perilous year that is before us?

Great changes are at hand. They are springing up about us, ripe with opportunities. Whether we shall reap these in a glad harvest, or see them blighted and scattered in hopeless ruin, who can tell us? What Commission will declare?

Without a Government that *can* govern—without a Legislature to legislate on our own soil, our fate may become whatever blind chance determines, if there be not native energy in the country to bring order out of chaos, and give a positive direction to its own future. If there *be* such energy, all may be well.

"Out of the peril and humiliation of the prosperous," says the Spanish proverb, "shall come the good of the poor." And, too surely, the prosperous, as well as the humble, will share this coming calamity. It will fall at once on both extremes of society, on the gay blossoms and the obscure root.

The first blow on the rich will be the inevitable reduction of rents. Heretofore, they have taken from the farmer and peasant *all* but a bare subsistence. They will take *all* but a bare subsistence now again. But that "all" is diminished. The "subsistence" *must* come mainly out of the corn—that is, out of the rent—out of the landlords' revenue.

This thing *must* happen, and never did the strictest poetic justice award a fairer punishment; for it is the landlords, not the blight, that make this famine. In other countries it will be a temporary privation; here it may be an absolute famine, because, living habitually within one degree of starvation, the People can endure no more, but must perish, or fall back on the rents. Thus injustice works its own punishment.

But this is not all. We hear glad shouts and clapping of hands because the Corn Laws must now quickly fall (and let them fall, for they are the crowning evil of a code of robbery). But surely their fall will be another heavy blow upon this country. A multitude of farmers with profitable leases, hundreds of the small gentry may be ruined. In the end all will, perhaps, fall on the great proprietors, but only after wide and bitter suffering. The whole landlord class will suffer a sharp and sudden reverse. The blight has consumed one moiety of agricultural produce; this repeal will be equivalent (as far as their interests are concerned) to a blight of the other also.

"But what of the landlords?" some angry tenant may ask. "Let them suffer." Alas, friend, in this strange net-work of society, one of the hardest problems to resolve is *how* to punish the wicked, without also punishing the innocent. How far this sudden stroke may penetrate from class to class—how deep—how wide—how vital; who can tell? What commission can even pretend to determine?

THE NATION, DUBLIN, 8 NOVEMBER 1845

TO THE FARMERS AND PEASANTRY
OF IRELAND

DIRECTIONS FOR MAKING WHOLESOME FOOD
FROM DISEASED POTATOES

1 st. The potatoes should be well washed with water, so as to cleanse them from all dirt.

2d. Grate down the potatoes by means of a grater, which may be made of a piece of sheet-iron or tin punched up into holes and fastened on a board; or a better machine may be had for four or five shillings, consisting of a cylinder of punched sheet-iron turned by the hand, with a hopper to hold the potatoes. This grater should dip nearly half into a bucket or tub of water, into which the pulp will fall according as it is produced.

3d. When the pulp has settled completely down, pour off the dirty reddish water, and put more fresh water on. Stir up all well together, and then let the pulp settle down again and pour off the liquor. If necessary, this is to be done again, if the liquor comes away reddish or brownish; but two washings will usually be enough to leave the pulp clean and free from the diseased parts, which all go off with the water.

4th. Recollect that the starch is not to be washed out of the pulp, but only the reddish diseased stuff. The starch must be let to settle down along with the pulp, for they are both required in the food.

5th. The wet pulp is then to be taken out of the tub, and is to be freed as well as you can from water, by draining and pressing it. To every three stone weight of this wet pulp is to be mixed one stone of oatmeal, and as much salt as you may think well. The mass is then to be rolled out into a thin cake, and this is to be baked on a griddle until it is quite dry and slightly browned on the outside.

6th. These cakes will keep for a very long time without souring or spoiling, if moderate care be taken to keep them dry. A good way is to put them on a string and hang them up to the ceiling near the fire.

7th. If you do not like to make all the potatoes into this sort of bread, dry the pulp on the griddle without the oatmeal, and do not let it brown. You will then get the pure potato meal, which will keep if you do not let the damp get at it. This meal will serve very well for making broth and soup, and for mixing with oatmeal to make bread.

In this way almost every diseased potato can be made into wholesome food.

THE VINDICATOR, BELFAST, 19 NOVEMBER 1845

THE MANSION HOUSE COMMITTEE

Your Committee report that a public meeting of the citizens and others interested, was called by The Right Honourable JOHN LADAVEZE ARABIN, the LORD MAYOR of the City of Dublin, on the 31st day of October, 1845, at the Music Hall, Abbey-street, to take into consideration the alarming accounts of the failure of the Potatoe crop, at which meeting it was resolved, that a Deputation be formed, consisting of the Right Honourable the LORD MAYOR, His Grace the DUKE OF LEINSTER, The Right Honourable The Lord CLONCURRY, ALDERMAN DANIEL O'CONNEL, M.P., The VERY REVEREND DR. YORE, V. G. & P. P., Rev. Charles Sheridan Young, &c. &c., to prepare and present an Address to HIS EXCELLENCY BARON HEYTESBURY, the Lord Lieutenant of Ireland, laying before His Excellency the awful state the kingdom was likely to become reduced to, if Government did not at once step in to prevent as far as possible, by all human means, the dreadful scourge of anticipated famine and pestilence.

An adjournment of the meeting above mentioned was held on the fourth day of November, 1845, at the same place, to receive the answer of His Excellency to the Address presented by said Deputation on the 1st day of November, 1845.

His Excellency's answer to the Deputation not being considered sufficiently satisfactory, it was resolved that a Committee be appointed to sit daily at the Mansion House, Dawson-street, and be called "The MANSION HOUSE COMMITTEE," each member of said committee to pay Five Pounds to cover the necessary expenses.

In pursuance of that resolution your Committee met at the Mansion House on the 5th day of November, 1845, when the following plan of proceeding was determined on—

First, to inquire into the extent of the calamity.

Second, inquiry as to modes of arresting or curing the disease, and especially as to the practical efficacy of each plan.

Third, modes of alleviation, by the introduction of food, and prevention of loss of food already in the country, and above all, the procuring of employment for the people.

Nos. 1 and 2, to be carried out by the following circular, addressed to the Clergy of all religious denominations, the Lieutenants, Deputy Lieutenants, Sheriffs, and Poor Law Guardians, throughout Ireland, amounting to Three Thousand Five Hundred and upwards: No. 3, to be carried out by

1st—That every effort should be made to increase the quantity of provisions.

2nd—That it is the unanimous opinion of this Committee that the ports should be opened for the free importation of all description of human food.

And resolved—That we forthwith write to Sir R. PEEL, pointing out to him the exact state of this country, and the pressing and imminent danger of famine, and calling on Government to take immediate and efficacious precautions to avert the otherwise certain and impending calamity.

Mansion House, Dawson-st. Dublin,
8th November, 1845.

Sir,

I am requested by the Committee appointed at the late Meeting held in this City, on the 4th instant, the Right Hon. the Lord Mayor in the chair, to submit the following queries for your consideration, and respectfully solicit a reply at your earliest convenience.

I have the honour to be, Sir,

Your obedient servant,

CLONCURRY,

Chairman.

1st—Whether the crop of potatoes was in point of quantity an average crop.

2nd—What proportion of the crop has been already lost to decomposition, or otherwise?

3rd—What is your opinion as to the probability of the remaining portion continuing sound during the year?

4th—What modes of preventing the disease, or of curing it if any, have been found practically efficacious in your district?

5th—Have any, and what modes been used for the above purpose, which have proved inefficacious or injurious?

REPORT OF THE MANSION HOUSE COMMITTEE ON THE POTATO DISEASE
DUBLIN, 1846

SIR ROBERT PEEL'S REPLY TO THE
MANSION HOUSE COMMITTEE

White-hall, November 10th, 1845

MY LORD—I have the honor to acknowledge the receipt of the communication of the 7th of November, which bears your Lordship's signature, earnestly calling the attention of Her Majesty's Government to the calamity with which Ireland is threatened by the failure, through disease, of the Potato crop, and suggesting for the consideration of the Government the following measures, [as already appear in the letter addressed to Sir Robert Peel].

I give full credit to the assurance that in making this communication your Lordship, and all those who are parties to it, are influenced by no other motive than the desire to aid the Government in the efforts which they are making to avert or mitigate the impending evil.

I shall without delay submit this, as I have submitted all other representations which have reached me on this painful subject, to my Colleagues in the service of Her Majesty.

Although considerations of public policy and of public duty prevent me from entering, in this acknowledgment of your Lordship's communication, into a discussion in respect to the advantage of the particular measures recommended for immediate adoption, yet I beg to assure your Lordship that the whole subject is occupying the unremitting attention of Her Majesty's confidential advisers.

I have the honor to be, my Lord,
Your most obedient servant,

ROBERT PEEL.

REPORT OF THE MANSION HOUSE COMMITTEE ON THE POTATO DISEASE

DUBLIN, 1846

THE MANSION HOUSE COMMITTEE

The following were among the latest letters on the potato crop, received by the Mansion-house committee:—

SHANAGOLDEN HOUSE

My Lord—In compliance with your request of the 4th instant, I forward you my answers to your queries as far as came under my notice in this locality:—

First query—Answer—The potato crop was more than an average one in this neighbourhood.

Second query—Answer—In some localities one-half are lost, in others fully one-third, from decomposition.

Third query—Answer—My opinion is, that the disease will progress.

Fourth query—Answer—The only mode of preventing the disease from spreading is by making small heaps and leaving them under stalks or straw, which has not proved efficacious. No cure has been found to prevent its spreading. The crop was nearly all dug out and heaped as above before the commissioners' report came out, and the late heavy rains got through the covering; so now the worst results are apprehended.

Fifth query—Answer—No modes have been used but those mentioned in the fourth query, which have proved inefficacious. Covering with earth immediately after digging has proved very injurious.

I remain, my lord, your obedient servant,

GEORGE VINCENT

Vicar of Shanagolden.

THE NATION, 13 DECEMBER 1845

FURTHER REPORT FROM THE
ARCHITECT TO THE
POOR LAW COMMISSIONERS

RELATING TO TEMPORARY FEVER WARDS

Architect's Office, Poor Law Commission,
Dublin, 22nd December, 1845

GENTLEMEN,

Referring to my Report of the 20th instant, on the subject of providing temporary Fever Hospitals in Union Workhouses. I beg to submit, for the information of your Board, a communication I have this day received, describing the temporary buildings which have been erected and put into use in the Galway Union Workhouse. The buildings being very similar in character to those described in my Report, my chief object in submitting the documents to your Board is to show in what respects those I have recommended for adoption, differ from the buildings which have been already built and occupied.

First, there is a double shed erected in the infirmary yard, in just the same position as shown on my plan (letter B), and recommended

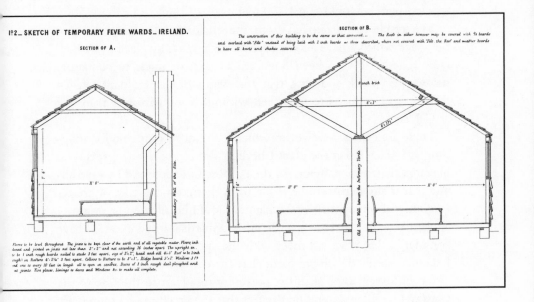

for adoption by my Report. The room erected differs from that I proposed, in being only nine feet wide, and six feet four inches high, instead of eleven feet wide, and seven feet six inches high, in the side-walls, as shown in my sketch.

The room is also without any flooring. I have, however, recommended that boarded floors be used.

In addition to the double shed in the infirmary yard, there has been also a single shed erected in the idiot's yard. This, however, has not been occupied. The double shed building (similar to that marked B in my sketch) appears to have been sufficient.

The cost of the double and single shed is about 100l.; and making allowance for the smaller size of the Galway sheds, and the absence of flooring, it will be satisfactory to your Board to find that the estimate I have given closely approximates to the actual cost of a similar extent of accommodation provided by the sheds in Galway Workhouse.

In the arrangement of the beds, it will be seen that two beds are put together in the sheds at Galway, and a space of one foot eight inches allowed on each side the double beds; this gives less than three feet in width to each bed; and multiplying the width of the building by the height,—namely, nine feet in width by nine feet in height,—a cubical space of 243 feet only has been allowed to each inmate. I have proposed four feet space for each bed; the width of the building being eleven feet, and the height upwards of nine feet six inches, the cubical space to each person would equal 400 feet.

The result to be derived from the enclosed information is, that the space which I have allowed for 45 beds, may, by placing the beds close together (as has been done at Galway), be made to contain as many as 55 beds; and also, that the width of the building (eleven feet) may be reduced to nine feet, without being narrower than that at Galway.

These are changes, however, which I do not recommend for adoption, as I believe that the plans I have made are not in any respect too liberal in their arrangements for the purpose intended; and I would advise that if any departure be made from them, for the sake of greater economy of outlay, that such changes should be allowed to originate altogether with the respective Boards of Guardians. In any case, I have considered that it would meet with the approval of your Board that I should submit the above particulars for consideration.

I avail myself, also, of this opportunity to advert to the case of the Galway Union, as exhibiting the fact that the erection of a temporary fever hospital appears likely, by the continuance of the temporary

49

building, to prevent the erection of a more suitable permanent structure.

    I have, &c.,

GEO. WILKINSON

To the Poor Law Commissioners.

TWELFTH ANNUAL REPORT OF THE POOR LAW COMMISSIONERS

LONDON, 1846

1846

UNION IS STRENGTH.

John Bull.—"HERE ARE A FEW THINGS TO GO ON WITH, BROTHER, AND I'LL SOON PUT YOU IN A
WAY TO EARN YOUR OWN LIVING."

ARE THE IRISH TO STARVE?

As yet, nothing has been done—nothing is being done, nor even in contemplation—calculated to meet, with efficiency, the coming danger. The country seems to be slumbering on the bosom of an earthquake. Politicians and journalists are engaged with discussions on the virtues and the vices of Peel's gigantic scheme of commercial policy;—there is a noise heard about relief, and the people, believing redress is at hand, remain tranquil, in silent expectation;—the public clamours deceive *them*, and *their* silence, being interpreted to mean the absence of danger, deceive the public; and thus we are hourly approaching nearer and nearer to a period when famine, if timely precaution be not used, must set in, with all its horrors—we are rapidly approaching to meet the attack of an enemy, more to be dreaded than armies in battle array, without having made any reasonable preparation...

We do not see any quarter from which we can calculate upon receiving food with certainty...This is just what we expected and feared. Confusion increases as danger draws near: when there is need of action, priceless time is spent in speculation; which, on turn, yields a new supply of barren conjectures.—There is now less hope than ever that the practical question, whence can the millions get food? will be speedily examined and settled...

Even if we had food landed on our shores, there is no machinery arranged for its satisfactory distribution under the extraordinary circumstances.—Did the people obtain employment and money before the famine set in, no difficulty would arise, as the food could be purchased in the usual way; but, if things be left as they are, until law is forced to yield to necessity—until ravenous hunger drives distracted millions to disregard the rights of property—until the rebellion of famine adds to pestilence, social anarchy and a forcible seizing of provisions—until the bonds of society are broken—who, then, will calm the stormy waters?—who will restrain the populace, protect life, and restore order?

THE VINDICATOR, BELFAST, 4 FEBRUARY 1846

Although we are not on the verge of famine in Ireland, as Mr. O'Connell has stated in the House of Commons, yet the fact that there will be scarcity in the summer months, owing to the progress of the potato taint, makes it necessary to consider how any deficiency in food may be supplied. Government, to their credit be it spoken, have not neglected necessary precautions at this emergency. Several bills, which will have the effect of giving employment to the people of Ireland, have been introduced into the House of Commons by Sir Thomas Fremantle, Chief Secretary for Ireland, and they have already made considerable progress in their respective stages.

The first is a bill for the extension of public works in Ireland. It authorizes the commissioners of public works to make additional grants to the extent of £50,000. Government have wisely adopted a suggestion made by the Land Commissioners, in their report, that money advanced for public works should be repaid within twenty years, instead of seven as before, and that the interest be "such as may be agreed upon," not five per cent. as before. This bill has passed the House of Commons.

A second measure of the same useful kind is the Drainage Bill. By this, money will be lent for the purpose of facilitating river drainages. It will enable landlords to improve their estates and give increased employment to the people. The bill has been read a second time.

A third measure is the Fisheries Bill. The object of it is to afford encouragement to the construction of small piers and harbours, calculated to extend the deep fisheries. It is proposed to expend £50,000 in five years upon such profitable works. The bill was read a first time on Monday.

These bills are so many steps in the right direction. They will tend to the improvement of the physical condition of the country. Such measures ought to stop the mouths of agitators; and the peasantry of Ireland are not so devoid of discrimination as not to perceive the difference between an English government which takes means to feed and clothe them, and those who despoil them of their hard-earned pence and shillings.

DOWNPATRICK RECORDER, 7 FEBRUARY 1846

Striding nearer every day,
Like a wolf in search of prey,
Comes the Famine on his way—

Through the dark hill, through the glen,
Over lawn, and moor, and fen,
Questing out the homes of men.

And a Voice cries overhead—
"Rend your hair—the hot tears shed—
Ye shall starve for want of bread.

"Though your wail be long and loud,
Hope for nothing from the Proud;
Dig the grave, and weave the shroud;

"Seek a place where ye may die—
Clench the teeth, and check the sigh—
Hope, but only hope on High.

"When the last hope fades in air,
To your hearts of grief and care,
Thus shall speak the fiend Despair:

'Cord and knife, and river deep,
Open paths for those who weep,
To a sweet and dreamless sleep.

'Though ye shun such thoughts at first,
When each hope you long have nurs'd,
Like a bubble shall have burst,

'Ye shall run to death, though He
Armed with double-terrors be;
Better death than misery.'"

'Tis a fearful sight to see,
Man, the equal and the free,
Kneeling at a Brother's knee;

When he knows a People's might,
Trained, directed, made unite,
Can do all things for their right.

Why then does he wail and weep?
Why does he supinely sleep,
And nor food nor vengeance reap?

'Tis not base and slavish fear
Makes him shun the sword and spear—
'Tis the Faith he holds so dear;

Faith, that turns a trustful eye
To the God that dwells on high,
In the bright and blessed sky.

But when thousands, day by day,
With the Famine pine away,
Will they own religion's sway?

Ah! ye mighty, ponder well;
If wild riot burst its shell,
Who its fearful flight can tell?

Men of wealth, in time be wise,
Lest they gather, with loud cries,
Round your well-fill'd granaries,

As the ravens, hunger hoarse,
Troop around the lifeless corse
Of a fever-stricken horse.

Give the wretched who complain,
And their rage you will restrain
With your love, as with a chain.

Brother, life is but a span—
See thou dost what one man can—
Help a fainting fellow-man;

While the magnates of the land
On their gilded titles stand,
Be thou called the "Open Hand."

And, when life is ended here,
In another, higher sphere,
Voices thus shall greet your ear:

"Without fear to judgment wend—
Here, the wretched toiler's friend,
Tastes the joy that has no end."

HEREMON

THE NATION, DUBLIN, 7 MARCH 1846

THE FAMINE

Mr. Justice Torrens, in opening the Commission at Omagh, incidentally alluded to the alleged failure of the potato crop in the following terms:—"I do not think, Mr. Foreman and Gentlemen, I should have had anything more to say to you respecting your duty as grand jurors, only that I have, this day, received by post, a copy of the statute on which grand jurors may now act in passing extraordinary presentments, and which has just passed the legislature and received the royal assent. It regulates the business usually transacted with contractors, for the purpose of a more ready circulation of money among those classes who are most in want of it, and has, as you are aware, been enacted for the relief of what has been called the starving population of the country. I must say, however, in relation to this subject, that, in passing through the country, I have not been greatly struck by any appearance of starvation or misery which may be said to be abroad.—I have observed the potato fields and the haggards of the farmers of the country as I have passed along, and I really must say—and I feel extremely

58 happy in being enabled to do so—that there is not more than the usual, if so much, appearance of misery or destitution throughout the country."

COLERAINE CHRONICLE, 21 MARCH 1846

GOVERNMENT SALE OF INDIAN CORN AT CORK.

INDIAN CORN IN CORK

On Saturday last, the Government Sales of Indian Corn and Meal commenced in Cork. Immediately on the depôts being opened, the crowds of poor persons who gathered round them were so turbulently inclined as to require the immediate interference of the police, who remained there throughout the day. Among the poor, who were of the humblest description, and needing charitable relief, the sales were but scanty. The occasion had become of necessity; for potatoes have risen to 11d. market price for 14lbs.; and, some of the leading commercial men in Cork have made a calculation, which shows that the Government can afford to sell the Indian Corn at a much cheaper rate. Our artist at Cork has sketched the crowd immediately on the opening of the store.

We feel gratified to learn that a steamer has been despatched from Cork to Dublin, laden with 600 sacks of Indian meal.

One half, by the orders, is to be despatched by the Royal, and the other by the Grand Canal, to the interior. It must be acknowledged that her Majesty's Government are executing their duty promptly and with energy.

The *Cork Examiner* of Tuesday, contains the following account of the sale:—

"The bakers in Dublin are selling India meal bread in large quantities to the better classes, as well as to the poor, and all consider it more palatable than the ordinary whole-meal, or brown bread.

"The price fixed on it was one penny per pound. The result of the day's sale is sufficient to dissipate all further doubt, and to demand the most serious attention of the citizens of Cork.

"We understand that 4480lbs. of the corn meal were sold on Saturday, at one penny per pound.

"The committee waited this morning on Mr. Hewitson, to grant them a further supply, they, of course, offering to pay the full price for it; but Mr. Hewitson was compelled to refuse the request, he having no orders from the Government to that effect.

"The people, supposing that the supply would be continued, assembled in hundreds round the depôts; but were informed of the fact of there being no more for sale. Considerable excitement was occasioned by the announcement, and the Mayor, fearing that a disturbance might arise in consequence, published a public notice, stating that when the order, which was daily expected, should arrive, further supplies would be distributed."

ILLUSTRATED LONDON NEWS, 4 APRIL 1846

THE FAMINE WAR COMMENCED

INCREASE OF DISTRESS—OUTBREAK AT CLONMEL

Letters have reached town to-day announcing that there was an outbreak of the people at Clonmel, the county town of South Tipperary, upon yesterday.—The people, who are reduced to the utmost extremity of distress, and whose bones protruded through

60 the skin which covered them—staring through hollow eyes as if they had just risen from their shrouds, cried out that they could no longer endure the extremity of their distress, and that they must *take* that food which they could not procure, and without which they could not live. They therefore assembled upon yesterday to the number of several hundreds and attacked the extensive and valuable flour mills situate just in the town. These mills are the largest, most valuable and perhaps the best stocked of any in Ireland.—They are the property of several Quaker gentlemen named Grubb, Malcomson, and Hughes. Fortunately, before the people could force their way into the mills the army, consisting of artillery and dragoons, had arrived at the scene of outrage, and succeeded in dispersing the rioters without loss of property, and happily without loss of life.—*Freeman of Tuesday*.

THE *VINDICATOR*, BELFAST, 18 APRIL 1846

FAMINE IN ULSTER

Gradually the fearful evil, hunger, that has long been preying in silence on the poor of Ulster, is attracting the attention of the humane. Lord Londonderry's prayer against relief committees, and the determination of the Grand Jury in Down not to appoint any extraordinary sessions, with some similar proceedings, to show, for Ulster's honour, that hunger had not visited it, stifled appeals for relief; for even the poor tried to make it a point of honour to bear up against destitution. The distress in Ballymacarrett was the first cry of want that unhinged the fine philosophy that would starve the poor for the honour of the rich. Another voice now comes to disturb the composure of those who hate distress, because it is a disgrace to the province, and wonder that persons will not be content to linger, sigh, and die in silence, sooner than sully the credit of Ulster. This wailing comes from Lisburn and its neighbourhood. A writer, whom the *Whig* calls a respectable correspondent, observes:—

"I believe that the wealthy inhabitants of this locality will not admit that distress (arising from non-employment) exists to any great extent. Should this indifference continue, there is no course left, for those who are suffering, but to resort to such steps as will force attention to their situation."

Of 285 looms in the neighbourhood, the *Whig*'s correspondent states that 164 are idle, and that it is very probable the remainder will soon be idle also, and that the people have nothing past them to live on. This mass of human misery is on the fertile estate of the Marquis of Hertford, an absentee landlord, who abstracts not less than seventy thousand yearly from Ireland. Would it be too much to expect he would send nine or ten thousand of such a large sum, to keep the life in the poor who labour to produce it for him?

THE *VINDICATOR*, BELFAST, 22 APRIL 1846

IMPERIAL PARLIAMENT

HOUSE OF COMMONS—FRIDAY, APRIL 17

The house to-day resumed its sittings after the Easter recess.
The SPEAKER took the chair at 4 o'clock.

DISTRESS IN IRELAND

MR. D. BROWNE wished to put a question to the right hon. baronet at the head of the government, to which, as it related to a matter of vital importance, he hoped no objection would be made on the ground that he had not given any notice.—What he wanted to know was, whether the right hon. baronet had received any official intelligence sufficient to convince him of the deplorable condition in which several parts of Ireland were placed from the want of sufficient food to support existence. Some accounts had become public, which stated that in some places the people had assembled in large numbers, had broken into mills, taking from them large quantities of corn and meal, and also attacking cars laden with flour, from which they also took a part of the contents. In other instances they attacked boats laden with corn and flour, part of which they had taken off, and it was said that they would have proceeded to greater lengths, but for the interposition of the civil and military authorities. He would ask, if, with such intelligence in their possession, the government had taken immediate steps for relieving the distress from which this violence had arisen? He had no wish whatever to embarrass the government as to the course they had taken or were about to take; but he thought it would be satisfactory to the public mind to know that active measures were in progress to relieve the fearful state to which the people were reduced by the famine which now prevailed in many places.

Sir ROBERT PEEL said, that the government had been informed of the circumstances to which the hon. member had alluded. There was no doubt that, on the whole, the people bore their distress with great patience; but disturbances had broken out in some places which had been repressed, and some of the authors of it taken into custody. He had long before this expressed his fears as to the coming distress, and the consequent necessity of taking active measures for facilitating the access of a supply of food to those districts where it was required.

PROTECTION OF LIFE (IRELAND) BILL

Upon Sir J. GRAHAM's moving that the orders of the day for the first reading of the Protection of Life (Ireland) Bill be read,

Mr. W.S. O'BRIEN made an appeal to the government on the deplorable condition of Ireland.—The people of that country were dying by starvation. Several verdicts had been returned by the juries serving on coroners' inquests to that effect.—In Kilkenny, and in Clare, the suffering was more intense than in any part of the country. In Cork and Waterford the distress was nearly as bad, and the prospect of the future was even worse than the present. He gave full credit to the government for their prudent forethought, in causing a large portion of Indian meal to be imported; but he wished to hear some explanations of the reasons which had induced the government, after it had distributed a certain quantity of that meal at Cork at reduced prices, to withhold a further supply of it. Did the government intend to withhold it until the whole country was one mass of distress and famine? If so, the government would have to deal with starving multitudes who would rather be shot than perish of starvation. After alluding to the riots which had taken place at Tipperary and Clonmel, where corn and flour had been taken away to a large amount, he asked whether there was in existence a fund adequate to the relief of the present awful state of famine? Sir James Graham had told them, on a former occasion, that he relied much on local aid for its relief. No doubt he might rely on the resident landlord, but why not place a tax for local objects on the absentee landlord;—The workhouse system could not and ought not to be relied on in such an emergency as the present. Surely the government ought to see that those who were willing to work had the means of procuring subsistence. (Cries of hear, hear.) After showing that the Drainage Act, the Public Works Act, the Grand Jury Presentment Act, and the Fisheries' Act could

not be rendered available for the relief of the existing distress, he expressed
his regret that the government had deemed it necessary to combine the
relief of just distress with the repeal of the corn-laws, as it had prevented
many persons who would otherwise have combined with the government from co-operating with it. The government ought also to have
disconnected the measures of coercion from those of a remedial
character.—An Irish Parliament would then have assembled in
November, and would then have considered the measures necessary to
meet a foreseen calamity.—Government must be held responsible for
all the loss of life which might occur from the scarcity of food, and for
all the outbreaks which might be occasioned by it.

Sir JAMES GRAHAM thought that he could not be accused either of
having concealed or having underrated the sad calamity with which
Ireland was at present afflicted. Nothing but the extremity of the present emergency would justify the measures of government in attempting to feed the entire people under the sudden calamity of approaching
famine; for its machinery was not adequate to any such object. No official account had yet been received of the occurrence of any death from
destitution. When it was stated that distress was now endangering life
in Ireland, it ought to be remembered that there were workhouses
throughout Ireland, and that in no one instance were they full.—It was
true that the government had ordered a large importation of Indian corn;

64   but it was not for the purpose of meeting the entire wants of the Irish people, but for the purpose of checking the markets and of preventing the price of corn from being unduly enhanced. (Hear, hear.) If the people of Ireland were starving in the midst of plenty, it was utterly impossible for the government alone to meet such an emergency, unless its efforts were assisted by the proprietors of the soil and the richer portion of the community. As Mr. S. O'Brien had asked him what the government had done, he would take the liberty of asking that gentleman in return what the landlords of Ireland had done? Government had done its very utmost. Had the landlords of Ireland done the same? After stating how far the different measures of government had failed and succeeded, he informed the house that the Irish government had been desired to investigate all the propositions made for new public works, and to undertake new public works, even if the sum granted for them was insufficient for their completion; for at a future period of the session, he should apply to parliament with confidence for any advance which might be necessary beyond the amount now specified in the public works act. He thought that an Irish parliament could not have dealt with a case of this description more generously than the British parliament had done. He hoped that the discussion on the first reading of this bill would now be allowed to proceed.

COLERAINE CHRONICLE, 2 MAY 1846

FAMINE

A letter from the special correspondent of the *Morning Chronicle* has appeared in that journal, dated April 20, from Limerick, detailing very minutely the result of a visit to the parish of Adare, the property of the Earl of Dunraven. He found at the very gates of this nobleman, among the labourers employed in the building of his "castle," destitution so complete, "that he could not make any one in England comprehend it." The houses are described as utterly unfurnished, save "a wretched apology for a bed, with a rag for covering," and the women as "bundles of rags." Some of the men, who were working for 7½d. a-day, had not tasted food up to the hour at which he saw them. In one cabin, of the smallest size, were domesticated fourteen persons, young and old; some slept on straw on the wet floor; some on a couple of dirty boards, with a few rags on them, which they called 65

beds. Two of the children were lying very ill, without assistance of any kind. They were paying 5d. a stone for diseased potatoes when they could scrape together a few pence; but, as they had no work, this was of rare occurrence, and the whole family might be said to be living on casual charity. The earl, to relieve the distress, had purchased half a ton of Indian meal, which was retailed at *two pence per pound* to his starving tenantry. This nobleman contrives to squeeze from the "roofless cabins" and elsewhere nearly 40,000*l.* a-year.

THE NATION, DUBLIN, 2 MAY 1846

FAMINE IN GALWAY

The remote portions of the county Galway are in a state of the most appalling destitution—whole families having neither employment of any kind nor the means of existence.

At a meeting of the inhabitants of Kinvara, to adopt immediate measures to relieve the pressing distress of that locality, the chairman stated that there were hundreds of their fellow-beings in the town and vicinity who had not a single day's support for themselves or their families, and unless something was done to assist them it was awful to contemplate the consequences likely to follow.

Captain Butler agreed with the chairman that distress of the most acute kind prevailed, and suggested a memorial to the Lord Lieutenant.

The Rev. Mr. Arthur said that while they were waiting for relief from the government (who appeared very tardy in affording relief to any district), the people would starve for want of the common necessaries of life. That very day he attended a family in fever who had no better drink than water—who had been reduced to that pitch of poverty, from very comfortable circumstances, in consequence of having lost all their potatoes by the rot.

A committee was appointed to carry out the objects of the meeting.

THE NATION, DUBLIN, 16 MAY 1846

POTATO DISEASE

A correspondent from Clogher informs us that the ravaging blight of the potato disease has done its work on the rising crops in his locality. He says that "in this parish an almost universal failure has already taken place. There is not a field which is not either totally or at least partially blasted. I do think that one-half of the crop is at present unfit for human use. In many instances the very swine, even when hungry, have refused to partake of the diseased potatoes."

THE VINDICATOR, BELFAST, 12 AUGUST 1846

ALMS FOR IRELAND

This day ends the Commission of one set of Government "Relief Commissioners." To-day they close their office, balance their books, and retire from their labours. The distress arising from *last* year's deficient potato crop is passed by: the state alms-givers shut their doors; because it is the 15th of August, and the new crop ought to be ready—the earth *ought* to be crowned with abundance.

And on this very day a cry of Famine, wilder and more fearful than ever, is rising from every parish and county in the land. Where the new crop ought to be, there is a loathsome mass of putrefaction: the sole food on which millions of men, women, and children were to be fed, is stricken by a deadly blight before their eyes; and probably within one month those millions will be *hungry* and have nothing to eat.

Yes; there have been, by this time, accounts received from every county in Ireland; and they all concur in representing the blight as being, even at this early period of the season, almost universal; for one family which needed relief during the past season there will now be three. Last year Government had to bethink themselves how to provide against a very general deficiency—this year they will have to consider how a starving nation is to be fed. All Relief Commissioners—all Commissioners of Public Works—Drainage Commissioners—Poor Law Commissioners—whatever machinery of public alms-giving there is, must not only be continued in operation, but get all powers, means, and appliances increased and extended; and it will be well, indeed, if with all possible efforts and furtherances in this direction, they may be enabled to stay the advancing Plague, and rob Death of his prey.

THE NATION, DUBLIN, 15 AUGUST 1846

THE POTATO PLANT.

THE POTATO CROP OF ULSTER

A friend writes to inform us of the state of the potato crop in Ulster. In the course of an excursion through Down, Antrim, Derry, Tyrone, Armagh, and Monaghan, he met with only two fields of potatoes still green. All the rest were, to all outward appearance, utterly destroyed, the leaves and stalks having a black coloured appearance, as if scorched up by fire. Of the two exceptions above referred to, one was on the Cave Hill, near Belfast; the other in the neighbourhood of

Glenarm. So much for the appearance presented by the fields. As for the roots themselves, in Down a few remained fit for use, but of so indifferent quality that in other years they would have been called "pigs' potatoes." In almost every other place visited by our tourist, potatoes

were not brought to table at all. At the hotels in the county Antrim rice is now customarily used in their stead. In the poorer districts it was quite heart-rending to see the wives and children of the peasantry vainly labouring to pick out of large creels full of the diseased roots a few not absolutely rotten, to maintain for another day their miserable existence. In short, the potato crop in this part of the country is gone. In the midst of this general desolation, one curious exception occurred. At Castleblayney, in Mrs. Rule's excellent hotel, "P.F." was surprised and gladdened to find potatoes at dinner, which "smiled as they were wont to smile" in former and happier years. Their flavour, too, proved excellent. On inquiry, it appeared that these potatoes had been planted in the beginning of January, and had been manured with horse-dung. Their stalks and leaves were blasted, as in other cases; but the roots had previously attained nearly to maturity, and up to this time the great proportion of them has remained sound.

DISEASED STEM.

THE NATION, DUBLIN, 19 SEPTEMBER 1846

TO THE LANDLORDS OF IRELAND

MY LORDS AND GENTLEMEN—You will, I trust, pardon me for claiming a few minutes of your time; the more especially as the subject on which I purpose to address you concerns your own interests. I am, it is true, one of the least distinguished of your body; but I am convinced you will not so much regard the insignificance of the advocate as the importance of the topic to which he solicits your attention.

I respectfully invite you to consider the present condition of Ireland; 69 to consider your own prospects, and to ask yourselves is there any mode open to you whereby you may essentially and permanently benefit both?

I venture to suggest that there *is* such a mode. The mode I propose to your consideration is, that you should enrol yourselves members of the Repeal Association, and work with that body for the restoration of the national legislature of Ireland. In other words, that you should struggle to recover for yourselves and for your countrymen, the exclusive control of your and their concerns; which, for the last forty-six years have been mismanaged by foreigners, always incompetent, and often hostile.

It may be asked, Why agitate Repeal at a period when our attention is engrossed by the heavy dispensation with which Providence afflicts the land? I answer—Because the Union is essentially connected with all Irish distress, either as a cause or as an aggravation. It is the direct source of much of the evil that our country suffers; and it aggravates all evils that spring from other sources, by diminishing or annihilating our power of self-protection.

The failure in the potato crop strongly illustrates the imperative necessity for home legislation. There is no self-governed country, the great majority of whose inhabitants habitually subsists on the lowest and worst sort of food, so as to leave nothing to fall back upon if that worst sort of food should be destroyed. And in no self-governed country do the sufferers in periods of scarcity experience, from any portion of their fellow-subjects, the heartless barbarity with which a part of the English press has treated the starving Irish population.

When the Repealers have assailed the Union as the source of national disaster, how have they been met? With allegations of the vast prosperity of Ireland—of her increasing wealth; and of the rapidly advancing comfort and happiness of her people.

Many of you implicitly believed those audacious falsehoods. You were predisposed to believe them in spite of your senses—partly by your prejudices, which led you to grasp at any statements that antagonised the assertions of O'Connell and his confederates. Many of you, also, were predisposed to believe that all went well with the people of Ireland, because matters went well with yourselves individually; for there is a strong propensity to consider other men's grievances apocryphal, when we are so fortunate as to have none of our own.

Well, it was alleged that the Irish people were so prosperous that they needed no Repeal. There were thousands of you ready to swear it. But what says Lord John Russell in his speech introducing the measure of relief? Why this—That the misery of the Irish masses is proved by the government commissioners to be excessive and nearly universal; that it almost transcends credibility, and that a vast proportion of our people are *ordinarily* destitute of the means to procure food. Mark, the Premier gives this fearful description of our state *as it has existed in past years*; and without reference to the awful visitation that has now overtaken us. The hired quacks, whose business was to write down and talk down Repeal, proclaimed, with brazen effrontery, our prevalent prosperity. The Prime Minister of England now proclaims our prevalent destitution.

It was impossible, Landlords of Ireland, that this appalling condition of affairs should not ultimately touch yourselves. The state of Ireland was like a rapidly extending gangrene which daily encroached upon the sound and healthy portion of the political body. It needed but a season of unusual dearth to precipitate the crisis. That crisis has arrived; and I earnestly implore, in a frank and friendly spirit, your best considera- tion of the duties which, as it appears to me, now devolve upon you. At a recent landlord-meeting in Cork, Mr. Sarsfield declared that the maltreatment of Ireland by England would tend more to make con- verts to Repeal than all the speeches in Consiliation Hall. I understand that Lord Mountcashel has expressed a similar sentiment. I am glad they have made the discovery. I tell them that the very nature of the con- nexion of the two countries *necessitates* the maltreatment of Ireland by England. It necessitates the intolerable pecuniary drain which leaves Ireland exhausted and helpless in the present emergency; it necessitates the suppression of Ireland's right to legislate for her own concerns; it substitutes the stranger for the native, in the management of Irish af- fairs; it consigns us, bound hand and foot, to alien control—of all which maltreatment the landlord body are henceforth likely to taste some of the worst fruits, unless they shake off their party prejudices, and com- bine in a vigorous and healthful effort for their country.

LETTER FROM W.J. O'NEILL DAUNT, ESQ., OF KILCASAN, COUNTY CORK, RE-PUBLISHED BY ORDER OF THE LOYAL NATIONAL REPEAL ASSOCIATION,

25 SEPTEMBER 1846

"GIVE US FOOD"

"Give us food, or we perish," is now the loudest cry that is heard in this unfortunate country. It is heard in every corner of the island—it breaks in like some awful spectre on the festive revelry of the licentious rich—it startles and appals the merchant at his desk, the landlord in his office, the scholar in his study, the lawyer in his stall, the minister in his council-room, and the priest at the altar. "Give us food, or we perish." It is a strange popular cry to be heard within the limits of the powerful and wealthy British empire. It is a cry not heard where civilisation is unknown. The red man of America flies before the advance of social life—slays the bison that grazes the prairie over which he roams, and fattens on untaxed, spontaneous plenty;—the sable son of Africa hunts in forests that own no lord but the Lord on high, and finds enough in their shadowy glades to raise him above the degradation of the cry of British subjects—"Give us food, or we perish;"—the Arab has his steed, his liberty, and fruit trees;—the Icelander his reindeer, its milk, and heaven's fee simple inheritance of the right to fish in the lakes and seas of his native land. No where round the world, from Pole to Pole, but within the limits of Britain's boasted empire, are millions reduced to the necessity of raising a public clamour of appealing to charity for the first necessary of existence—food. In other countries, there are wants—wants of valuable, social institutions—wants of arts and sciences—wants in laws, in education, in comforts, refinements, and luxuries; in the British empire alone, in isolated Ireland alone, is there a want of the necessaries of life. Russia wants liberty, Prussia wants a constitution, Switzerland wants religion, Spain wants a king, Ireland alone wants food. The public cry in every other country argues an advance in the social system; the public cry in ours betokens and presupposes a state of misery unknown on the other side of civilisation—a deepest depth of human wretchedness, to which the tame slave of the "white face" and the wild man of the woods are utter strangers. "*Give us food, or we perish!*" Social life, if properly managed, could not yield such a national cry. From barbarity it could not spring. Nothing but a state of being, in which the crimes of civilisation and barbarity had united to banish the virtues of both, could reduce a whole nation to a huge, untended poor-house, from which one only prayer ascends— "*Food; food; give us food, or we perish!*"

THE VINDICATOR, BELFAST, 3 OCTOBER 1846

CONFIDENCE BETWEEN
MAN AND MAN

The great tendency among public men of all parties in Ireland, to look to parliament and the government of the day, as the source from whence relief is to be expected, must be regarded as a great evil. It evinces a want of self-dependence, it betokens a want of moral training, and until it be in some sort modified, forbids us to hope for effectual improvement. The wisdom of the legislature and the beneficent intentions of the minister, important as it is that such wisdom and such beneficent intentions should exist, play but a secondary part in the development of the resources of a nation ... It is, therefore, especially desirable, that the relations of landlord and tenant in Ireland, should be placed upon a better than its present footing; the real interest of all parties, excepting the mere grievance monger, with whom no one would sympathise, would be promoted by it, and the country would become prosperous from the only sure source of prosperity—confidence between man and man.

DUBLIN UNIVERSITY MAGAZINE, OCTOBER 1846

The accounts which reach us from several localities in Ulster represent distress as becoming general, and, in many instances, heart-rending. It is time that, in every district, the humane should be actively engaged in making preparations to meet the spreading calamity. The subjoined communications prove that not even is Belfast or the county of Down—the two places in Ireland in which it was least expected the famine would immediately set in—free from the common misfortune:—

TO THE EDITOR OF THE VINDICATOR

SIR,—The number of poor who are at present going about this town saying that they are starving, is truly distressing. All that the inhabitants have in their power to do should be done, to ensure the certainty that none need die of hunger, and, at the same time, to secure themselves from imposition. The best means of accomplishing this object would be, it appears to me, to commence a subscription forthwith, for the purpose of establishing a depot, where any one might, on application, procure a comfortable meal, to be eaten on the spot. If the food was not allowed to be taken away, few would apply who were not actually in want; and it would be an unspeakable relief to know that all who are in want could obtain food. Should this suggestion meet with approbation, no time should be lost in calling a public meeting, to carry this or some similar plan into execution. I know of many of our townspeople who are both able and desirous to forward such a plan.

The immediate insertion of this letter in your journal will greatly oblige.

AN INHABITANT
Belfast, October 22, 1846

FAMINE IN COUNTY DOWN
TO THE EDITOR OF THE VINDICATOR

DEAR SIR,—I have not troubled you for a length of time with anything relative to the state of the poor in and about the Seven Towns; indeed, it appeared almost an act of supererogation to talk of their condition at all, seeing that it could not be worse than that of their fellow-sufferers in other parts of the county; nor would I refer to it now but that there seems to be a total disregard, or, to say the least of it, apathy, on the part of the wealthy of the district in question. We had a relief meeting in Castlewellan, to be sure, but, literally speaking, nothing was done. The landlords were, as they ever have been, absent when either honour or duty calls; let it not be disguised, there is no real sympathy among them for the starving people. Mr. Moore tested them to the core, and showed that what I have stated is a simple fact. The able-bodied men are going about idle; every day adds to their misery. Their wives and children are becoming feeble and weak, through sheer hunger. Owing to the extraordinary wetness of the season, turf cannot be procured— coals are out of the question, and the poor have thus the double pressure of hunger and cold to bear up against; while the rich wrap themselves up in their own importance, and shun their dependants as a plague. The continual cry among the small farmers is, "What in the world are we to do!" The rent is being called for, in some instances, with merciless perseverance. Add the prospect of being turned out of their holdings, to that of depriving themselves of the means of sustenance, and you will be able to form an opinion of the feelings of the poor farmers in this district. The bodings of the cottiers and day labourers are melancholy in the extreme; their accustomed food is gone, and no substitute forthcoming. Their usual wages would require to be trebled to be of any sufficient service whatever; it is provokingly barbarous to offer them 8d or 10d per day, and yet none of the farmer class is able to pay more. My own impression is, that a regular list of all the landlords of the locality should be made out, and each of them called on to attend another meeting, to be convened in the same place, as soon as possible, so as to see their tenants in person, and hear what is the real state of the question. It will not pass to "shab" away to England, with their people's money in their pockets, and leave them to the tender mercies of heartless, ignorant bog-bailiffs, and screwing agents, whose pay depends on the amount wrung from the unfortunate class committed to their charge.

A COUNTY DOWN MAN

Castlewellan, October 22, 1846

We have no doubt that the Lord Lieutenant will, in compliance with the request of the resolution passed at the late meeting in Castlewellan, order an Extraordinary Presentment Sessions for the district to which our correspondent alludes. But, as experience proves that the fruit of Presentment Sessions ripens but slowly for the people, a relief committee should be formed, if such is not already done, to provide for the immediate support of the hunger-bitten poor, and call upon the heartless 75 landlords, whom "A County Down Man" reproves, for subscriptions to aid in the generous work of rescuing them from death by destitution.

THE VINDICATOR, BELFAST, 24 OCTOBER 1846

DISTRESS—STARVATION—DEATH!

AWFUL STATE OF NENAGH

The number of families on the relief list of the Nenagh committee is six hundred and seventeen—the average number of each family is six; thus making three thousand seven hundred and two destitute persons in the town of Nenagh receiving meal under first cost. There are in the Nenagh Union Workhouse at present between seven hundred and eight hundred persons; the number is augmenting every week; and with the present prospects, we should not wonder if the house were crowded beyond the number for which it was built, namely, one thousand, within three or four weeks. Meanwhile, starvation presents its fearful appearance in many districts; and the wail of despair is commencing to be heard!

The Rev. Mr. Stoney, rector of Castlebar, writes in reference to the wretched victims of hunger in his district:—"Never has such a calamity befallen our country. The whole staff of life is swept away; the emaciated multitudes are to be seen looking in vain for food, with hunger depicted in their countenance."

DEATH BY STARVATION!!!

We (*Tipperary Vindicator*) have received the following truly afflicting and terrible statement from the Rev. Cornelius O'Brien, the respected parish priest of Lorha and Durrow:—

SIR,—I have to inform you of another victim of starvation. A coroner's inquest was held on the lands of Redwood, in the parish of Lorha, on yesterday, the 24th, on the body of Daniel Hayes, who for several days subsisted almost on the refuse of vegetables, and went out on Friday morning in quest for something in the shape of food, but had not gone far when he was obliged to lie down, and melancholy to relate was found dead some time afterwards. He was well able to work before starvation fastened upon him, and plenty of public works were struck in the neighbourhood by the 'extraordinary road sessions,' but not yet commenced. How long, Mr. Editor, are we to be deluded by this neglect? Our relief committee has been formed and sanctioned three weeks, and the names of persons in need of employment returned to the proper officers; but scarcely any notice has been taken of our returns. Ere many days I fear there must be need of an increase of coroners and a decrease of civil engineers, if matters go on in this way—Yours truly,

CORNELIUS O'BRIEN

Lakeen, October 25, 1846

THE VINDICATOR, BELFAST, 31 OCTOBER 1846

SUSPENSION OF PUBLIC WORKS
IN CLARE

TO THE INHABITANTS OF THE BARONY OF UPPER TULLA, COUNTY OF CLARE, AND THE ADJOINING DISTRICTS

The Lord Lieutenant has learned with the deepest concern that occurrences have taken place in the barony of Tulla, and part of the adjacent districts, which have obstructed the operation of those means of employment for the labouring poor in their present distress which the legislature intended to afford. Large presentments have been made for public works in that barony, a great proportion of which (exceeding 20,000*l*.) has already received the approval of the proper authorities.

His Excellency looked with confidence to the commencement and progress of those works, as affording to the industrious and well-disposed the means of immediate employment, and a prospect of continued support during the approaching winter. Competent officers were provided and employed in the necessary arrangements for setting the works in operation, some of which have already commenced.

His Excellency has, however, learned that the preparations made have for the present been frustrated by a system of insubordination and outrage, which endangers the lives of the officers and overseers, and deters the poor and peaceable inhabitants from labouring on the works.

The Lord Lieutenant desires most earnestly to point out to the people the serious consequences to themselves from such a course of conduct. The obstruction of officers in the discharge of their duties creates, in the first instance, confusion and alarm; it has the ulterior effect, already apparent, of necessarily suspending all further progress in the works; and, combined with the outrages committed on private persons and property, must preclude any attempt for the continued employment of the destitute poor. The works in the district have, in consequence, been suspended.

Ample arrangements have been made, and all the powers placed at the disposal of the executive will be exerted for preserving the lives and properties of the peaceable inhabitants, repressing outrage, and bringing to justice the disturbers of the public peace and the perpetrators of crime. But his Excellency would hope that the good sense of the people will resume its influence—that they will see the folly and the crime they are guilty of in thus wantonly interfering with the means provided *for the support of the destitute* in this time of distress, and that he will have the satisfaction of receiving full assurance of their return to a better course of conduct—of their cordial acquiescence in the arrangement made for their employment, and of their determination to refrain from further obstruction or injury to persons engaged in laying out or superintending the public works.

His Excellency will then gladly direct the immediate resumption of those works, in the conviction that they will prove the means of preserving the people from that destitution and ruin which a perseverance in their past line of conduct must, he fears, inevitably produce.

By his Excellency's command,

T.N. REDINGTON

Dublin Castle, 21 November 1846

THE NATION, DUBLIN, 7 NOVEMBER 1846

TO THE MAGISTRATES
AT PETTY SESSIONS

GENTLEMEN—His Excellency's attention having been directed to the frequent outrages committed by armed parties in various parts of the country, and to the appearance of persons armed, as well by day as by night, to the terror and alarm of her Majesty's subjects, and who, there is good reason to believe, do not bear arms for any legitimate purpose—I am directed by the Lord Lieutenant to state, for your information and guidance, that:

Under 15 and 16 Geo. III., c. 21, p. 2 (the Whiteboy Act), any person or persons being armed with fire-arms, firelock, pistol, or any offensive weapon, who shall rise, assemble, or appear by day or by night, to the terror of her Majesty's subjects, is guilty of a high misdemeanour, and punishable by fine and imprisonment.

This section is still in force, and there can be no doubt that, in a district where outrages have been committed of a Whiteboy character, any person so appearing may be committed under this section, unless it be shown that he was out on a lawful occasion.

By the 6th section, every magistrate or any other peace officer, within the limits of his jurisdiction, is authorised to apprehend, disperse, or oppose any person or persons so appearing armed.

This section should be acted upon if there is reason to think that the parties are not in arms on some lawful occasion, and more especially at night, when there is less reason to suppose that such is the fact; but whenever the parties are distinctly known to the police, informations should be sworn against them, upon which they should be arrested, and if the case require it, be committed for trial. If the person or persons so appearing armed are not known, or if, being known, there be an apprehension that he or they are engaged in the prosecution of some illegal act, the constables would be authorised to arrest them, and bring them before a magistrate.

His Excellency is desirous of calling the attention of the magistrates and peace officers to the provisions of the law with respect to persons appearing armed, and the power which it gives of punishing those who, by such conduct, create terror and alarm in the minds of the well-disposed; and he trusts that, by a vigilant and prudent application of those enactments, the proceedings to which he had referred may be effectually checked.

You may rely upon the cordial support of his Excellency in your efforts to prevent the right of carrying arms for lawful objects, which every Irishman now possesses, from being perverted to purposes which are contrary to law and dangerous to the peace of the country.

I have the honor to be, gentlemen, your obedient servant

H. LABOUCHERE

DUBLIN CASTLE, 3 DECEMBER 1846

Emigration.

For Sydney, New South Wales,
TO CALL AT HOBART'S TOWN,
AND SAIL FROM BELFAST DIRECT,

THE New Brig E M M A, in preparation to class A 1 at Lloyd's, will Sail in all December (the day of intended Sailing will be advertised at a future period).

This Vessel will be fitted up in a very superior manner for the accommodation of Passengers, and every attention will be paid to their comfort, in the finding of suitable Stores for the Voyage.—Apply to

SINCLAIR & BOYD, Donegall-quay.
1st December.   (62

THE EVILS OF EMIGRATION

Our paper of Monday contained a set of resolutions by the guardians of Kilrush Union, in which the government is urged to devise and carry into effect some plan of extensive emigration, as a remedy for Irish evils. Kilrush is in the county of Clare, in which one-third of the adult male population is receiving pauper allowance, under the name of government employment. No wonder that the guardians should be anxious to rid themselves of this terrible incubus, which, if it continues a single year, bids fair to imbue the whole labouring population with the feelings of sturdy beggars for the remainder of the present generation at least. But it is a wonder that people shou'd persist for ever in looking five thousand miles off for what they have at their doors. The Kilrush guardians would not send their sheep or their oxen across the Atlantic to graze, when there is ample pasture on the other side of the brook. Why is there a different rule for human beings? Why so anxious to send fellow-creatures out of sight, where their success can be a benefit to nobody but themselves—where no one can be either taught or inspired by their example? A large body of the peasantry are to be drafted off and made comfortable, or put in the way of making themselves so, by giving them land, we suppose, and tools to cultivate it. Is there any peculiar propriety in selecting the Antipodes as the scene of this very simple work of justice and beneficence? Is the light that is to be kindled one that should be hid under a bushel? Ought it not rather to be made to shine before men?

We are as favourable as any one to measures for facilitating emigration. We think that all persons who desire to remove to the colonies should have every kind of information given them for their guidance, and every needless difficulty removed from their path. We would have the system of landed property and the distribution of population in the colonies so regulated as to afford the greatest possible field of employment for emigrant labour. We would give every facility to the formation of a colonial fund for importing labour from the mother country; and we would even advance for the purpose, from the national treasury, any sum which the colonies desired, and could be expected to repay. We would do everything in aid and support of *voluntary* emigration; but that which is now urged upon the government is compulsory—for what compulsion is stronger than that in which the alternative is starvation?—*Morning Chronicle*

THE VINDICATOR, BELFAST, 9 DECEMBER 1846

PUBLIC WORKS

RELIEF DEPARTMENT

Board of Public Works, 9th Dec., 1846

The employment of the destitute on roads and other public works must soon terminate, and reproductive works be substituted for them. To render such works really beneficial and morally useful, the landed proprietors must join hand in hand with the Board of Works. Every proprietor or farmer will be interested in the practical success of some local work, and as the number will be great, the success will be

in proportion to the zealous co-operation which the board may 81
receive.

Works connected with thorough draining and subsoiling with the spade must be executed systematically and calmly—no external force, no hurry, can be admitted. The number of labourers required for each particular work can be accurately known, and each individual labourer should have a task allotted to him, say, sufficient for a fortnight or three weeks.

To enable each labourer to till his own farm, or that of a neighbouring farmer, and at the same time earn the support of his family through employment on drainage works, it is proposed that the task to be allotted to each labourer should consist of a certain length of drain, and the collection and breaking of stones for the drain; where the stones are to be gathered from the same or neighbouring fields, the children of the labourer may be employed by him in collecting them into heaps, and if sufficiently near, depositing them on the side of the drain cut by the father.

If, with the assistance of his children, the task, sufficient for a fortnight, be completed in six or eight days, the labourer will receive his money and be at liberty to devote the remainder of the fortnight to farm labour, and still will have earned sufficient to support his family until the time arrives for commencing a second task, and so on.

To render the drainage works substantially beneficial to the landed proprietors, it is necessary that the most approved system of thorough draining should be adopted. To effect this object, the commissioners of public works mean to appoint district inspectors of drainage, whose duty will be, in the first instance, to examine the site of every work presented for; to determine the extent of land to be drained, and mark its boundaries on the ordnance plans; to lay out the works connected with the main or open drains; to determine the depth and all the detail belonging to the covered drains; to estimate the cost of the drainage per acre; to value the land in its present state, and give his opinion as to the increased value which will result from the drainage; and report on the whole to the commissioners.

During the time occupied by the inspector of drainage in the performance of this duty, the landed proprietor, the agent, or steward, should attend for the purpose of receiving instructions as to the particular works to be executed in each case, and should recommend suitable persons who may be employed as local overseers to carry them out.

The stewards or farmers, as the case may be, to act without salary;

but the local overseers recommended by them, when approved of by the inspector of drainage, will be paid according to their qualifications and exertions.

The sanction of the treasury having been received for the drainage works of any district, and the number of labourers to be employed in each determined, on due notice being given to the relief inspecting officer of the Board of Works, he will name labourers for each from the list of the destitute residing within the electoral division or barony, as is usual for the road works; and it is expected that the landed proprietors, farmers, and stewards connected with each work will use every exertion to scrutinise the list of the destitute, to insure that none who have other means of support be employed. The land will be assessed for the expenditure, and, consequently, the admission of persons not requiring relief, by adding to the number, will proportionably increase the assessment; hence it becomes the interest as well as the duty of all cess-payers to limit the admission of labourers to those who are wholly destitute.

By order,
JOS. C. WALKER
Secretary

DOWNPATRICK RECORDER, 19 DECEMBER 1846

EMPLOYMENT OF THE DESTITUTE POOR

The distress occasioned by the disease in the potato required the Board to direct all its energies in affording employment to the destitute poor, under the respective Acts of 9th Vict., chapters 1, 3 and 4, which were passed early in the session of 1846, for the special purposes of affording relief by employment.

The greatest number of persons employed by us, on a daily average, amounted to 88,340...

The disease again appearing, and much more general, required that greater aid should be afforded to meet the distress this continued calamity would produce; and it was in August considered necessary to furnish the Government with additional powers to meet the crisis, and the Act 9 and 10 Vict., c. 107, was passed for this purpose, by which considerable labour was thrown upon this Board, who thus became the department charged with the execution of the Act.

To enable us to carry out the new measures for relief, as well as the other services which were added to our ordinary duties, your Lordships were pleased to alter the establishment of the Board, by adding two members, and consolidating the duties performed by us as Commissioners under special Acts of Parliament, such as Drainage, Fisheries, Shannon Improvement, &c.

This arrangement has been found to work extremely well, giving thereby increased strength to every branch; but without such addition to the number of members, it would have been physically impossible to have surmounted the task which devolved upon us in providing employment for the number of labourers who required it.

The number employed on the works during the week ended 26th December was 398,231, and the expenditure 154,472*l*.

FIFTEENTH ANNUAL REPORT FROM THE BOARD OF PUBLIC WORKS IN IRELAND

LONDON,1847

DESTITUTION AT SKIBBEREEN

We take the following from the *Cork Examiner* of Friday evening:—

"Disease and death in every quarter—the once hardy population worn away to emaciated skeletons—fever, dropsy, diarrhoea, and famine rioting in every filthy hovel, and sweeping away whole families—the population perceptibly lessened—death diminishing the destitution—hundreds frantically rushing from their home and country, not with the idea of making fortunes in other lands, but to fly from a scene of suffering and death—400 men starving in one district, having no employment, and 300 more turned off the public works in another district, on a day's notice—seventy-five tenants ejected here, and a whole village in the last stage of destitution there—relief committees threatening to throw up their mockery of an office, in utter despair—dead bodies of children flung into holes hastily scratched in the earth without shroud or coffin—wives travelling ten miles to beg the charity of a coffin for a dead husband, and bearing it back that weary distance—a government official offering the one-tenth of a sufficient supply of food, at famine prices—neither mill nor corn store within twenty miles—every field becoming a grave, and the land a wilderness."

THE VINDICATOR, BELFAST, 23 DECEMBER 1846

PROCEEDINGS IN IRELAND

We now proceed to report the progress made since the date of our last Report in the administration of the laws for the relief of the poor in Ireland.

The amount of expenditure for the year . . . was 435,001*l*., and the number of poor persons relieved in the workhouses during the same period was 243,933 . . .

Since our last Report, the Guardians of the Tuam, Castlereagh, Cahirciveen, and Clifden Unions have opened their respective workhouses for the relief of the poor, and a rate has now been made in the Clifden Union. All the workhouses in Ireland, therefore, are now opened for the relief of the poor, and there is no union in which a rate has not been made . . .

The number of workhouse inmates . . . underwent a gradual decrease from the 13th of June [and] reached its minimum on the 29th August, the return for the week ending on that day, being 43,655.

From that point of time the number gradually increased, and on the 17th October we reported four workhouses as already full to His Excellency the Lord Lieutenant . . .

In the months of October and November, the pressure upon some of the Workhouses was already so great that the Guardians of the Cork Union, and several other Unions in the county of Cork, were induced to attempt a system of out-door relief, by giving food daily on the workhouse premises to persons not admitted as inmates; and this example was followed at Kilkenny, and a few other unions in the county of Tipperary and elsewhere.

We felt bound to oppose the introduction of the new system; and in adopting this course we were influenced by the following considerations;—1st. It appeared to us certain that the system was

contrary to the intention of the Legislature in passing the Irish Poor Relief
Act, and we were desirous of reserving for the Legislature alone the
question of whether it was or was not desirable to alter the existing law.
2ndly. We entertained no doubt that the Unions in Ireland (with a few
exceptions) were not in such a financial condition as would enable them
to defray from their own resources the expenses which the new system
would involve. 3rdly. If the system were to be introduced at all, we
knew that it would lead to great abuse and confusion, unless accompanied by checks and precautions, which the existing state of the law
did not enable us to adopt. We therefore deemed it our duty to point
out to the Guardians the inevitable evils of endeavouring to give relief
in a manner not contemplated by the Legislature, and we urgently requested the Guardians, in every instance in which the practice was
adopted, to discontinue it. The Guardians of such unions, partly moved
by these remonstrances, and still more by the abuses and tendency to
confusion (involving danger even to the public peace), which a short
trial of such a system showed to be practicably inseparable from it, one
by one abandoned it, and reverted to the legal course of administering
relief only in the workhouse. In the case of the Cashel Union only have
we issued an order directly prohibiting the continuance of the new
system . . .

That which we believe to be the right course, under such trying circumstances, is the course least in accordance with the feelings of the
parties locally conducting the administration of relief;—eye-witnesses
of the distress endured, they find it difficult, almost impossible, to resist
the immediate impulse of the desire to relieve the individual cases brought
before them; thus applicant after applicant is admitted to the workhouse
by the Guardians, long after the limit of sanitary safety has been reached.

In the operation of such benevolent but dangerous impulses, it is
forgotten that the very object sought, that of making the limited means
of relief available to the utmost extent, is most surely sacrificed by this
course of proceeding; that effectual relief, even to the extent of the
existing accommodation, cannot be given, if contagious disease takes
possession of the workhouse; that the relief purported to be afforded
in an establishment, when once so infected, is not relief, but a delusion
fatal to the recipients; and that the Guardians, in attempting to go beyond
due sanitary limits, turn what was designed and adapted for good
purposes, into active evil, and deprive themselves of the power of
using effectually those means of relief which have actually been placed
at their command . . .

86   We regret to say that in many of the workhouses, more especially some in Connaught and some in the south of Ireland, such has been the frightful state of distress, that all precautions of this nature have been borne down, and the workhouses crowded to an extent far beyond their calculated capacity; and the consequences have been in some cases most disastrous. In all these cases the seeds of contagious disease have been introduced by persons suffering under dysentery or fever when first admitted; and the diseases so introduced have spread to inmates previously healthy, and also to the officers of the workhouse. Not only has the overcrowding of the workhouses been favourable to the spread of contagion, but the amount of hospital room provided has been totally inadequate to a due separation of the diseased from the healthy. The workhouse hospitals were, it will be remembered, provided to meet the casual sickness arising in a number of inmates generally presumed to be healthy, and in ordinary circumstances they have been usually found proportioned to those requirements; but in the present state of things nearly every person admitted is a patient; separation of the sick, by reason of their number, becomes impossible; disease spreads, and the whole workhouse is changed, by rapid transition, into one large hospital, without those preparations and means of arrangement which are essential to the conduct of such an establishment.

In a few cases, this state of things has been aggravated to a most serious extent by the illness, retirement, or death of all the principal officers of the workhouse.

THIRTEENTH ANNUAL REPORT OF THE POOR LAW COMMISSIONERS

LONDON, 1847

NOTICE.

THE TENANTS OF THE
VISCOUNT DUNGANNON,

On the BELVOIR Estate, comprising the Townlands of *Moneyrea, Munlough, Bal-lyknockan, Ballynavally, Ballynahatty,* and *Gallwally,* are requested to pay their respective Rents at the Office, at Mr. Pos-NETT's House, *Rose Lodge,* on

FRIDAY, the 23d January, 1846.

3d December, 1845.   R. GEORGE JEBB.

The Tenants are also requested to come prepared to produce their last Receipt.

J. SMYTH, Printer, Belfast.

1847

TO BE SOLD
BY PUBLIC AUCTION,

At DENVIR'S Hotel, in DOWNPATRICK, on
TUESDAY the 23d MARCH, instant, at One
o'clock, afternoon;

THAT FARM

In Ballykinlar, about five miles from Down-
patrick, now in the possession of ELIZABETH
MAGINNIS,

CONTAINING about 31A. 2R. 0P. (Irish plantation
measure) held by Lease under the Marquis of DOWN-
SHIRE, for two good Lives, still in being, at £46,
18s. 2d. yearly rent.

There are upon the Lands a good DWELLING-
HOUSE, two stories high, with Office-houses. all
lately built and slated. The Farm is in the highest
state of cultivation, and there are already sown in it
3½ acres of Wheat, one acre of Oats, and 1A. 1R. of
Peas, and the remainder of the Farm is all ploughed.

A deposit of £50 will be required, on the purchaser being declared. For particulars of Title,
apply to Messrs. H. WALLACE & Co., Solicitors,
Downpatrick.

Elizabeth Maginnis.

Ballykinlar, 10th March, 1847.

BAZAAR

FOR THE FAMISHING POOR IN CONNAUGHT
WILLIAM M'COMB

There is wailing on the mountains—
    Want in cottage, glen, and hill—
    Broken pitchers by the fountains—
Present evil—threatened ill!

Bread there's none to buy or borrow,
    Fathers, mothers, children cry!
Woman weeps the tears of sorrow—
    Man the tears of agony!

Ye whom God hath blest with fulness
    Hasten to the rescue soon;
Linger not with selfish coolness—
    Help in time is double boon!

Many a needle has been plying
    For our cause in many a home;
Come and buy, and save the dying;
    Judgment—mercy bids you come.

BELFAST, 1847

THE FAMINE IN IRELAND

The following circular has been addressed by the Right Rev. Dr. Griffiths to his Clergy:—

Golden Square, December 29

REV. DEAR SIR—Although we have lately forwarded to you our pastoral letter on the approaching jubilee, which has been already announced to your flock, we deem it advisable to address some directions personally to yourself, leaving the manner of communicating them to your flock to your own prudence.

"We send herewith a copy of the apostolical letter of his Holiness Pope Pius IX, that it may be read to your flock on the Sunday after you receive it.

"As we have been informed by private letters, as well as by the public papers, that the state of destitution in some parts of Ireland is very appalling, thousands suffering acutely the miseries of hunger, and many dying in consequence; and as we learn likewise, from our beloved clergy who have the best opportunity, whilst visiting the sick poor, of ascertaining their real condition, that the sufferings and miseries of the destitute are painfully shortening their days in London itself; we feel it our duty, in conformity with the undoubted principles of Christian morality, alluded to in our pastoral, and well known to yourself, to remind you of the obligation of exhorting the members of your flock, who have the means of complying with the great precept of almsgiving which is so peculiarly imperative in the present distressed circumstances of the poor.

"In order that the condition of the jubilee, which prescribes almsgiving, and the exercise of this most acceptable branch of charity may be attended to on the same occasion by all the members of the London district; we direct that on Sunday, the 10th of January, an appeal be made from the pulpit of your own chapel, for the two fold object of relieving the distress in Ireland, and in your own congregation. And we recommend that the money collected in consequence of your appeal be divided into two equal portions, of which one may be retained for your own poor, and the other either forwarded direct to Archbishop Murray, of Dublin; or, in order to save his Grace the trouble of receiving several small sums, placed to an account at the Commercial Bank, in our name, for the Irish poor.

"As many members of your flock may not have the opportunity of visiting your chapel except during the time of the adorable sacrifice on Sunday mornings, to enable them to fulfil the third condition of gaining the jubilee, we direct that the hymn *Veni Creator Spiritus*, and the psalm *Miserere*, be recited either in Latin or in English, either before or after every mass for the congregation on each of the four Sundays comprised within the time of the jubilee. This union in prayer with the priest will likewise draw down more abundant blessings upon his Holiness and the faithful.

"In conclusion, we call your attention to those words of his Holiness, in which he recommends that the faithful should be properly prepared by the preaching of the Word of God, for partaking of the blessings of the jubilee. We advise you, therefore, so to arrange your instructions and exhortations for the next four Sundays, that the faithful entrusted to your charge may be enabled to fulfil with due attention and devotion the five conditions imposed by his Holiness for gaining the effects of the jubilee.—We remain, &c., your faithful servant in Christ,

"THOMAS GRIFFITHS."

FREEMAN'S JOURNAL, DUBLIN, 9 JANUARY 1847

THE FUTURE POTATO CROP

The following letter appears in the *Dublin Evening Mail*

SIR—The year which has passed has been momentous to Europe from the scarcity of food occasioned by the preternatural abundance of the Aphis Vestator. Let us now forget the sarcasms of the journals of the unsuccessful investigators, and take advantage of the knowledge acquired during the past year to regulate the measures for the ensuing season.

I examined the subject as a scientific recreation for the summer evenings, and having discovered the cause of the disease, it now becomes my duty to point out in the public journals how the crops are in future to be treated, as my work on the potato plant is not likely to be perused by the poorer agriculturists; and, it is manifest, that those who were unfortunate enough not to see the insects cannot render information on the matter.

The Vestator attacks many plants, and kills whatever it attacks. It destroys the potato, spinach, turnip, carrot, beet, and clover, &c. It will even live upon the wheat, and I am now writing with a wheat plant before me on which the creature is feeding.

Notwithstanding rain, snow, and frost, the Vestator is still alive and active, and it is uncertain to what extent it may appear next season; on the one hand it may destroy all our crops, on the other it may be swept from the face of the earth, and produce no further mischief.

The potato plant, like all organic bodies, when disased, retains its tendency to disease in future growths, which is not singular when we remember that the scrofulous father is liable to produce a diseased offspring.

The Vestator has heretofore not appeared, in profusion till July or August, hence we may, in some degree, prevent its ravages by getting our potatoes ripe before the Vestator comes in great abundance.

All succulent and cellular growths are prejudicial, as liable to favour the disease; but, on the contrary, the early deposition of fibre is calculated to enable the plant to resist the injurious action of the Vestator.

From the above statements, we may deduce the following line of treatment applicable for practice during the next two or three months:—

1. Cultivate all crops to the usual extent.
2. With regard to potatoes, use sets from former healthy plants.
3. Select early varieties.
4. Plant early.
5. Use but little or no manure.
6. Choose a sandy or peaty soil.
7. Destroy the plants the Vestator is now living on.

I call the attention of the benevolent to the above rules, and recommend them to circulate these short directions throughout Ireland, the poor parts of Scotland and England; I also beg to recommend them as true charity to send sound sets of early kinds to those districts. I myself am against the overculture of the potato, for reasons which I have elsewhere stated, nevertheless as a secondary crop, too little culture will always be attended with great privations to the poor.

At the early period of the year, it is desirable to destroy such plants as the creature likes. It lives freely upon the Shepherd's Purse, Mallow, and Turnip; on this account the husbandman should destroy these plants as well as possible before spring advances to furnish it with abundance of food. The Vestator causes the first damage to vegetables it attacks, and is thus the cause of the disease from which all subsequent changes take place as a consequence. Every farmer should know the form and habits of the creature, and every one should assist him to kill this destroyer of human food.—I am, Sir, your obedient servant,

ALFRED SMEE

DOWNPATRICK RECORDER, 9 JANUARY 1847

HUNGER AND DESTITUTION
OF THE PEOPLE

THE PEASANTRY IN THE CITY

The pangs of hunger appear to have driven a number of the country people to seek relief in the city. On yesterday morning between seven and eight o'clock a number of able-bodied men evidently from the rural districts, amounting to between forty and fifty in number, came in a body down Great Britain-street. They surrounded a bread cart belonging to Mr. Walsh, baker, of No. 3, Dorset-street and at once commenced rifling its contents. In spite of the resistance of the driver they succeeded in taking away forcibly twenty loaves of bread and about a dozen rolls, value about ten or eleven shillings. They then went off, some devouring the bread with evident voracity.

Afterwards between one and two o'clock a body of twelve peasants assembled in Marlborough-street in front of the house of a provision dealer named M'Coy, living at No. 20 in that street, and afterwards at the houses 91 and 92 in the same street, tenanted by Mr. Cavanagh and Mr. Fitzharris, bakers, and demanded bread. The men were relieved at each place, and some gentlemen passing by at the time gave them some money.

Inspector M'Mahon dispatched Acting-sergeant Petit after them with four police constables who followed them to watch their further movements.

They proceeded down Marlborough-street to Eden-quay, and again stopped before the door of Mr. Coyne, the bread and biscuit baker residing there, and repeated their demand for bread; but on seeing the police approaching they retired, and passed over Carlisle-bridge in the direction of Westmoreland-street.

A mob surrounded the shop of Mr. Jeffers, baker, of Church street; but the police being in the vicinity, they were called on, and succeeded in dispersing the mob.

Several bread-carts were stopped in the outlets of the city, and their contents taken.

There is a rumour afloat about the town that the peasantry in vast numbers are approaching the city. This, however, does not appear to

94 be substantiated. We ourselves are not inclined to give much credence to the report.

Government will offer inducements to able bodied and industrious farm labourers from Ireland to emigrate as settlers to New Zealand, with farmers of small capital.

WEEKLY FREEMAN'S JOURNAL, DUBLIN, 9 JANUARY 1847

DISTRESS AND DESTITUTION IN ARRAN

In the remote and sequestered isles of Arran we lament to hear that the most deplorable destitution prevails—aggravated in no small degree by the want of anything in the nature of a local institution, or means to meet the calamity. These remote islands, from the rocky character of their agricultural surface, admit but of little, if of any, improvement in the way of drainage. Some employment might be afforded in the completion of a main road, commenced in the summer of the last year, but which still remains unfinished. Owing, however, to the shallow surface of the soil, those means of employment and relief which may be applied in more favoured districts, cannot be available in Arran; and hence, notwithstanding what is known of the primitive independence and spirit of those virtuous islanders, we lament to be informed that, whether as regards public works, or labour of a productive nature, very little can be accomplished, and that their only hope of subsistence depends upon eleemosynary relief.

Harrowed by the afflicting scenes which he was doomed to witness, and bestowing upon his suffering flock the only pecuniary means at his disposal, the estimable and truly benevolent parish priest of these islands, the Rev. Mr. Harley, has come to Dublin in the hope of exciting some attention to the condition of his famishing parishioners. He has already waited upon the Irish Relief Committee, in Sackville-street, and the General Central Relief Committee, and we sincerely hope that to neither will his appeal prove abortive. It is gratifying to us to be able to add, that since his arrival in town he has happened to come into communication with the officiating Protestant curate, the Rev. Mr. Cather, and with the son of Mr. Thompson, agent to the property, who

accompanied him to both committees, and there took occasion to
impress upon them the afflicting sufferings of the people of Arran.

WEEKLY FREEMAN'S JOURNAL, 9 JANUARY 1847

THE FAMINE IN IRELAND
AND SCOTLAND

U p to yesterday (Thursday) the total amount contributed towards the relief of the distress in the remote parishes of Ireland and Scotland was 13,651*l.* 14s. 6d., of which her Majesty contributed 2,000*l.* and Prince Albert 500*l.* To the Irish and Scotch Famine Relief Society 1,152*l.* 10s. 3d. has been recently forwarded, making 6,934*l.* 15s. 2d. placed at their disposal. In addition, penny subscriptions are actively carried on by tradesmen in the metropolis, the sums thus raised being also weekly forwarded to the distressed districts.

DAILY NEWS, 10 JANUARY 1847

FAMINE AND STARVATION IN
THE COUNTY OF CORK

V ery lamentable accounts are given from various parts of the county of Cork. From Bantry, Skibbereen, Crookhaven, Castletown, and Tracton, the reports present the same gloomy features. The intelligence from these scenes of misery is summed up by the *Cork Examiner* as follows:—

"SKIBBEREEN.—In the parish of Kilmoe, fourteen died on Sunday; three of these were buried in coffins, eleven were buried without other covering than the rags they wore when alive. And one gentleman, a good and charitable man, speaking of this case, says—'The distress is so appalling, that we must throw away all feelings of delicacy;' and another says—'I would rather give 1s. to a starving man than 4s. 6d. for a coffin.' One hundred and forty have died in the Skibbereen Workhouse in one month; eight have died in one day! And Mr. M'Carthy Downing states

THE CORK SOCIETY OF FRIENDS' SOUP HOUSE.

that 'they came into the house merely and solely for the purpose of getting a coffin.' The Rev. Mr. Clancy visits a farm, and there, in one house, 'he administered the last rites of religion to six person.' On a subsequent occasion, he 'prepared for death a father and a daughter lying in the same bed.' Dr. Donovan solemnly assures a public meeting that the people are 'dropping in dozens about them.' Mr. Marmion says that work on the public road is even more destructive than fever; for the unfed wretches have not energy enough to keep their blood in circulation, and they drop down from the united effects of cold and hunger—never to rise again.

"In Tracton, deaths, it appears, are occurring too. Mr. Corkoran, P.P., in a letter to Mr. Redington says: 'Over *sixteen deaths occurred in my parishes for the last ten days*. I am morally certain that each and every one of them was occasioned and accelerated by *want of food and fire*. Buckley, of Ballyvorane, and Sullivan, of Oysterhaven, died suddenly. Buckley dropped dead on the works, after a journey of *three miles before day*. His wife will make affidavit, that he had not sufficient food the night before he died, and that she and the rest of her family lived thirty-six hours on wild weeds *to spare a bit of the cake for him*. (In this case, a Coroner's verdict was given without sight of the body.) This horrifying economy is practised by scores of families in this district. Similar effects must be expected from similar causes. I fear we must bury the dead *coffinless* in future. My God! what a revolting idea! *Without food when alive, without a coffin when dead.'* "

The Rev. Robert Traill, chairman of the Schule Relief Committee, county Cork, states that 15,000 persons in that wide district are destitute; of this 5000 are entirely dependent on casual charity; fifty deaths have resulted from famine and "hundreds" are so reduced that not food or medicine can restore them! The deaths, he adds, now average 25 daily!!

Ten additional deaths by starvation have occurred in the barony of Bantry. The Jury at the inquests at Bantry handed in the following remonstrance, by their foreman, Mr. E. O'Sullivan:—"That we feel it our duty to state, under the correction of the Court, that it is our opinion that, if the Government of the country shall persevere in its determination of refusing to use the means available to it for the purpose of lowering the price of food, so as to place it within the reach of the labouring poor, the result will be a sacrifice of human life from starvation to a frightful extent, and endangerment of property and of the public peace . . .

The Illustration shows a benevolent attempt to mitigate the suffering in the city of Cork, viz., the *Society of Friends' Soup House*. There are many similar establishments in operation through the county; but, we prefer the annexed because the idea originated with the Society of Friends. The funds for its support are chiefly raised among this charitable class; and we are happy to state that the establishment is now in a position to supply 1500 gallons of Soup daily, at a loss, or rather cost, of from £120 to £150 per month to the supporters of the design. The present calls are for from 150 to 180 gallons daily, requiring 120 pounds of good beef, 27 pounds of rice, 27 pounds of oatmeal, 27 pounds of split peas, and 14 ounces of spices, with a quantity of vegetables. Tickets, at one penny each, are unsparingly distributed, on presenting one of which, each poor person receives one quart of soup, with half a small loaf of bread; and both are of good quality.

In the making of the Soup, the greatest possible cleanliness is observed; attention is paid to the poor, who throng the place daily, for their cheap supply of food; as well as to the visitors, who go to see the soup made, and who are requested to test its quality, and suggest any improvement. The vats, which are shown in the Sketch, are worked by a steam-engine, in an adjoining house; and, to ensure cleanliness, as well as sweetness, they are used alternately. Too much credit cannot be given to this establishment, and to the exertions of the Society of Friends in general; for, not content with originating these Soup Establishments, they have also raised a sum of money for distribution in the west, so as the more effectually to relieve the poor in distant districts.

ILLUSTRATED LONDON NEWS, 16 JANUARY 1847

DEATHS FROM STARVATION

AWFUL STATE OF SLIGO

It is our painful duty to record the deaths of *fifteen* persons within one week in this small county, from *absolute starvation*! We give the names of the victims of famine, and the verdicts of the coroner's juries; the evidence, if published at full length, would disclose an amount of human misery such as, perhaps, was never before known to exist in any other county. We have neither space, nor indeed spirits, to go through these shocking details, and we shall, therefore, be as brief as possible in our announcements.

The following inquests were held by Alexander Burrows, Esq., coroner for this county; the cases all occurred in the barony of Tirerill.

An inquest was held on the 8th inst., on the body of Mary Cunningham, of Carrickbanagher; it appeared that she and the other members of her family were obliged, for some weeks past, to live upon one meal of gruel in the twenty-four hours. Verdict—"died for want of sufficient food."

An inquest was held, same day, upon the body of James M'Garry, at Ardcurly. Verdict—"died of insufficiency of food and clothing to support life."

An inquest was held on the 9th instant on the body of Patrick Ward, Tunagh. Verdict—"deceased came to his death by starvation."

An inquest was held on the 13th inst., on the body of Michael Kilmartin, Emero. Verdict—"deceased came by his death by starvation."

An inquest was held same day, on the body of Catherine Kilmartin, of Emero. Verdict—"died of want of food."

An inquest was held same day, on the body of Bridget M'Dermott, of Doonskeen. Verdict—"died of want of food, and we regret to say the other members of the family are likely to follow, if not speedily relieved." When this verdict was pronounced four of the M'Dermotts were in bed unable to get up from want of food!

An inquest was held same day, upon the body of Patrick Dyer, Ardagh. Verdict—"died of starvation and want of proper clothing."

THREE DEATHS IN ONE FAMILY FROM STARVATION!—An inquest was held at Aughanah, upon the bodies of Edward Tighe, John Tighe, and Anne Tighe—brothers and sister. Verdict—"died of starvation and want of proper clothing."

HORRIBLE!—An inquest was held on the 12th instant, upon the body of Thomas M'Manus, of Kilmactranny—verdict. "Deceased came to his death by hunger and cold." This wretched creature was observed by a man lying in a muddy ditch; he was raised up, and the man went to two or three houses in the neighbourhood, and asked the people to admit deceased, but they refused, alleging that he had typhus fever. He then carried deceased to a haggard and placed him upon some straw, where he was found dead on the following morning, and dreadfully mutilated. We copy the evidence of Thomas Burrows, Esq., M.D.— "Examined the body of Thomas M'Manus; both the legs, as far as the buttocks, appeared to have been eaten off by a pig; is of opinion his death was caused by hunger and cold." There was not a particle of food found in deceased's stomach or intestines. Those who saw the body were of opinion, from the agonized expression of M'Manus's countenance, that he was *alive* when the pig attacked him.

The following inquests were held before Meredith Thompson, Esq., coroner:—On the 12th instant, on the body of a man not known— verdict, "Died of the want of sufficiency of food." On the 13th instant, at Curry, on the body of George Cuff—verdict, "Died for want of food."

But the above list is not complete, as more deaths occurred during the week than are recorded in it.—A correspondent says, "six persons have died here for want of food, but we had no inquests, though a requisition was sent to the coroner; he was, however, unfortunately too much employed in the upper part of the barony to attend. I fear that half our people will die unless government do something very quickly to relieve us."

Let Lord John Russell read the above, and then say, if he can, that he is justified in keeping the government stores closed against the people.—*Champion.*

THE VINDICATOR, BELFAST, 20 JANUARY 1847

With regret we have to add another name to the melancholy catalogue of the dead from starvation in this district, in the person of an aged poor woman named Mary Commins, who, while on her way on Wednesday last to seek for admission in the workhouse, expired on the side of the road near Dangan, within about a mile of the town. When she was discovered, life was found extinct, and her remains were taken to the workhouse, where an inquest was subsequently held upon the body, by Michael Perrin, Esq., deputy coroner, and a verdict returned of "died from want and the inclemency of the weather."

GALWAY VINDICATOR, 23 JANUARY 1847

THE ENGLISH PARLIAMENT AND
THE IRISH PEOPLE

Ten days ago—surely we did not dream it—there was a mighty assemblage here in Dublin of the nobles and landed men of Ireland, who announced, in six-and-thirty unanimous resolutions, the measures which in *their* opinion ought to be instantly adopted for the rescue of their perishing country. They met amidst high excitement and joyful expectation; amidst the applauses of the Press and the blessings of the People; proclaiming to all the world that the peril of Ireland was imminent and deadly, relating tales of such unheard-of horror, such desperate, and hitherto fabulous misery, that the hair of men bristled on their heads,—and demanding prompt and extensive measures of redress. Men said, surely the Queen's English Ministers, cold-blooded and stupid as they are, will not dare to set at nought this singular unanimity amongst the magnates of Ireland, this fearful desolation which their own hands have wrought—will not dare *this time* to utter the usual meaningless mockeries of a Royal Speech through the mouth of their Queen!

It was a signal mistake. In Dublin, it is true, the voice of Irish gentlemen sounded bold and high—their array looked potent and grand. But they have gone to London—where they are one to six—and behold how they have dwindled! It does not even seem to be known in those parts 101

that such a meeting assembled:—there is in Ireland, her Majesty has been advised to say, a complete "absence of political excitement;" and so she invites her faithful Commons to "take a dispassionate survey of that country." Yes; from that distance they can take a dispassionate survey:—there are no verdicts of Death from Starvation ringing in their ears there; no wasted corpses searing their eye-balls, and grinning frightfully through their dreams there. Before Heaven, they disbelieve all this, and have taken care not to admit the horrid tale. Hear how they have made the Queen speak of the famine which they have created:—"The loss of the usual food of the people has been the cause of severe sufferings, OF DISEASE, and of greatly *increased mortality* among the poorer classes." A small matter this: the human frame is liable to "disease" at all seasons, and "mortality" is the lot of humanity; and sometimes there is more of it in a season and sometimes less, a mere statistical fact either way. Even in London there is "mortality," and the very best-fed men will die, of gout, or indigestion, or *delirium tremens*:—and shall Ireland be exempt from the doom of man? Ah! most gracious Madam, beware of lying councillors! The "disease" is sheer Hunger—the "increased mortality" means that thousands of strong and healthy men and women have been slaughtered more cruelly, more surely, more hideously, than if your Royal troops, Oh gracious Queen! had swept their villages with shot and shell. Nay, your Majesty's ministers have so ordered matters with the help of Political Economy, that there are now walking or tottering upon this land hundreds of thousands of doomed wretches, who must surely die—for whom, as for the man of Uz, "the graves are ready," and whom it would be *mercy*—mercy to themselves and the survivors—to slay at once and bury out of sight—to bury, however, without coffins, on account of the expense.

THE NATION, DUBLIN, 23 JANUARY 1847

INQUEST—STARVATION

On Sunday, an adjourned inquest on the body of a woman named M'Cabe was held at Drumclay. In consequence of a report of her having been poisoned by her husband, a *post mortem* examination and analysis of the contents of the stomach was ordered, which were minutely performed by Doctors Rodgers and Ball. No food was discovered in the stomach or intestines, except a few grains of unmasticated and undigested wheat, and five or six ounces of greenish fluid. No traces of poison were discoverable. Verdict—destitution and neglect.—*Fermanagh Reporter*.

THE VINDICATOR, BELFAST, 30 JANUARY 1847

THE IRISH POLICY

Rendered forbearing by the presence of difficulties, the Legislature has given an almost unanimous approval to Lord John Russell's measures. The Irish policy of the Government has been submitted to Parliamentary and public opinion, and has borne the test of both far better than Whig measures in general, and Whig Irish measures in particular were accustomed to do in years not long passed by. In the palmy days of the Grey and Melbourne Ministries, when the party was strong in numbers and influence, a cry of spoliation and revolution would have burst forth from one end of the kingdom to the other, on the announcement of such a scheme as the Premier laid before the Legislature on Monday. Now that a Whig Ministry, by a curious combination of circumstances, holds office, while actually in a minority, they deal with hostile interests, and depart from old principles, not only without being denounced, they do it with general assent, and something very like general applause. How is this? Why has opposition ceased? Why are those once so "willing to wound," now "afraid to strike?" Because a common calamity hangs over all and differences must be sunk in the great emergency. So Protectionists give their aid in abolishing the last relic of Protection; and political economists acknowledge there are exceptional circumstances in which rigid principles cannot be applied; and Conservatives alter and destroy, unscared by that word of fear, "innovation," and all men and all parties are seen doing the things most opposite to those which, from their avowed opinions, might be expected of them; we are, politically, gathering grapes from thorns and figs from thistles.

The fact is, the consciences of our statesmen of both parties are somewhat weighed down and oppressed by the memory of former errors and short-comings towards Ireland. None have so fully discharged

their duty, as to have acquired the right to accuse another. As Lord John
Russell said on Monday last, "there have been errors, there have been defects," and they must be shared, not in exactly equal proportions, perhaps, but still shared, between the two great English parties who have by turns governed for the last century. Sins, both of omission and commission, lie at the door of both. The two sides became champions of political or religious questions, which aroused fierce hatreds and passions, which continued to be fought almost through generations, and by the noise of the conflict drew attention from the awful abyss of social misery that existed dark and silent beneath the feet of the combatants. If they, in the intervals of the struggle, legislated at all for the social condition of Ireland, it was by passing laws that increased the power of property, placed the Executive above the Constitution, filled the statute book with Arms Acts, Insurrection Acts, Ejectment Acts, and swelled the records of the country with tithe massacres, proclamations of martial law, and suspensions of the Habeas Corpus. In the midst of all these things came periods of famine—precursors of the heavier visitation that has now befallen us; but they were met by temporary expedients: England sent money and food, and, with more or less of suffering, the crisis passed away. But why all these things occurred—why Ireland was an exception to all Europe besides—no party, no statesman enquired; a fear of touching such a mass of evils seemed to outweigh the acknowledged necessity of "doing something:" the something was never done. So all parties now find themselves placed face to face with the most terrible of national calamities—Famine: with every difficulty aggravated tenfold, they must go to work at once; and England learns with dismay, that millions of men are dependent for life on its Treasury—that its Exchequer must freight ships with food—must frame a machinery of relief and distribution—must, for a long time to come, send out grants, loans, advances—must pay the wages of half a nation for this year—must even provide the seed for the harvest of the next. To all the objections made on principle, to all allegations of difficulty in practice, there is but one answer—it must be done! It is the general conviction of this necessity that silences opposition to the Government and its plan.

The details of that scheme do not challenge much criticism: it is rather a modification and extension of former expedients than anything wholly novel. Grants for Public Works, Loans, and all this class of measures, are familiar features of Irish policy. The only difference is, that the Exchequer is compelled to open the whole hand, where it formerly only unbent a finger. Half of what has been lent to the landed proprietors is made a free gift, provided they will pay the other half: further aid is promised them on better terms. Some abuses in the system of employment will be corrected; the proposition to reclaim waste lands is good in itself, but the Government has its hands too full to undertake it at present; what is done for Emigration will not amount to any practical change in the present system; and, of all the alterations, that which extends the operation of the Irish Poor-law is the most important, and shows that the Government is on the right road, but advances as yet timidly. The absurdity of Boards of Guardians not having the power, under the law, to give relief, even in food, out of the workhouse, though it might be crowded to excess, was too glaring, and the Irish law is now assimilated more to the English system, which, Heaven knows, is harsh and restrictive enough. We alluded to this subject last week, and need only remark here, that Lord John Russell might have gone farther in this direction with more effect. The appointment of Local Committees, who are to have some mixed and not very clearly-defined functions, in conjunction with the Boards of Guardians, but, as it seems, independent of them, will, we fear, prove a failure. Public rates, private subscriptions, and Government advances, cannot well be mixed up together, we think we see the elements of endless confusion in these committees, but are willing to hope the best from them. In principle, they acknowledge the necessity of an extension of the relief of the poor by rate on property; to this the land of Ireland must come at last; everything tends to hasten the period; and we will give our reasons for thinking so.

In the first place, public opinion in England is awakening to the subject. Ireland is beginning to create a formidable balance against us in the national account; neglect, carelessness, and *laissez faire* do not make a cheap system of Government but a very costly one. Absorbed in business as we are, and rather indifferent to abstract rights, Ireland might have been governed as a Colony till the end of time, if it could have been done without estblishing a drain on the Imperial Exchequer, to which John Bull, by the Income Tax and otherwise, is so large a contributor. Former famines only roused an uneasy suspicion that all was not quite sound; but with the disappearance of the evil, he relapsed into carelessness—forgot Ireland altogether, and sunk as many millions in Mexican Mines as would have turned Tipperary into a market garden; for John, though immensely enterprising, is not perfectly wise in all his speculations. But this last call is too much for him. There is one book in which Englishmen devoutly believe, and that is the Ledger; its teaching may often be sordid enough, but it is useful—in some cases, indispensable: it is not safe to scorn even the Evangel of Mammon. By that light, such as it is, England is now reading what she has lost by her positive enmity or careless neglect of Ireland: we are paying dearly for the errors of our fathers, which meet us on many a page of the journals of our Legislature. When Ireland had trade and industry, the merchants and manufacturers of England petitioned William the Third to "discourage" them; and the Dutchman did it. With the consent and applause of Parliament, the rising manufactures of Ireland were destroyed; it was made felony to weave and spin, and enterprise was punished as a crime. So capital went elsewhere; Ireland sunk; no middle class grew up; and slowly, but surely, the bulk of the nation was flung upon the Land alone, millions depending for existence on the lowest vegetable produce, while they exported cattle and provisions of all kinds to England, whose Parliament once voted even that importation "a nuisance." No poor-rate attached a portion of the rents of the soil, and appropriated it to the poor; the Landlord swept all, according to law, returning what he chose—according to conscience. Next to crushing the manufacturing industry of Ireland, our greatest error was allowing the land to go untaxed, for the support of the destitute. Both mistakes combined have obliged us to deal, for the last century, with a state of discontent, poverty, rebellion, anarchy, and crime, that has cost us—we return again to the money argument—millions upon millions. Grants, loans, subscriptions, have followed each other in rapid succession, and these have been but a slight outlay, compared to the continual expense of keeping up there a greater military force than in all the rest of the Kingdom besides. And past expense, again, will sink into a trifle in comparison with that of the future, if half the nation is to come to the Government pay-table. All this is beginning to alarm the tax-payers of England; and it is through the ledger—through the columns of profit and loss—that we shall be taught the wiser policy of encouraging industry, instead of blighting it, by "Act of Parliament." In the early part of the last century, it was the leading idea of the statesmen of England, that commerce and manufactures, in all the dependencies of the Empire, ought to be discouraged, and, on principle, crushed and destroyed. In this respect, Ireland and the Colonies of America were treated exactly alike. The laws against the industry of the "plantations," as they were called, are almost beyond the belief of the present age; yet, there they are, on the Statute Book— laws forbidding manufactures of all kinds, down to hats and nails, lest those of England should be injured; laws petitioned for by the people, deliberately passed by the Legislature, and supported by the public opinion of the time. This was the narrow policy of the age; it lost us America, but there its effects have long since disappeared; not so in Ireland, where the consequences of those errors still remain, and where we but reap the bitter fruits of the follies and crimes of our fathers. We can no more escape those consequences than we can repudiate the debts they handed down to us as a legacy of embarrassment. We must deal with the difficulties as we best can; any effort must be made for the present, and as soon as a better state of things is brought about, we must provide for the future. In doing that, we must depart as widely as possible from the precedents of the last century. Lord J. Russell quotes the descriptions of England and Scotland as they once were, to show that we should never despair of improvement. It is sad to think that if we progress no faster, a century hence is the earliest period at which a satisfactory state of things can be looked for in Ireland; but if a beginning is not made, the better time will never come at all.

ILLUSTRATED LONDON NEWS, 30 JANUARY 1847

THE FAMINE

It seems to be admitted upon all hands that this country is on the eve or in the midst of social changes, the ultimate issue of which is beyond human foresight. The time for measures precautionary or palliative is gone. The Divine infliction—the calamitous state of the poor—the embarrassment of property—the perplexity and dismay which prevail everywhere—the absence of any distinct and generally approved plan

to meet the emergency, or any sagacious and ruling mind to guide us through it—the land uncultivated—the daily employment (last month) of a quarter of a million of human beings, paid out of the public funds,—present a combination of circumstances that may well appal the boldest mind. A desperate exigency will not wait upon deliberation, and as yet there has been little else. The crisis has come suddenly and terribly; and, to all appearance, will be left to work its own ends unarrested.

At such a time, it is at once a duty and a relief to stand aside from the din and darkness, and contemplate what is passing by a light which earthly policy is incapable of yielding. We ought to do so, for it is only thus we can expect to learn how, individually, we should think and act for the occasion; and it is a relief, amid the bewilderment of human counsels, to trace the purposes of Providence, even though their language to ourselves be awful and humbling.

The perils and sufferings of the country have arisen immediately out of the destruction of a crop, upon which it is stated that about one-fourth of the population were dependent for their food. Moreover, it was the food of the poor—the food of those who, in losing this, lost what was to have been their support until another harvest. The produce of other crops may have been defective or abundant; but to the sufferers the potato was at once food and money; and when this perished, it was the same to them (so far as any power of commanding a supply), whether plenty or dearth reigned in the country. The owners of corn might export it, might hoard it up, might expose it for sale; but as the poor had no means to buy, there was no interval between the consumption of the few and half poisonous potatoes they could save, and the actual presence of famine.

And this visitation came suddenly, and bearing upon it all the marks of Divine infliction. Last year there was a hint and rumour of the danger, yet not sufficient to lead to any extensive precautions, or to prevent the husbandman committing the same seed to the ground in hope. Summer came and disclosed the terrible reality of blasted tracts, and the root rotted in the earth. And the immediate cause of the calamity is as secret as its presence was sudden. Inquiry and speculation have been actively at work; scientific men have investigated, and practical men have tried experiments; one theory has been set up against another, and one remedy after another has been tried; and yet after all the main result which theory and experiment have elicited is the same which the poor labourer had already reached when he gazed upon his black and withered field—that the crop had hopelessly perished. Conflicting opinions declare that the physical causes of the blight are as yet a mystery.

And the universal consternation which prevails speaks as if men's hearts were secretly smitten with similar convictions. This shews itself remarkably in the way in which persons of all parties seem to have forgotten their differences, and to be drawn together as in the sense of something dreaded which is approaching. A few weeks have done more to soften down old feelings of antagonism, to produce extraordinary changes of opinion, to ripen matters for new political combination, than could have been accomplished in many common years. And still, with all this, no answer to the two pressing questions of the day has yet come out; how are the poor to be fed? how is the country to be extricated from its present difficulties? As if it were the will of Providence that we should suffer more, be brought through greater straits, and were not yet to see the end of what is destined for us.

Such considerations alone are probably enough to shew that there is something in the present visitation which peculiarly addresses itself to every serious mind. It is in this view we desire to place it before our readers. It would exceed alike our province, and the limits to which we are confined, to discuss any of the various projects to which the present crisis has given occasion. Some suggestions, however, naturally occur to us as churchmen, one or two of which we shall mention.

In a time of public trouble the Church occupies a conspicuous and responsible position. It is an especial time for proving, amid those less privileged, the reality of our exalted claims. With all allowance for exaggeration in one place, and imposture in another, of this there can be no doubt, that the poor in parts of this country are actually suffering most dreadfully. It is a horrible thing to be said in a Christian country, where, taking the whole, there is, we believe, no positive lack of food, *that Christian people are dying of hunger.* No words could make more or less of this fact; and if it be a fact, the call which it makes upon the Church must supersede all others. Self-denial is at all times an essential part of Christian duty, at such a time it is only an aspect of common humanity— nay, even of self-interest. Let every one who knows this fact that the *poor are starving*—wasting by a shape of death so merciless, if food could be reached, so agonizing to the body, so cruelly tempting to the soul— well consider whether they can be clear as long as they leave any superfluity wilfully unretrenched, so long as they do not endeavour to bring their habits and expenditure into harmony with the miserable time. And we may add a practical hint to all members of the Church, suggesting at least one obvious way by which, while they are humbling themselves before God, they can sympathize with and assist the suffering poor, namely, that they should strictly observe the fasts appointed by their Church, and give what they save in expenditure to feed the hungry; thus literally complying with the direction of Scripture,—"is not this the fast that I have chosen, . . . to deal thy bread to the hungry? . . ." Any one who takes the trouble of calculating will be surprised to find what the amount of contribution would be, if every adult member of the Church gave the cost *even of a single meal every Friday* (without reckoning the occasional fasts) into a common fund.

But, in every way, the Church is called on this occasion to a manifestation of unity and life, for the storm may be upon her before we are aware. There are past sins to deplore, fresh struggles to prepare for. The clergy have already suffered; now the laity are threatened. The miserable policy which allowed or forced the expatriation of a Protestant peasantry, and stimulated the frightful competition for land—land, to the highest bidder, no matter who or what he was or by what means the price was to be wrung,—is bearing rapid fruit. And if in the social changes which impend, the Church is likely to be driven into a new position, there is surely no time to be lost in considering how her position may be maintained under altered circumstances. Is the distinctive churchmanship, which now prevails among us, sufficiently vigorous to hold the body together, if outward support were withdrawn? are the principles of the Church so established in the understandings and hearts of the people, that a mere worldly reverse could not uproot them? Or is there, indeed, danger that if the State machine were broken up, the inward fabric might dissolve with it, and many of our members fall away—some to Romanism, some to the various classes of dissent—when the main bond of union was broken; when they had no deep principle to hold them together, and were at liberty to follow the leadings of inclination, fear, or worldly interest, without restraint?

IRISH ECCLESIASTICAL JOURNAL, JANUARY 1847

TO LORD JOHN RUSSELL

PRIME MINISTER OF GREAT BRITAIN AND IRELAND

MY LORD,

Whenever I have dedicated any of my Works hitherto, I have always prefixed to them the name of some personal friend: in dedicating the following Work to your Lordship, I would fain hope that I dedicate it to a friend of my country.

This is an Irish Book, my Lord, to which I would respectfully solicit your Lordship's attention; it is painful to me to be obliged to add, that it is written upon an exclusively Irish subject.

It is in your character of Prime Minister that I take the liberty of prefixing your Lordship's name to this *Tale of Irish Famine*. Had Sir ROBERT PEEL been in office, I would have placed his name where that of your Lordship now stands. There is something not improper in this; for although I believe that both you and he are sincerely anxious to benefit our unhappy country, still I cannot help thinking that the man who, in his ministerial capacity, must be looked upon as a public exponent of those principles of Government which have brought our country to her present calamitous condition, by a long course of illiberal legislation and unjustifiable neglect, ought to have his name placed before a story which details with truth the sufferings which such legislation and neglect have entailed upon our people. This, my Lord, is not done from any want of respect to your Lordship, but because the writer trusts that, as it is the first Tale of Irish Famine that ever was dedicated to an English Prime Minister, your Lordship's enlarged and enlightened policy will put it out of the power of any succeeding author ever to write another.

Permit me to say that your Lordship need not call in question the facts and circumstances depicted in it. It is, as I have stated, a tale of Irish suffering and struggle; and you may rest assured, my Lord, that there is no party in this country so well qualified to afford authentic information on this particular subject, as those who have done most in giving an impulse to and sustaining the literature of their country.

I have the honour to be, my Lord,
Your Lordship's obedient servant,
THE AUTHOR

THE BLACK PROPHET BY WILLIAM CARLETON

BELFAST, 1847

SKETCHES IN THE WEST OF IRELAND

BY MR. JAMES MAHONY

The accounts from the Irish provincial papers continue to detail the unmitigated sufferings of the starving peasantry. Indeed, they are stated to be on the increase, notwithstanding the very great exertion of public bodies and individuals to assuage their pressure.

With the object of ascertaining the accuracy of the frightful statements received from the West, and of placing them in unexaggerated fidelity before our readers, a few days since, we commissioned our Artist, Mr. James Mahony, of Cork, to visit a seat of extreme suffering, viz., Skibbereen and its vicinity...

"I started from Cork, by the mail (says our informant), for Skibbereen and saw little until we came to Clonakilty, where the coach stopped for breakfast; and here, for the first time, the horrors of the poverty became visible, in the vast number of famished poor, who flocked around the coach to beg alms: amongst them was a woman carrying in her arms the corpse of a fine child, and making the most distressing appeal to the passengers for aid to enable her to purchase a coffin and bury her dear little baby. This horrible spectacle induced me to make some inquiry about her, when I learned from the people of the hotel that each day brings dozens of such applicants into the town. *See the Sketch*.

WOMAN BEGGING AT CLONAKILTY.

"After leaving Clonakilty, each step that we took westward brought fresh evidence of the truth of the reports of the misery, as we either met a funeral or a coffin at every hundred yards, until we approached the picturesque country of the Shepperton Lakes. *See the Sketch* [on p. 112]. Here, the distress became more striking, from the decrease of numbers at the funerals, none having more than eight or ten attendants, and many only two or three.

"We next reached Skibbereen ... and, it being then late I rested until Monday, when, with the valuable aid of Dr. D. Donovan, and his assistant, Mr. Crowley, I witnessed such scenes of misery and privation as I trust it may never be again my lot to look upon. Up to this

FUNERAL AT SHEPPERTON LAKES.

morning, I, like a large portion, I fear, of the community, looked on
the diaries of Dr. Donovan, as published in *The Cork Southern Reporter*,
to be highly-coloured pictures, doubtless, intended for a good and
humane purpose; but I can now, with perfect confidence, say that neither
pen nor pencil ever could portray the misery and horror, at this
moment, to be witnessed in Skibbereen. We first proceeded to
Bridgetown... and there I saw the dying, the living, and the dead,
lying indiscriminately upon the same floor, without anything between
them and the cold earth, save a few miserable rags upon them. To point
to any particular house as a proof of this would be a waste of time, as
all were in the same state; and, not a single house out of 500 could boast
of being free from death and fever, though several could be pointed
out with the dead lying close to the living for the space of three or four,
even six days, without any effort being made to remove the bodies to
a last resting place.

"After leaving this abode of death, we proceeded to High-street, or
Old Chapel-lane, and there found one house, without door or window, filled with destitute people lying on the bare floor; and one fine,
tall, stout country lad, who had entered some hours previously to find
shelter from the piercing cold, lay here dead amongst others likely soon
to follow him. The appeals to the feelings and professional skill of my
kind attendants here became truly heart-rending; and so distressed Dr.
Donovan, that he begged me not to go into the house, and to avoid
coming into contact with the people surrounding the doorway.

"We next proceeded to the Chapel-yard, to see the hut, of which
Dr. Donovan gives the following graphic account in his diary:—

'On my return home, I remembered that I had yet a visit to pay; having in the morning received a ticket to see six members of one family, named Barrett, who had been turned out of the cabin in which they lodged, in the neighbourhood of Old Chapelyard; and who had struggled to this burying-ground, and literally entombed themselves in a small watch-house that was built for the shelter of those who were engaged in guarding against exhumation by the doctors, when more respect was paid to the dead than is at present the case. This shed is exactly seven feet long, by about six in breadth. By the side of the western wall is a long, newly-made grave; by either gable are two of shorter dimensions, which have been recently tenanted; and near the hole that serves as a doorway is the last resting-place of two or three children; in fact, this hut is surrounded by a rampart of human bones, which have accumulated to such a height that the threshold, which was originally on a level with the ground, is now two feet beneath it. In this horrible den, in the midst of a mass of human putrefaction, six individuals, males and females, labouring under most malignant fever, were huddled together, as closely as were the dead in the graves around.

'At the time (eleven o'clock at night) that I went to visit these poor sufferers, it was blowing a perfect hurricane, and such groans of roaring wind and rain I never remember to have heard.

'I was accompanied by my assistant, Crowley, and we took with us some bread, tea and sugar; on reaching this vault, I thrust my head through the hole of entrance, and had immediately to draw back, so intolerable was the effluvium; and, though rendered callous by a companionship for many years with disease and death, yet I was completely unnerved at the humble scene of suffering and misery that was presented to my view; six fellow creatures were almost buried alive in this filthy sepulchre. When they heard my voice, one called out, "Is that the Priest?" another, "Is that the Doctor?" The mother of the family begged in the most earnest manner that I would have them removed, or else that they would rot together; and they all implored that we would give them drink. Mr. Crowley produced the tea and sugar, but they said it was of no use to them, as they had no fire or place to light it in, and that what they wanted was *water*; that they had put a jug under the droppings from the roof, but would not have drink enough for the night. The next day I got the consent of the Poor Law Guardians to have my patients removed from this abode of the dead to the fever hospital, and they are since improving.'

"To complete my melancholy visit to this scene of horror, and to visit every corner of Skibbereen, next morning, accompanied by a Mr. Everett, whose knowledge of the country I found most useful, I started for Ballidichob, and learned upon the road that we should come to a hut or cabin in the parish of Aghadoe, on the property of Mr. Long, where four people had lain dead for six days; and, upon arriving at the hut, the abode of Tim Harrington, we found this to be true; for there lay the four bodies, and a fifth was passing to the same bourne. On hearing our voices, the sinking man made an effort to reach the door, and ask for drink or fire; he fell in the doorway; there, in all probability to lie; as the living cannot be prevailed to assist in the interments, for fear of taking the fever.

"We next got to Skull, where, by the attention of Dr. Traill, vicar of the parish (and whose humanity at the present moment is beyond all praise), we witnessed almost indescribable in-door horrors. In the street, however, we had the best opportunity of judging of the condition of the people; for here, from three to five hundred women, with money in their hands, were seeking to buy food; whilst a few of the Government officers doled out Indian meal to them in their turn. One of the women told me she had been standing there since daybreak, seeking to get food for her family at home.

"This food, it appeared, was being doled out in miserable quantities, at 'famine prices,' to the neighbouring poor, from a stock lately arrived in a sloop, with a Government steamship to protect its cargo of 50 tons; whilst the population amounts to 27,000; so that you may calculate what were the feelings of the disappointed mass."

ILLUSTRATED LONDON NEWS, 13 FEBRUARY 1847

SKULL, FROM THE BALLIDICHOB.

IRELAND again! Yes, dear readers, you must not be weary of Ireland; the Christian Ladies' Magazine has always peculiarly belonged to the cause of Ireland. What would our honored predecessor say, could she know that it was even one month silent in this hour of Ireland's bitterest woe? 1822 was, as an Irish Clergyman writes, nothing to 1847.—Besides what have we to do with weariness?—weariness is the child of despair, and we are full of hope. When our resources are quite exhausted, when every means of relief has failed, then it will be time to be weary, and we will beg to be spared from tales of woe. Just now a more than usually bright ray of hope beams upon us, and in case the proposal is unknown to some of our readers, we must bring it before them. The Irish Clergy now especially claim the sympathy of their protestant brethren in England; they are doing their very utmost to relieve the wretchedness around them, and doubtless their influence over their flocks is thus widening and deepening, for it is in the hour of distress, men find out who are their true friends; but the burden is too great for them to bear. Many of them, with small incomes, have themselves suffered severely from the potato failure. The plan proposed is this, that each wealthy English parish should select some starving parish in Ireland; in many cases local connections which had excited previous interest, would determine the choice, in others, information with regard to the most distressed localities, might be obtained from the Irish Society. Weekly collections would then be made, the English Clergyman would enter into communication with the Clergyman of the Irish parish, stating what sum he hoped to be able to remit weekly, (which would enable the other to make the most advantageous arrangements with regard to meal, &c.,) and requesting weekly statements of progress—a detail both of their wants and of the amount of relief afforded. In some cases, this might lead, where funds allowed, to the establishment of Scripture readers. This scheme would give us almost the interest of personally administering our food to the hungry. The adopted parish would be to us almost as a child; we should learn to know and love it, its temporal and spiritual wants would be often on our minds, and often we trust borne before our God in prayer...

Courage, then, dear friends, this is no time for weariness, we can do much, and by God's grace, or to use the Irish beggar's plea, "for the

116 love and mercy of God," we will. "Freely we have received, freely we will give."

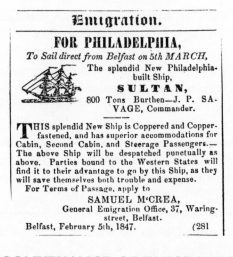

CONVEYANCE OF EMIGRANTS
TO AMERICA

In THE NATION of the 14th November last, I endeavoured to point out the infamous conduct adopted towards the great majority of emigrants, from the moment they leave their native soil to that on which they land on the shores of a new world. The time is now rapidly approaching when emigration on a far greater scale than ever has been known before will be commenced; it may, therefore, be of use to elicit opinion on the subject.

Many persons who believe that the present system of conveying people to America is improperly carried on, declare that the interference of parliament is imperatively necessary to effect an improvement, and that laws of a stringent character should be passed to remedy the evil. They do not reflect that the legislature has already deliberated upon the matter; that the statute book bears on its pages a highly salutary enactment on this head; and that it is partly because the persons entrusted with its execution have omitted their duty, and partly from the contracted jurisdiction of the act, that the grievances now complained of exist. It shall be seen presently how both these causes operate.

I have glanced at some of the judicious regulations framed for the protection of the emigrating community, and intended to prevent in some degree the designs of interested men. By the second section of the act, which came into force on the 1st October, 1842, it is provided: that no ship carrying passengers on a voyage from any port in the United Kingdom to any place out of Europe, and not being within the Mediterranean Sea, shall proceed, with more than three persons to every five tons of her registered burthen, to each of whom shall be allotted on the lower deck, the space of ten superficial feet; and the master of any ship exceeding these proportions is liable to a penalty of 5*l.*, in respect of every passenger constituting the excess.

Sec. 4. That such ship shall be of the height of six feet at the least between the upper and lower decks; and shall not carry passengers on the orlop deck, unless the height between such deck and that immediately above it, be six feet at least.

Sec. 5. That no ship shall have more than two tiers of berths, and that the intervals between the floor of the berths and the deck beneath shall not be less than six inches; that the berths shall be securely constructed, and their dimensions not under six feet in length and eighteen inches in width for each passenger.

Sec. 6. That there shall be issued to the passengers daily a supply of water, at the rate of at least three quarts to each; and that there shall be also issued, not less often than twice a week, a supply of provisions, at the rate of seven pounds of bread, biscuit, flour, oatmeal, or rice, per week; and that no ship shall be cleared out until there shall be on board such quantity of pure water and provisions as may be sufficient for the voyage.

Sec. 10. That the government emigration agent, at ports where there is such an officer, or, in his absence, the collector or comptroller of customs, shall survey the provisions and water required, and ascertain that the same are in a sweet and good condition.

Sec. 11. That these officers shall see that the other directions of the act be complied with, so far as can be done, before the departure of the ship.

Sec. 12. That these officers shall also, if any doubts should arise as to the seaworthiness of the ship, cause her to be surveyed by two competent persons; and, if they shall report her unseaworthy, such ship shall not be cleared until the report be disproved, or till she be rendered fit for the voyage.

Sec. 13. That every ship shall have good, sound boats, in proportion to her tonnage: two boats, if under 250 tons; three boats, if 250 tons and upwards; and four boats, if 500 tons and upwards; one of such to be a long-boat of suitable size.

Sec. 14. That two copies of this act be kept on board, one of which is to be produced to any passenger for perusal upon request made to the master at any seasonable time.

Sec. 15. That no ship shall clear out until she shall have on board such medicines, with directions for using same, and other things necessary for the medical treatment of the passengers during the voyage, as may be available for that purpose.

Sec. 21. That any licensed broker (for without having a license none can act) who may receive money from any passenger, without having a written authority to act as agent from his assumed principal, or, by fraud or false pretence, induce any person to engage a passage, is liable to a penalty of 10*l*.

Sec. 22. That if any person who shall have contracted for his passage, and be at the place of embarkation at the time appointed, and not obtain his passage, either from the circumstance of the ship having already sailed, or in consequence of the neglect or refusal of the owner or master; or shall not in a reasonable time obtain a passage in some equally eligible vessel, and meanwhile be supported as the act directs, he will be entitled to recover the money he may have paid for passage, and a moderate compensation for his loss and inconvenience.

Sec. 23. That if the ship shall be detained by any cause but wind and weather beyond the time agreed to with any passenger, the master shall victual such passenger in like manner as if the voyage had commenced; and after the lapse of two days without sailing, he shall pay to such passenger, instead of victualling him, one shilling per day until the actual departure of the ship.

Sec. 24. That the master shall not land any passenger without his consent at any place other than that at which he may have contracted to do so.

Sec. 25. That at the close of the voyage every passenger shall be entitled to remain on board, and to be maintained in the same manner as during the voyage for the space of 48 hours after arrival.

Sec. 27. That in the event of the provisions contained in this act for the security of passengers not being carried into effect, the master renders himself liable to the payment of a fine not exceeding 50*l*.

Sec. 29. That the penalties imposed by the act may be recovered to the use of her Majesty by any government emigration agent or any collector or comptroller of the customs; and all sums due, as return of passage-money, subsistence-money, or compensation, may be recovered by any passenger entitled thereto, or by such officers before mentioned for his use, before any two justices of the peace in any part of her Majesty's dominions in which the offence shall have been committed, the cause of complaint arisen, or in which the offender may happen to be.

From this brief abstract, it will appear that, with the exception of having caused no arrangements to be made with regard to light, ventilation, and fuel, parliament has not neglected its duty to the emigrant. Yet it is undeniable that the state of things which preceded this law, and absolutely demanded its enactment, has been very little, if at all, improved. It is not difficult to see why this is. By the 10th, 11th, and 12th sections above referred to, the government emigration agent, or, in his absence, the collector or comptroller of customs, is required to ascertain that the directions of the act are, as far as possible, complied with, before a ship leaves port. If this were regularly done, no vessel could go to sea that was not properly constructed, fitted for the voyage, capable of accommodating passengers, and provided with all such requisites as by law are specified. But even after these precautions, the emigrant may incur bad treatment—and herein consists the chief cause of the comparative failure of the law—namely, its applicability solely to her Majesty's dominions. For example, persons going to the United States, who have been deprived during their voyage of some of the benefits which it guarantees to them, must return to this country in order to obtain redress. It is true, that any compensation they may be entitled to can be recovered by the proper authorities at home, who are authorised to proceed on behalf of the injured absent; but the means of proof can rarely be supplied, save by the complainant's presence.

WILLIAM POWER

THE NATION, DUBLIN, 27 FEBRUARY 1847

IRISH DISTRESS IN CONGRESS

On the 26th of February, in the Senate of the United States, Mr. Crittenden rose to introduce a bill for the relief of Ireland and Scotland. After remarking upon the extent and depth of the famine in the British Islands, particularly in Ireland, he referred for constitutional authority for this bill to the act passed May 8, 1812, for the relief of the people of Venezuela, who had recently suffered from a dreadful earthquake; and to the great constitutional men of that day, who had united in the passage of that bill, including Mr. Macon, Mr. Randolph, and Mr. Calhoun. Here was a much stronger case; that was a partial calamity—this is a general and all-pervading famine. The fruits of the earth have been cut off by a pestilence, and death stalks abroad over the Green Island in his most horrid form. We are, moreover, not only bound to render this relief by the ties of common humanity, but by the ties of kindred blood. We are, to a great extent, the descendants of these very people; we are under a family obligation to relieve them. The day when the principle of hate and the work of bloodshed alone controlled the relations of nations to each other has passed by, and a better state of things has succeeded; and what more beautiful example could be given of the Christian principle that is diffusing itself among all nations—the principle of a common humanity—than the employment of the public ships in this great national movement of fraternal relief. He had no idea that the federal constitution, in its design or in its spirit, was inconsistent with the principles of common humanity, or of the great laws of our common nature. He eloquently appealed in behalf, too, of the public policy of passing this bill. He passed up the bill to the secretary, and it was read. It provides:—

"1. That the President of the United States shall be authorised to purchase such provisions as shall be deemed suitable and proper for the relief of the poor of Ireland and Scotland; said provisions to be rendered over to the British government for distribution.

"2. Appropriates 500,000 dollars, to be set apart for this object.

"3. Authorises the President to employ the public ships of the United States, at his discretion, in the transportation of said provisions to the British government, for distribution."

Mr. J.M. Clayton said he would give the bill his most hearty support, and adverted to the resolutions adopted by the legislature of Delaware on the subject, in which they recommend their representatives in Congress to support any movement here for the benefit of Ireland, and give their sanction to it; and recommend that the U.S. ship Pennsylvania be employed in the transportation of bread to Ireland, or such war steamer as may be spared. Mr. Clayton appealed that the bill be passed without delay, and dwelt upon the extent of famine prevailing in Ireland and Scotland as the stern necessity.

Mr. Cass said he should give this bill his cordial support. The famine prevailing in Ireland was unexampled in the history of modern times. While our land was abounding in plenty, starvation was stalking abroad over the nations of Europe. It was such an universal destitution that no private efforts were sufficient to relieve it. Ireland had no Egypt to go to for corn, that "she might live and not die." After adverting to our kindred relations with the British islands, and to the services which the people of Ireland had rendered to the United States in peace and in war, from the heights of Abraham to the walls of Monterey, Mr. Cass approved the national plan of relief proposed. Let us convert our ships of war into ships of peace—our messengers of death into messengers of life—our instruments of destruction into agents of preservation. He would support the bill of the senator from Kentucky with great pleasure.

Mr. Niles thought they ought to pause a little. Does any national movement belong to us? Did it not rather belong to the government to which Ireland belongs to make this movement? He considered this bill as a pernicious precedent, and that the proceeding in itself was not authorised by the constitution.

Mr. Bagby, without committing himself upon the bill, was not prepared to give it three readings in one day.

The bill was then read a second time, and laid over till the 27th. Congress was to rise on the 4th of March.

THE NATION, DUBLIN, 3 MARCH 1847

REPORT ON MATTERS REQUIRING ATTENTION

IN THE MANAGEMENT OF THE WORKHOUSE BUILDINGS IN IRELAND

BY GEO. WILKINSON, ESQ.,
ARCHITECT OF THE POOR LAW COMMISSION

ARCHITECT'S OFFICE, POOR LAW COMMISSION OFFICE,
DUBLIN, 10TH MARCH, 1847

GENTLEMEN,

Under the extreme pressure brought upon the Irish poorhouses, and the present overcrowded state of many of them, I beg to submit to your Board some observations with reference to some regulations of a practical kind which in a sanatory point of view seem to me to require particular attention at the present time.

The matters to which I have to allude are, chiefly, the ventilation of the buildings, the state of the manure-pits and cesspools, and ground around the workhouse sites.

VENTILATION

The doors of the several wards almost all of them open into what is technically called the well-hole of the staircase, over which is a turret or lantern light, made to open so as to occasion a free circulation of air upwards from the doorways of the several wards opening into it. The doorways of the wards are almost all formed with semicircular arched heads, the door being made only so high as the springing of the arch, leaving therefore the upper space quite open, occasioning a free circulation of air.

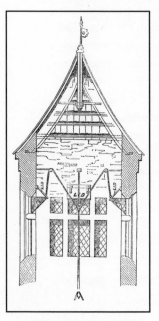

A.—VENTILATING TOWER OVER WELL-HOLE OF STAIRCASES

In some of the houses the openings on the turret and lantern lights are much neglected, and where this is the case the ventilation of the building is very much prejudiced; this is a matter, therefore, requiring particular attention, and I would recommend that in those houses which have the stone towers (being those houses originally built for accommodating a less number than 700 persons) the wood lids for regulating the admission of air should be altogether removed from the opening lights.—Sketch (A) of the inside of the tower, shows the lids proposed to be removed.

In those doorways formed without open circular heads over them (as those which adjoin the passages near the master's apartments in the children's dormitories of the smaller-sized houses) I would recommend the doors being pierced with circular holes, cleanly formed, according to the accompanying sketch (B)—the holes at the bottom of the doors might be introduced to all the doors of wards, whether with open circular heads or without them.

In the infirmary wards the rear walls, being those which adjoin the men's and women's yards, have

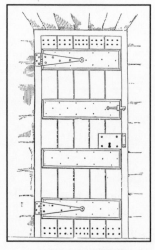

B.—DOOR OF THE WARDS.

no windows in them for certain reasons, which

influenced their constructive arrangement in the original plans.
In about one half the buildings large ventilators, similar to the accompanying sketch (C), have at various times within the last three years been

introduced in several of the Unions; where they have not been introduced they have been recommended to be so, and drawings have been furnished in several instances for that purpose. Their advantage is so great, and in the present crowded state of many of the hospitals their want is so much felt, that I

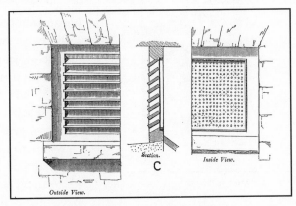

C.—VENTILATOR FOR INFIRMARY.

would beg to advise efforts being made for their insertion in every infirmary which is without them. The same kind of ventilators may with much advantage be introduced in the side walls of the wards in the wing buildings of the poorhouse, more particularly in those houses where there are no outside windows in the flank walls of wings. In the infirm rooms on the ground floor two in each room would be desirable, placed at equal distances about 12 inches below the ceiling joint.

Sketch (D) is a ventilator also applicable to the wards of the poorhouses generally, where the cost of obtaining zinc plates is objectionable, or where a somewhat less costly construction is required; but these latter are not so suitable for the infirmary as the former drawing (C).

Pierced zinc plates inserted in the panes of glass of the windows, as shown on the accompanying drawing (E), will occasion a considerable circulation of air and very little admission of driving rain: where zinc may not be conveniently procured, I have found the old tin cans of the poorhouses have been beaten flat and punched with regular-formed holes; holes one-twelfth of an inch in

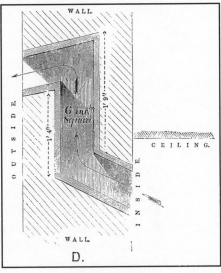

D.—VENTILATOR.

E.—WORKHOUSE WINDOW—SHOWING ZINC
PLATES SUBSTITUTED FOR GLASS.

diameter and half an inch apart are found to have answered the purpose very satisfactorily. Zinc for plates, however, of the required size, already punched, may be obtained of Mr. Loftus Bryan, Bride-street, and may be also procured from other places in Dublin, and in most of the large towns in Ireland. It is recommended that the zinc plates should be punched, and the birr or rough side be put outwards, which will the better prevent driving rain from entering.

Where from the above cause any driving rain may find its way inside the windows, I have to recommend a catch-water slip like sketch (F) being fixed to the inside lower part of the window-frame, and also for catching the condensed water which frequently runs down the inside of the windows on the floor of the room in cold and frosty weather.

THIRTEENTH ANNUAL REPORT OF THE POOR
LAW COMMISSIONERS

LONDON, 1847

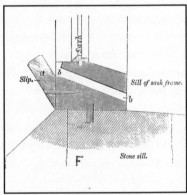

F.—SLIP FOR CATCHING WATER ON
INSIDE OF WINDOWS.

THE NEW POOR LAW

Lord John Russell, in trying to produce a poor law for Ireland, has manifestly failed to please either of the two great classes into which the old feudal institutions have divided society. The failure may, with some show of reason, be attributed to the difficulty of the subject, to the present ill-temper of all parties concerned, to ignorance

of the condition and of the peculiar habits and tastes of this nation, or
to all these causes combined. To whatever cause, however, the failure
is to be attributed, it is plain that to landlords and merchants—farmers
and citizens—clergy, aristocracy, and people—the proposed new poor
law is alike distasteful. On one point only do all agree, and that is, that
the present bill will be acceptable to none.

WEEKLY FREEMAN'S JOURNAL, DUBLIN, 13 MARCH 1847

NEXT YEAR'S FAMINE

One paragraph from a letter of Mr. FITZPATRICK, Parish Priest
of Skibbereen, published in the *Freeman* of yesterday, includes
within it the whole history of Ireland for the year 1847, and,
by anticipation, of the two or three years following:—

"The ground continues unsown and uncultivated. *There is a mutual
distrust between the landlord and the tenant.* The landlord is in dread, if he
gives seed to his tenant, that the tenant will consume the crop and not
pay him his rent; and the tenant is in dread that, if he himself sows seed,
the landlord will pounce on the crop as soon as it is cut. Thus there
is a mutual distrust; and, therefore, the ground *remains uncultivated.* The
landlord would wish, if possible, *to get up his ground,* and the unfortunate
tenant is anxious to stick to it as long as he can. A good many, however,
are giving it up, and preparing for America; and these are the substantial farmers, who have still a little means left."

THE NATION, DUBLIN, 13 MARCH 1847

SOUP STORE AT CORK

The benevolent attempts to alleviate the present scarcity are
specially worthy of illustration in our pages; since they, doubtless,
in many instances, prompt the reader to aid directly or indirectly
in the good work, "all mankind's concern"—charity. The annexed
Illustration is of this class of subjects; it represents the Soup Depôt, in
Barrack-street, Cork, stated to be the first establishment of the kind

THE CENTRAL SOUP DEPÔT, BARRACK-STREET, CORK.

opened in Ireland for the distribution of food to the poor, gratuitously. Our artist (Mr. James Mahony) assures us that 1300 poor persons are thus relieved daily; and that the establishment has effected more good among the wretched than any other means of relief yet suggested. The rush to obtain a place in one of the partitions (eight in number), so as to be in time for the distribution, is surprising; as is, also, the quiet, peaceable demeanour of the poor people.

The spot where this large Depôt has been fitted up was, until this year, one of the principal potato markets, and is, therefore, well calculated for the purpose; it being well walled in, and surrounded with sheds, which afford shelter to the poor applicants. The food is cooked in an upper building, and handed down for distribution, as shown by our artist. Previously to this, an equally large quantity of capital meat soup is distributed at one halfpenny per quart, to such as choose to purchase it. It is worthy of remark, that, from the opening of this Depôt to the present time, not an act of dishonesty has been known to take place; Alderman Roche stating that not a spoon or vessel to be missing.

ILLUSTRATED LONDON NEWS, 13 MARCH 1847

DISMISSAL OF THE LABOURERS

MINISTERIAL PLEDGES AND
MINISTERIAL PERFORMANCES

We were not a little astonished to read the reply which is reported to have been given by Mr. Labouchere, in his place in the House of Commons, to the question put by Mr. W.S. O'Brien, on Monday night, with respect to the dismissal of the people employed on the public works. Mr. Smith O'Brien asked if the government intended "to adhere to the rule laid down" for the dismissal of "20 per cent" of the labourers. The English Chief Secretary for Ireland replied that the government had, indeed, issued such an order, but "had not thought proper to adhere to this plan throughout the whole of Ireland."

WEEKLY FREEMAN'S JOURNAL, DUBLIN, 27 MARCH 1847

BENEFICIAL EFFECTS OF
RELIEF AFFORDED

BY THE HIBERNIAN FEMALE SCHOOL SOCIETY

Many of our readers have been interested in the accounts we have given of the labours of this Society...

FROM A LADY IN SLIGO

"Dec. 24th, 1846.—As you enjoy so much the luxury of doing good, you may form some right conception of my delight yesterday, after having 100 articles of dress made in the school, and distributing with them fifty more with my own hands to our children. Think of the joy and gladness with which each little one returned to her own home. It was a jubilee indeed. Oh! what a gracious God we have to do with! Who serves him for nought! I received your second welcome half note to-day. When a supply comes, I think I am passing rich; but, to my surprise, I find myself, on the arrival of a new announcement, actually in need!

"Jan. 5th. 1847.—How good God is in thus bringing into such active operation the benevolence of comparatively unknown friends. I include

128 in this remark the £5. of your last remittance, and all the other marks of God's tender pity through the instrumentality of our humane and munificent English sympathizers. It is amazing the regularity with which my charity purse is supplied. When I begin to calculate on withholding my hand, as its contents begin to run to a close, I am that very day put to shame for my unbelief, by the delivery of some new packet of help. My God, where shall I thy praise begin? We are not now suffered to complain."

CHRISTIAN LADIES' MAGAZINE, LONDON, MARCH 1847

CALL TO PRAYER

WILLIAM M'COMB

SUGGESTED BY A PROCLAMATION FROM THE QUEEN FOR A GENERAL FAST, ON THE 24TH MARCH, 1847

Heralds, as in days of Esther,
    Make the Royal Message known,
    Day of solemn prayer appointed—
God acknowledged from the throne.

Fathers, mothers, sisters, brothers,
    Every family apart,
Bow before the throne of mercy,
    Bend the knee and lift the heart.

Queen of England's proud dominions,
    Princes, nobles of the land,
Pastors, people, ruled and rulers,
    Bend the knee and lift the hand.

When Jehovah hath withholden
    From the poor their daily bread—
When the famishing are dying—
    Bend the knee, and bow the head.

Rich and poor obey the summons—
  Loud the message comes to all—
When the Lord in wrath hath smitten,
  Prostrate at His footstool fall.

In the hour of tribulation,
  To the house of God repair;
Lay your gifts upon the altar,
  Faith, and penitence, and prayer.

BELFAST, MARCH 1847

A SERMON

BY THE REV. THOMAS HANLEY

Ireland's harp is unstrung—her minstrelsy is silent—"The mirth of the land is gone!"

Why is this? Why this perplexity and difficulty among our statesmen? Why this painful anxiety and apprehension among our gentry? Why these cries of distress, and looks of destitution, among our peasantry? Why these records of mourning and lamentation? Why this national gloom?—JEHOVAH, the Creator of the universe, the King of kings, the Lord of nations, the Providing God—He is angry; and he has manifested his anger by laying bare his arm, and taking away from upwards of three millions of our people their "stay and staff, their whole stay of bread." Famine, disease, and death are the consequence. This the Queen of these realms acknowledges—the government of our country acknowledge—and you, my dear friends, by your attendance here this morning, acknowledge the same truth. On this solemn day, then, set apart as it is for national humiliation, it will not, I sincerely hope, be unprofitable for us to enquire, *What it is* that has so displeased Jehovah . . . Give me your serious attention while, in the plainest language, I lay before you the cause of this national calamity . . .

Now, dear friends, we hesitate not to affirm, that the Lord is in our own day and nation publicly carrying out this retributive system . . . It behoves us to examine ourselves, and enquire what are the sins which have thus incensed Jehovah against us, and brought down this manifest token of his displeasure . . .

Bear with me while I endeavour, faithfully, to expose a few of the sins and shortcomings of which many of the disciples of Jesus are guilty . . .

First, I shall notice their *Divisions.* You are, doubtless, aware that there are among the professed disciples of the same Lord many divisions, which have been the cause of much scandal among the adversaries of his cause, which divisions are probably, by these adversaries, in no small degree amplified and exaggerated, and which are to be condemned as being both offensive and sinful . . .

Besides the divisions existing among the disciples of Jesus, look at their *Worldliness.* It was a main design of Him who is the author and finisher of our faith, that his disciples should be as far separated from the world, as their residence in the world could by possibility admit . . .

I must notice the *Inactivity* that exists among the disciples of Jesus. When we estimate the magnitude and nature of the objects for which the activity of the Church is demanded, and compare these objects with the amount of activity really and actually rendered, we have reason to be astonished and confounded at the splendid position of the one, and the complete insignificance of the other; and even with regard to those who are esteemed diligent in the Gospel cause, would not the labour which they are accustomed to give to the Church, be esteemed little better than sluggishness and idleness if given to the world . . . *Infidelity* has still many votaries—men who entirely reject the record of divine truth, trample on the Christian doctrine of the omnipotence of God, and reduce the mighty principle of a future existence to the mere non-entity of the fancy . . .

There is the *filthy conversation* of the multitude . . .

There is the *want of principle*, too, that characterizes the vast majority of the population . . .

And there is *Sabbath-breaking*, and *neglect of Church ordinances* . . .

But examine this still blacker catalogue of crime, those iniquities which our courts of justice are obliged to take cognizance of and to punish . . . *Drunkenness*, that meanest and most dangerous of crimes— mean, because it degrades man below the level of the brute creation; and dangerous because by reason of its maddening and reason-dethroning influence, it exposes men to the perpetration of guilt from which they would otherwise shrink and revolt. *Robbery*, that most cowardly and dishonourable of crimes . . . And *Murder*, that most treacherous and damnable of crimes—treacherous, for the assassin walks abroad wearing the day-light robe of charity and peace—salutes you by the way—engages in conversation—watches his opportunity—plies his secret dagger—effects his deadly purpose—then flies back to his hiding place, glutted, but marked with blood—damnable, for if there is one more than another, who, should he die unrepenting and unforgiven, shall suffer the extreme of hell's torment, and hell's punishment, it will be the assassin, who, unprovoked, and with cool, calculating premeditation, waylays his fellow-man, and sends the innocent victim to an unmerited and untimely grave.

'THE FAMINE—ITS CAUSE AND CURE': A SERMON PREACHED IN THE PARISH CHURCH OF MULLABRACK, DIOCESE OF ARMAGH, ON WEDNESDAY 24 MARCH 1847

DEAD—TWENTY PER CENT MORE

We would write with our heart's-blood, if the writing could waken you who read to that frightful spectacle—our country. If every man in the land see it not very soon, she will be as a howling solitude. From South to North spreads over her the shadow of death, and the air smells of the charnel-house. In Munster the living are not there to bury the dead. In Ulster, where tenant-right and plenty once reigned, gasping men totter like ghosts along the roads. All who can are flying from the land as they would from a pest-house. The poorhouses are become mere vents of death for the unfortunates who must emigrate—to another world. Everywhere thousands of thousands have been sacrificed to the Moloch of English economy. Others are on intermediate stations to the altar. And now, at this moment, sentence of doom, without appeal, has gone forth against every fifth man of those recently kept by "public work" between life and death. The order just issued by the English Government, and which has been carried out in every locality with which we are acquainted, adjudges "Death by starvation" to 20 per cent. of the *heads* of families—a most impartial and systematic murder.

The pretence of it—the motives assigned by its originators—considering them, as we are willing to do, true and real—display more than anything else their utter apathy to the tremendous responsibility with which they are trifling, and their utter ignorance of the ruin which that trifling has induced upon our people. While the "public work" was in its fullest swing, men have died in nearly every county through sheer want. Was this the time to make supernumerary starvelings—to drive men into the market where there was no market? During the week previous to this order there were more unsuccessful applicants for public work than would till all the land yet turned in Ireland. Was this the time to increase the number? When the farmers of twenty and thirty acres had discharged their servants through incapacity to feed them, was this the time to throw into the market of death 20 per cent. more of the labouring? Where are the farmers to employ a fraction of these? In America—on the Atlantic—in the poorhouse—in the same "labour-market," or in the churchyard. All small farmers who could amass the means have fled, or are flying, the country. All who could not were themselves driven to "the work," or the poorhouse, or death. And now the English Government turns round on these public paupers, nominally holders of land under ten acres, saying, "Go ye, who have not a dinner for to-day, become capitalists, and grow wheat for next year." Is not this the most murderous absurdity it has perpetrated yet?

THE NATION, DUBLIN, 27 MARCH 1847

FINALE OF A COOK'S TRIUMPH

FROM THE PACKET OF TUESDAY NIGHT

Cooks are looking up—the kitchen is prospering—soup-makers are the fashion—"turnspits are," as *Goldfinch* says, "the go, the gape, the stare, the gaze"—scullions strut about with heads erect, and *High Life Below Stairs* is no longer a farce, but a real occurrence. We have a railway king, and we have also a king of the dish-covers; and, while the aristocracy of wealth licks the dust beneath the feet of the former, the great and the titled celebrate the triumph of the latter. Since Easter Monday M. Soyer has enjoyed a succession of ovations. Fair ladies have smiled upon him while wielding his ladle, as a conqueror wields his baton, and their only rivalry has been who should receive most attention from this emperor of grease. Fashion, in her wildest caprice, never dreamed of such a fancy as has been exhibited in this worship of a cook—inventive cruelty could not imagine a more inhuman proceeding than the parading of wretched thousands to render his glory more complete.

We learn from *Saunders*, which really deserves, from its painstaking

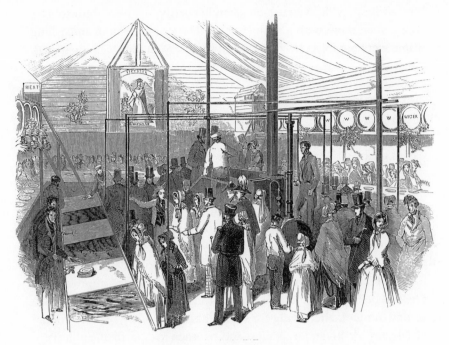

M. SOYER'S MODEL SOUP KITCHEN.

reports of the sayings and doings of this Soyer to be called the cook's
oracle, that "at the particular desire of several charitable ladies" the model
kitchen was set to work on Saturday last, and that these "charitable ladies"
attended and served out the slop with their own fair hands, while, by
an advertisement in the same journal, the general public were offered
a treat in beholding these "charitable ladies" ladling out the soup to the
poor. We think it a pity to withhold this document from our readers:—

"Soyer's Model Kitchen.—By the special desire of several charitable
ladies who have visited and paid particular attention to the working of
the model kitchen, it will be opened again on Saturday next, from two
to six, on which day those ladies, under the direction of Mrs. La Touche,
will attend and serve the poor; the admission for the view on that day
will be 5s. each, to be distributed by the Lord Mayor in charity; after
which the kitchen will be closed, M. Soyer being obliged to leave for
the Reform Club, London."

Five shillings each to see paupers feed!—five shillings each to watch
the burning blush of shame chasing pallidness from poverty's wan
cheek!—five shillings each! when the animals at the Zoological Gardens
may be inspected at feeding time for sixpence! We hope that, as these

"five shillings each" were to be given in charity, the poor unfortunates who earned them with scalding tears and bitter humiliation and galling shame were not forgotten; and that on this occasion they were presented, when the performance was over, with something more than a "fine cake"!

We are also informed by *Saunders*, that the friends of M. Soyer entertained him at dinner on Saturday, in the Freemason's Hall, College-green, when the chair was filled by T.M. Gresham, Esq., who in the names of the city cooks generally, we presume, presented him with an "elegant snuff box," and declared, with the gravity of a Solon, that "although his exertions were not approved of by all parties, they were fully appreciated by those who were the best judges of what was most likely to improve the condition of the country." Now we are not maliciously inclined; but we would dearly like to dose these "best judges" for a week with no aliment but Soyer's soup, and ask them, then; did they find this improver of the "condition of the country," improve their physical being? We should like to see the chairman and vice-chairman of this banquet, after living for seven short days solely on the product of M. Soyer's inventive genius, and try then would their enthusiasm lead them to the dictation of such an inscription as this:—

"PRESENTED TO
MONSIEUR ALEXANDER SOYER,

In testimony of the high sense entertained of his valuable, scientific, and philanthropic services, while engaged in this country on his mission of good in behalf of the destitute poor, by some of his admiring friends, who gladly avail themselves of an early opportunity to mark their regard for himself personally, and the esteem in which his beneficent and truly useful labours have been held by them.—Dublin, April 10th, 1847."

In responding to his health, M. Soyer modestly alluded to his own "profound knowledge of the culinary art," and delicately hinted that he deserved the title of a "true philanthropist" (?)

So has ended, for the present, the cook's ovation, in order that the poor's probation may begin. He has departed, bearing glory with him, and a gold snuff box—they remain, that experimentalists may test whether or no hunger has left the *dura ilia messorum*.

FIRST REPORT OF THE IRISH
POOR RELIEF COMMISSIONERS

The Right Honourable the Lords Commissioners of her Majesty's Treasury have received from the Irish Poor Relief Commissioners their first report, and our London Correspondent informs us that it was to have been presented to both houses of parliament on Monday evening. We are unable to print the document *in extenso* to-day; we will, however, endeavour to convey to our readers a correct idea of what the Commissioners allege to have been done in furtherance of the act up to the date of the report.

The report is dated 10th April, 1847, and begins by stating that, "As Commissioners for Relief under the Act of 10th Victoria, cap. 7, we submitted a preliminary report of our proceedings *on the 27th February*, 1847," and that, in compliance with the Treasury instructions, they now proceed to present their first monthly report. Let us see, then, what has been effected under the temporary Relief Act since it has become law, and what has been done in the interval between the *27th of February* and *the 10th of April*, an interval of *forty-one days*, being just seven weeks less by one day.

We have read the report through with unwonted care, and instead of informing us, as we naturally expected, that thousands and tens of hundreds of thousands of rations were being daily distributed under the act to the wretched labourers who were disbanded by scratch of pen, the Relief Commissioners report, as the boasted labour of the enormous and expensive machinery put in motion by them, that they have distributed *fourteen* tons—of food? No, but fourteen tons *of paper!*

The following is the passage in the report. Speaking of the distribution of "documents," the Commissioners say:—

"The distribution is now nearly completed, and your lordships may conceive the mass of labour, in many branches, on this head, when informed that these documents comprised upwards of 10,000 books, 80,000 sheets, 3,000,000 card tickets, and that their gross weight was not less than 14 tons."

It does not appear from the report that previous to its date one ounce of food had been distributed under the act.

WEEKLY FREEMAN'S JOURNAL, DUBLIN, 24 APRIL 1847

ROYAL IRISH ART-UNION

EXHIBITION OF PICTURES BY ANCIENT
AND CELEBRATED DECEASED MASTERS, FOR
RELIEF OF THE DISTRESS PREVAILING IN IRELAND

One of the most remarkable and gratifying Exhibitions ever opened in Ireland is now attracting great and well-deserved attention in Dublin. It appears that the Royal Irish Art-Union, like many other public establishments and institutions, were called on to contribute towards the relief of the urgent and deplorable destitution now prevalent throughout Ireland; but found that, constituted as they were, they had no right to divert any of their fund from the specific objects for which it was originally subscribed. When, however, a good and energetic spirit is not wanting, there is not much difficulty as to the proper method of proceeding. In a happy moment it was suggested that, previous to the opening of the modern Exhibitions of the year, a project which the Committee had long contemplated using their influence to have revived, viz., an Exhibition of the Works of Ancient Masters, might, at the present juncture, be brought forward with peculiarly beneficial effects.

Mr. Stewart Blacker moved this resolution, the Committee recommended it, and the Society enthusiastically adopted the proceeding at a full and general meeting. The consequence has been, that in three weeks, by well-directed energy, judgment, and taste, such an exhibition of paintings has been collected and presented to the Irish public as must surprise every one—even those best acquainted with the resources of Ireland in this department—and this is the more remarkable, as it appears that, in order to save time and expense of carriage, the Committee restricted themselves almost altogether to Dublin and its immediate vicinity.

Very often in such undertakings—charity concerts and so forth—the expenses swallow up all the proceeds. The Committee and some members of the Art-Union determined this should not be the case as far as their speculation was concerned: for, by a spirited private subscription, they took the contingent expenses (no trifling matter) on themselves; and thus allowed the public the great additional gratification of feeling that every shilling given for admission went direct and unencroached on, to feed the hungry and comfort the destitute.

We used the word *speculation* advisedly: for although amateurs,

connoisseurs, artists, and so forth, might very highly appreciate such an 137
undertaking, and value it in an aesthetic point of view very highly, still
it was a question yet to be decided, how it would *take* with the public
in general. This has been answered in a manner most creditable to the
discrimination of the Irish metropolis, and beneficial to the charity.
Independent of the expenses, paid as mentioned before, three or four
hundred pounds have been sent to the general relief fund in a few weeks;
and, in order to satisfy ourselves that this has not arisen from a mere
occasional impulse, we have inquired and ascertained that already nearly
1500 season and family tickets have been issued! and are glad to find
that many, who go at first from mere curiosity, pay additionally in order
to study at their leisure.

Beneficial as the idea has turned out, as far as charity is concerned,
the advantage taken by the Committee for the advancement of a true
taste and genuine feeling for Art is deserving, in our opinion, of peculiar
commendation, and this especially in two particulars. First, the very full
and judicious explanatory catalogue they have published at so cheap a
rate, so as to place within the reach of the many who have neither opportunity, means, or leisure, to cull for themselves the mass of information that is brought so concisely and readily within their grasp. Instead
of the usual mere list of dry names of masters and proprietors, a short
historic sketch of the progress of painting is given, the various schools
and their principal characteristics, a classification of the works exhibited,
the whole concluding with an ably-condensed notice of each artist. It
is, in short, a model catalogue; and, considering the brief time there
must have been to arrange, write, and compile it, required no small exertion of both body and mind.

The second grand achievement for which we must give the Committee full credit is the establishment of a Morning Academy, for the
free and exclusive study of artists and properly-qualified students. We
are glad to find all the noble and distinguished proprietors have given
full permission for studies to be taken from their valuable works, under
the care and surveillance of the Committee; and that from thirty to five-
and-thirty artists and students attend every morning from six o'clock
till ten, after which the public are admissible. The hours of study are
under the direction and control of the members of the Royal Hibernian
Academy and leading artists—a member of Committee also attending
to afford any accommodation required; and nothing, we understand,
can be better regulated or more satisfactorily conducted.

ROYAL IRISH ART UNION MONTHLY JOURNAL, LONDON, 1 MAY 1847

LETTER OF THE POPE
ON THE STATE OF IRELAND

The Paris *Univers* publishes the encyclical letter addressed by the Pope, on the 24th ult. to all the patriarchs, primates, archbishops, and bishops, directing them to implore the divine aid in favour of the kingdom of Ireland. After some prefatory observations, in which the Pope states that he had already caused relief to be sent from Rome, and prayers to be offered up in that city, on behalf of Ireland, his holiness thus proceeds:—

"We exhort you to ordain that in the dioceses or countries subjected to your jurisdiction, as has already been done in our city of Rome, there shall, during three days, be recited public prayers in the temples and other consecrated places, in order that, touched with these supplications, the Father of Pity may deliver the Irish nation from this cruel calamity of scarcity, and keep away so frightful a calamity from the other kingdoms and countries of Europe. And in order that this desire may be more fully and usefully accomplished we accord our indulgence of seven years for every time, to all those who shall be present at such prayers; and to those who during the three days shall have been present at the prayers, and who during the week of this *triduo* having been purified by the sacrament of penitence shall receive the most holy sacrament of the eucharist, we give, by our apostolical authority, plenary indulgence. Next, we recommend more strongly to your charity, venerable brethren, that, by your exhortations, you incite the people submitted to your jurisdiction to aid Ireland with liberal alms. We undoubtedly know that we have no need to remind you of the virtue of alms-giving, nor of the abundant fruits which it produces in obtaining the pity of the Very Good and Very Great God. You will find in the Holy Fathers of the Church, and especially in most of the sermons of St. Leon the Great, learned and magnificent praises of alms-giving. You have before you the admirable letter written by St. Cyprian, martyr, Bishop of Carthage, to the bishops of Numidia, a letter which contains a remarkable testimony of the singular zeal with which the people confided to his pastoral care came by abundant alms to the help of the suffering Christians. You may, besides, recall to mind the words of St. Ambrose, Bishop of Milan—'The beauty of wealth is not to reside in the money-bags of the rich, but to serve as an ailment to the poor; treasures shine with greater brilliancy when distributed to the infirm and indigent; Christians ought to know that they should employ money to seek, not what is of them, but what is of Christ, in order that in his turn Christ may seek them.' For these motives, for the others that we have recalled to your benevolent minds, we firmly hope that you will afford powerful help to the poor of whom we speak. We might here terminate this letter; but at the moment at which, in deference to our intentions, you are about to order public prayers, we shall not forget what inspires us day and night, our pre-occupation of every moment—the welfare of all Churches. We have, in fact, incessantly before our eyes this cruel and terrible tempest which has risen against the universal Church—our mind trembles with dread in thinking how the 'enemy rises with malignity against the saint of saints,' and how odious his machinations are 'against the Lord, and against his Christ.' Therefore, we recommend you, above all, on the occasion of the public prayers to be ordained for Ireland, to engage the people submitted to your power to supplicate the Lord at the same time in favour of all the Church.''

BELFAST COMMERCIAL CHRONICLE, 3 MAY 1847

DREADFUL LOSS OF AN EMIGRANT SHIP

To the kind attention of Captain STEWART, of the *Thetis*, and Captain BROWN, of the *Glow-worm*, steamers, we are indebted for copies of the *Glasgow Herald* of Monday, in which are related the fearful details of the loss of the emigrant ship *Exmouth*, from Londonderry to Quebec, on the coast of Islay, with the loss of upwards of *two hundred and forty lives!* But three persons (sailors) escaped, all else— the greater proportion being women and young children—were in a moment engulfed in the pitiless and insatiable deep. We have seldom had to record so dreadful a calamity, or one involving so large an amount of loss of life; but it seems to have been one which no human wisdom could foresee, nor nautical experience obviate.

BELFAST COMMERCIAL CHRONICLE, 5 MAY 1847

WRECK OF "THE EXMOUTH"
EMIGRANT-SHIP

The details of this deeply lamentable catastrophe were given in our Journal of the 8th instant. We are now enabled, by the aid of an obliging Correspondent, to furnish some additional account of the recovery of a number of bodies from the wreck, together with the two annexed views.

By the exertions of Mr. Campbell, of Ballinabey, and Mr. Henry Campbell, of Rockside; aided by three men, whose names are Turner, McNeivin, and Macdonald (the latter one of the gamekeepers of Campbell, of Islay), no fewer than 108 bodies have been recovered and interred. These persons, slung over the rocks by turns, succeeded in hooking the bodies in the surf; and the two gentlemen named above wrapped the women, all of whom were naked, in sheets, and had them thus hoisted up to the summit of the cliff.

The bodies were dreadfully mutilated; some without faces, others without heads or limbs, and all in a far advanced state of putrefaction. The country people would not touch the bodies, and this threw this heavy and most painful duty entirely upon these five fine fellows, who had, up to May 14, decently buried no less than 108.

The conduct of the Messrs. Campbell, who are small proprietors in Islay, is very warmly spoken of; and, if they had not the strength and nerve of two ordinary men each, they could not have borne the fatigue and horrors which they have endured. The three fine fellows, also named, are very little behind the gentlemen in their most meritorious exertions; and they deserve a higher reward than mere praise.

Very few men have been found; the bodies are almost all those of women and children. The body of the Captain has been found, the only one with a stitch of clothes on; all the others were quite naked.

The last report adds the names of John McCaffer, Donald McLaughlin, and Dugald Fergusson (workmen of Campbell, of Ballinabey), as having added their exertions in preparing graves, and hooking the bodies; although still averse to handling them. They are all buried in a beautiful spot—soft green turf, surrounded by wild rocks.

These sketches have been made by Mr. J.F. Campbell (of Islay), the son of the noble-

WRECK OF "THE EXMOUTH"—RECOVERY OF BODIES.

spirited Lord of that domain; who, with his cousin, Mr. W. Campbell, have had some share in the good work.

We understand that her Majesty's Government has been pleased to notify to these gentlemen their sense of such meritorious example and exertion, and to add a gratuity to the men engaged in assisting them.

One of the Illustrations shows the spot where most of the wreck came on shore; the other, a deep chasm, from which the greater number of the bodies were recovered.

ILLUSTRATED LONDON NEWS, 29 MAY 1847

With feelings of profound grief we have to announce the death of THE GREAT CHIEFTAIN—an event that will fill not Ireland alone with sorrow, but will send a shock throughout the civilized world, and mark an epoch in the history of mankind. For this crushing event the physicians and friends of The Mighty Dead were better prepared than was his country. With anxious solicitude they watched the progress of his malady, and in some degree expected the melancholy catastrophe; but the country could not bring itself to believe that He who made our millions free, and for half a century led them on from triumph to triumph was about to be numbered with the dead, and to pass to the cold and silent grave ere he had accomplished the great object of his ambition—the final liberation of the land of his love and of his labours. But, alas! the painful truth must come home to the country—our O'Connell is, indeed, no more. His magic voice will never again be heard on earth, and there remains to us now of our Mighty Champion nothing save his imperishable deeds—his fame, and his glory.

WEEKLY FREEMAN'S JOURNAL, DUBLIN, 29 MAY 1847

THE BURIAL IN GLASNEVIN CEMETERY.

THE CONDITION OF THE COUNTRY
AND THE DUTY OF THE CHURCH

In the discharge of what we feel to be a duty, we return to a subject upon which a suggestion was briefly offered in the last Number of this Journal.

The visitation under which the country suffers is not abated; on the contrary, it is assuming more complicated and threatening features. Disease has followed upon famine; fever rages in many places, and has now entered the metropolis. The wasted strength of the poor quickly sinks under it, and its ravages are beginning to extend to the upper classes. And still the prospect darkens. It is with the commencing summer that sickness has commenced; serious apprehensions are entertained that the supply of food which can be obtained between the present time and the coming harvest, will be insufficient for the demand; and the harvest itself, with all that the fact involves, is yet future.

Now, let us put a few plain questions in reference to this whole state of things:—

Can it be agreeable to the will of God, that, when His judgments are thus around us, we should still continue to live as we have been in the habit of living in ordinary times? While famine and sickness are sweeping away multitudes, are we to go on eating and drinking, and partaking of all customary enjoyments, without hindrance or abatement? While the country rings with the sounds of suffering from one end to the other, is there to be no permanent and public acknowledgment of God's Hand; no special and constant supplications offered by those who are spared, for themselves and for those who suffer? Are the events which now happen really to be regarded as chastisements for sin, public as well as private, and can we expect any mitigation so long as we exhibit so little consciousness of our actual condition, so few evidences of repentance? The very life of the country seems to be bound up in the results of the coming harvest; but what has been done to shew our profound conviction that those results are altogether at the disposal of Him "who giveth fodder for the cattle, and the green herb for the service of men?"

And in what quarter is a movement to be looked for at such a time? Is the Church, or is she not, the religious teacher and guide of the people? And, if she be, has she no distinct and urgent duty to perform in connexion with the terrible crisis? Is it not the office of the Church to give audible echo to the voice of God's providence; to lead the way, and supply the helps of repentance? And has she fulfilled her duty in this regard? Are the two Fast Days which have been already observed, and the use of the short Collect (which is still continued, at least in some churches), to be considered sufficient for the exigencies of a time like the present? Is there to be no definite recognition of the new element which God has been pleased to introduce into the sufferings of the country,—the disease which is sweeping away those whom hunger had brought low; no prayers for a fruitful harvest; no stated and solemn humiliation for sin, commensurate with the continuance of the chastisement?

We do most earnestly commend these plain queries to the attention of our readers. No doubt, many amongst us fulfil the duties to which we refer, in private, as far as they can be so fulfilled, yet even they would derive help from some stated public observance. We become insensibly and desperately familiarized with events such as are now passing, and require every religious help that can be afforded to enable us to feel as we ought respecting them. If we had been told a twelvemonth since that we should be actually living among scenes which are now, alas! of daily occurrence in this country, we should have regarded it as incredible, or thought death to be preferred. Yet we now hear of crowds of our countrymen dropping by the road sides; of others seized by a new and incurable sickness, of whose swift and silent issue the victim is incredulous, but which never spares: we hear of horrors almost too great for mention,—of parents wishing for their children's death,—of men eagerly scrambling for fragments of putrid carrion,—of dogs devouring Christian flesh,—and yet how inadequately do we feel, compared with the dread reality of our position! Many, again, because the blow has not yet reached themselves in any shape, live on, unconscious of God's judgments,—their indulgences undiminished, their very amusements uninterrupted. These surely need something to awaken them,—some plain and faithful voice to recall them to the truth of things. To these and to all the voice of the Church could scarcely fail of bringing salutary warning. The very sound of the church bell would be as a sermon, startling the world's forgetfulness, and forcing men to think, if it were but for a moment, of the dread occasion.

While thus suggesting the necessity of some stated observance during the continuance of the present visitation, we are not unmindful of the difficulty which lies in the way of introducing any change into our public services; but this difficulty might, perhaps, be avoided in the present case, by taking advantage of the provision which the Church has made in the Prayer Book for extraordinary occasions. Thus, for instance, the Commination Service, which is appointed for the first day of Lent, may be used "at other times, as the Ordinary shall appoint." This service is in itself very suitable to the time, and might be employed without alteration as long as the visitation continues: and even if so much as this could not be accomplished, still individual clergymen might, in their own parishes, induce their people to a more solemn observance of Fridays: in public, by attending church (the prayers against dearth and sickness being used on that day, along with the Litany); in private, by keeping the fast in their families, and thus endeavouring to humble themselves before God, and sympathize with their suffering countrymen.

IRISH ECCLESIASTICAL JOURNAL, DUBLIN, 1 JUNE 1847

THE CROPS

From every part of Ireland come good tidings of the crops now growing—*all* the crops, potatoes and all. Of potatoes, from every account we collect that about one-sixth of the usual quantity has been planted in the present year; and the remainder of the potato-ground is occupied by grain or by some profitable green crop. In every province of Ireland there is considerably more ground under corn crops *than ever there was before*. On the whole, therefore, we have no scruple in asserting that there is now on Irish soil, in one shape or another, *food enough* to feed all the survivors of the Irish people who will be alive to gather in the harvest.

Nay, there will be *more* than enough. We have already twice proved in THE NATION that, even last year, without the potatoes, there was *still* food enough for us all: and we were then eight millions.

And now the thing for Irishmen to consider is this—no people on the globe was ever put to the solution of such a problem before—how to get leave to eat the bread that God has sent them. It will be no easy matter, we can tell them, to come at this. Already the English are counting on the appearance of our food, as usual, at their tables; and if the ordinary commercial intercourse between the two islands shall be in operation at October next, another million of the Irish must perish.

Let us describe to you, Irish farmer, Irish landlord, Irish labourer, and

Irish tradesman, what became last year of your harvest, which is your only wealth. Early in the winter it was conveyed, by the thousand ship-loads, to England; paying freight: it was stored in English stores; paying storage: it was passed from hand to hand among corn-speculators; paying at every remove, commission, merchants' profit, forwarding charges, and so forth: some of it was bought by French or Belgian buyers and carried to Havre, to Antwerp, to Bordeaux,—meeting on the way cargoes of other corn coming from Odessa, or Hamburg, or New York, which other corn was also earning for merchants, ship-owners, and other harpies, immense profits, exorbitant freights, huge commissions, in all latitudes and longitudes—and whatever corn *you* eventually got to eat, came to you loaded with all those charges to increase the price. In other words, you sent away a quarter of wheat at 50 shillings, and got it back, if you got it at all, at 80 shillings.

This kind of traffic is termed "civilization," and the "enlightened spirit of commerce," and other respectable names; so that whoever dies of it may congratulate himself that he is a martyr to the cause of human improvement and progress of the species.

If any of you should think it desirable to retrograde in civilization, and save yourselves and your children alive, (as is not impossible,) we shall endeavour to expound next week how this may be done. In the meantime, we desire all our readers to ponder on the fact that there is now, within our four seas, food enough growing up to feed all Irishmen next year.

THE NATION, DUBLIN, 12 JUNE 1847

POOR LAWS—PUBLIC WORKS

The Ministerial Poor Law for Ireland received the Royal assent on Tuesday last, and is now the "Law." That there will be objects enough for this law to operate upon, there can be no doubt. The eight hundred thousand paupers, many of them farmers and comfortable cottiers once,—now all *paupers*, and representing about two million other paupers,—will form one part of the Poor Law machinery quite ready to the Commissioners' hands. And it will be seen, by the letter of Mr. "Jos. C. WALKER," in another column, that all the remainder of the Public Works labourers, the last 200,000, are all to be discharged on the 15th of August next.

So there are to be "paupers" in abundance; there are no poor honest countrymen in Ireland now,—all that class have become Government "paupers:"—there will also be officials enough, all gentlemanly persons, and many with moustaches: and then there will be nothing to provide but the *rates*. But out of what funds? "Government" apparently has forgotten to arrange this. The nation is bankrupt; the landlords (who are expected to "absorb" all this labour) have scarce money enough to pay interest on their incumbrances; the tradesmen are in the hands of the Sheriffs and Bankrupt Commissioners; the banks have no gold; the farmers have neither money nor credit; and although the crops may turn out abundant, there will be no medium through which to exchange them, and pay a money-rent, as usual: insomuch that we are credibly informed the farmers mean to pay their rents *in kind*, and that the "paupers"—in other words, the population—mean to divide the rest. "Government" ought to look after *its* share in time.

THE NATION, DUBLIN, 12 JUNE 1847

APPALLING SCENES OF DESTITUTION IN KILGLASS

THE UNBURIED DEAD

TO THE EDITOR OF THE FREEMAN
KILGLASS, ROOSKEY, COUNTY OF ROSCOMMON, 14TH JULY, 1847

SIR—There is not in Ireland any parish where fever and destitution prevail to so fearful an extent as here. We have about 800 sick of fever just now, without the advantage of an hospital, a medical officer, or, I may say, a committee, to stay the progress of disease or provide coffins for the dead. By the bungling of some government official, one half of this parish is annexed to the Elphin committee, which meets near twelve miles distant therefrom, whilst the other half is joined to the Kilmore committee, that meets near eight miles off. Little or nothing is doing to relieve the sufferers. By this time fever has made its way into almost every house. The poor creatures are wasting away and dying of want. In very many instances the dead bodies are thrown in waste cabins and dykes and are devoured by dogs. In some parts the fields are bleached with the bones of the dead that were previously picked by dogs. About a month since two died in a waste house near my residence. I have made many fruitless attempts to procure persons to bury these bodies. There was such a terror over all of going into the infected cabin that even for money I could not get them to comply with my wishes. About two days ago my curate and myself succeeded in prevailing on two little girls who are recovering from fever, to drag out the second body. Now both the bodies are lying in a drain, to the rear of the house, with a slight covering over them. The body was covered with worms, and had one of its thighs devoured by dogs. On behalf of the parishioners I have been all the season applying to the government, and the Relief Commissioners, for a local committee in Kilglass, for these two electoral divisions into which our parish is divided. We held a meeting at which we adopted three petitions, one to the Lords' Justices, one to the Commissioners, and the third to the House of Commons. The two former we forwarded to their proper destination. We sent off the third petition also, and posted it to Mr. Collett, the member for Athlone, to whom we entrusted it for presentation to the house. But strange to say, Mr. Collett has neither acknowledged the receipt of it, nor has as yet presented it, nor even replied to two letters I have addressed to him on the subject within the last fortnight.

Since the Earl of Clarendon has come over to Ireland I wrote to him to request that the just and necessary demand of the parishioners would be acceded to, but his Excellency has not condescended a reply. Had we got the district committee, we would undertake to remedy the evils complained of and endeavour to have the Temporary Relief act *administered pursuant to its spirit and letter,* and that in a retired miserable locality, where the poor are neglected, famine and disease stalk abroad with uncontrolled sway, and death most successfully doing its work of desolation. The only alternative now left us is to appeal to the public sympathy through the columns of your excellent journal, one of the faithful mirrors of public opinion in Ireland.

I shall repair to London with the humble address of the poor afflicted
sufferers of Kilglass, and with it lay before our gracious Queen the wants
and tribulations of this ill-fated portion of her Majesty's dominions.

I have the honour to be, Sir, your most obedient, &c,

HENRY BRENNAN, P.P., of Kilglass.

WEEKLY FREEMAN'S JOURNAL, DUBLIN, 17 JULY 1847

THE POTATO CROP

We still hold our opinion that the potato crop is upon the
whole in a favourable state, notwithstanding the rumours
to the contrary; and as time is safety in this case, each day
adds to security. A most careful scrutiny of the reports which have reached
us from all parts of Great Britain leads to this conclusion . . .

As to Ireland, it is hard to say what will be the fate of the (comparatively
insignificant) crop planted in that country. It is to be anticipated that
large losses must be there sustained, because of the late planting, and
the natural dampness of the climate. Nevertheless, we cannot say that
the intelligence which we have received is materially different from that
of England. A friend who has been yachting round the coast finds the
crop a month earlier than last year, and heard of little mischief except
about Bantry Bay. Waterford and Cork seem in the worst plight; but
even in the latter county one of our correspondents describes the disease
as being much mitigated and not inclined to spread . . .

All these circumstances lead us to the conclusion that, although we
are not justified in declaring the crop to be out of danger, yet that the
symptoms are much more favourable than they have been since 1844.—
Gardeners' Chronicle.

BELFAST COMMERCIAL CHRONICLE, 13 AUGUST 1847

On this subject, the following circular, conveying important information, has been issued to the inspecting officers of unions:—

Relief Commission Officer, Dublin Castle, 6th August, 1847

"SIR—The Relief Commissioners have received many communications from committees remonstrating against closing the temporary relief in their respective districts on the 15th of August. The objections advanced are:—1. That the harvest will not be in full operation by that period. 2. General want of means of the poor. 3. That the poor law guardians have no funds.

"With regard to the first, the Commissioners wish it to be understood that they do not consider the actual state of the harvest, in the precise locality, to be the only datum for discontinuance of relief to the able-bodied, since it is clear that the reduced price of provisions, together with the general, if not local, increasing demand for labour, must afford means of earning a subsistence to many who are now dependent on public support. That this is the case, and that many who ought not, have been still lingering on the gratuitous relief, has been proved in several places by very light tests. Many have given up the rations for themselves and families, rather than perform three or four hours' labour, and others rather than enter the poor house.

"The temporary relief act was passed, not as a remedy for any financial embarrassments in the union, nor for any general poverty in the country, but solely to replace, for one season, the food of which the people were deprived by the failure of the potato crop, and the operation of the act was to be discontinued as the different crops of the ensuing season should come forward, and provisions become more abundant. As these are gradually in course of being realized, the Commissioners feel that their functions must close, and the poor law guardians must make the necessary efforts for such partial early collection as may be sufficient to meet the first emergency.

"There are still some remote districts where the relief may be continued by special permission after the 15th Aug. for limited periods, on account of the peculiar extent of the distress in them, added to an unhappy neglect of that cultivation which might have provided an earlier and more general stock for the support of the people, but even in these the scale must be very much reduced.

"The period for the revision of the lists, in reference to individuals only, is now passed, and they must be reduced by classes even where the relief is allowed to be partially continued.

"It must be recollected, that nothing but compelling men to make greater efforts for self-support, and to avail themselves of means that are really within their reach, will prevent the great amount of disastrous results that must otherwise ensue from a sudden stoppage, on a great scale, at the end of September, after which all advances under the temporary act must cease.—(By order of the Relief Commissioners),

"R. HAMILTON."

BELFAST COMMERCIAL CHRONICLE, 15 AUGUST 1847

EXPULSION OF TENANTRY

A most afflicting case of eviction, on a large scale, has been communicated to us. The scene of the expulsion is Tonny-mageera, near Mount Nugent, in the county Cavan, where ninety-nine houses were pulled down, and the unfortunate occupants sent adrift upon the world. Five houses upon the property have for the present escaped; they have not as yet been levelled, because the occupants are afflicted with the pestilence which has so effectually aided the "clearance system."

The estate in question is, for the present, under the administration of the Court of Chancery; but, we need scarcely say, the case is one in which that court had no discretionary power; neither had the receiver in the cause any option. He had postponed the evil day as long as he could, and, furthermore, we understand, did all in his power to alleviate the sufferings of the mass of human beings thrown out on the highways, without a home—without shelter or sustenance.—*Evening Post.*

WEEKLY FREEMAN'S JOURNAL, DUBLIN, 18 SEPTEMBER 1847

THE CLERGY OF KILLALA

PROSELYTISM

In another column will be found a resolution and a letter, emanating from a meeting of the Catholic bishop and clergy of the diocese of Killala, held at Ballina on the 7th instant. The object of these documents—classical, eloquent, argumentative, and high-toned as they are—is to expose the nefarious, unchristian wickedness of a pre-concerted system of proselytism now in active operation in that district, and to invoke public assistance to save famine-orphans and other destitute creatures from the claws of the proselytising vultures that are pouncing upon them.

It appears that the stoppage of all government relief was the signal for a general attack on the consciences of the poor. The agents of the charitable associations, who hitherto appeared as angels of light, no sooner got the field of destitution to themselves than they opened a slave market of immortal souls, and held up, to tempt the passions of ravening hunger, the mess of pottage, which was only to be obtained at the price of what the poor, sorely tried creatures believed to be truth, on the profession of which their eternal salvation depended.

The guilty agents in this immoral traffic are chiefly the almoners of the Society of Friends—but it is hoped without the consent of the Society—and emissaries from the Exeter Hall Society, the Orphan Association, and the Belfast Society for the Relief of Distress in Connaught. The sphere of their operations is as unlimited as the ruin of the famine in the locality. The population of the diocese was 160,000 souls. Of this number no less than 100,000 were receiving government support, and are consequently now to be fed on the bread of proselytism or die.

WEEKLY FREEMAN'S JOURNAL, DUBLIN, 25 SEPTEMBER 1847

A LETTER, &C.

JAMES H. TUKE

When I had the pleasure of meeting you, a few weeks ago, in Dublin, on my return from a journey through a considerable portion of Ireland, you expressed a wish that I should communicate to you the result of my observations on the condition of those parts of the country which I had visited, and their prospects during the coming winter. To gain information on these points, and to ascertain the working of the new Poor-Law, and the probability of its being brought into efficient action in the worst districts of Ireland, were the chief objects of this tour. I thought these objects would be most effectually attained by devoting my attention chiefly to Connaught; and accordingly, though I visited several other districts, my time was mostly passed in that western province.

This province being, as a whole, by far the poorest and most destitute in Ireland, I thought that it was most important to ascertain particularly its condition and prospects . . .

It is probable that one-fourth, *at least*, of the whole population of Connaught will require to be supported during the coming winter; in Mayo, as well as in some of the Unions of Galway, Leitrim, Roscommon and Sligo, nearer one-half. The total inability of many of these Unions to collect a rate, at all commensurate with the wants of their population, may be easily shown by the instance of the Union of Westport, which with a population, in 1841, of 77,953 persons, is valued for the poor's-rate at £38,876, giving little more than 10s. per head for every person in the Union; a rate of 7s. in the pound had just been struck . . . The value which the farmers place upon agricultural knowledge, or upon skilled agriculturists, has been shown in the few instances where agricultural schools have been established, by their great anxiety to obtain, as servants, the boys educated in them. This subject seems to be well deserving the notice of the Commissioners.

The enormous size of the Unions of Connaught is also a subject which deserves attention . . . The barony of Erris alone is clearly large enough for one Union, and ought to have its poor-house at Belmullet.

I must be allowed to dwell at some length upon the peculiar misery of this barony of Erris, and parish of Belmullet, which I spent some days in examining. Afflicting as is the general condition of Mayo—fearful as are the prospects of the province in general, there is here yet a lower depth in misery, a district almost as distinct from Mayo as Mayo is from the eastern parts of Ireland. Human wretchedness seems concentrated in Erris, the culminating point of man's physical degradation seems to have been reached in the Mullet. It may seem needless to trouble you with particular descriptions of the distress I have witnessed; for these descriptions are but repetitions of the far too familiar scenes of the last winter and spring; although the present seem aggravated by an earlier commencement; nevertheless, such a condition as that of Erris ought, however painful, to be forced on our attention until remedies are found and applied.

This barony is situated upon the extreme north-west coast of Mayo, bounded on two sides by the Atlantic ocean. The population last year was computed at about 28,000; of that number, it is said, at least 2,000 have emigrated, principally to England, being too poor to proceed to America; *and that 6,000 have perished by starvation, dysentery, and fever.* There is left a miserable remnant of little more than 20,000; of whom 10,000, at least, are, strictly speaking, on the very verge of starvation. Ten thousand people within forty-eight hours' journey of the metropolis of the world, living, or rather starving, upon turnip-tops, sand-eels, and sea-weed, a diet which no one in England would consider fit for the meanest animal which he keeps. And let it not be supposed that of this famine diet they have enough, or that each of these poor wretches has a little plot of turnips on which he may feed at his pleasure. His scanty meal is, in many cases, taken from a neighbour hardly richer than himself, not indeed at night, but, with the daring of absolute necessity, at noon-day.

On entering the houseless and uncultivated region of Erris, the traveller is reminded of the wilds of Canada: for some miles hardly an acre of cultivated land or the appearance of human residence greets the eye . . .

One poor widow with a large family, whose husband had recently died of fever, had a miserable patch of potatoes seized, and was thus deprived of her only resource for the ensuing winter. What could she do? The poor-house was thirty miles distant, and it was full. Though many of these ruined creatures were bewailing their cruel fate, I heard nothing like reproach or reflection upon the author of their misery, and the bailiff told me that he had no fear of molestation in pursuing his calling.

In this village fever was terribly prevalent, and the food such as before described, but wanting the sand-eels and sea-weed. Advancing further

in Erris, the desolation and wretchedness were still more striking. One
may indeed at times imagine oneself in a wilderness abandoned to
perpetual barrenness and solitude. But here and there scattered over this
desolate landscape, little green patches appear unexpectedly where no
other sign of man presents itself to you; as you walk over the bog, and
approach nearer to the spot, a curl of smoke arises from what you suppose
to be a slight rise on the surface.

A VISIT TO CONNAUGHT IN THE AUTUMN OF 1847

LONDON, 1847

THE FAMINE YEAR

LADY WILDE

Weary men, what reap ye?—Golden corn for
the stranger.
What sow ye?—Human corses that wait for the
avenger.
Fainting forms, hunger stricken, what see ye in the
offing?—
Stately ships to bear our food away, amid the stranger's
scoffing.
There's a proud array of soldiers—what do they round
your door?
They guard our master's granaries from the thin hands
of the poor.
Pale mothers, wherefore weeping? Would to God
that we were dead—
Our children swoon before us, and we cannot give
them bread.

Little children, tears are strange upon your infant
faces,
God meant you but to smile within your mother's soft
embraces.
Oh, we know not what is smiling, and we know not
what is dying;

But we're hungry, very hungry, and we cannot stop
      our crying.
And some of us grow cold and white—we know not
      what it means;
But, as they lie beside us we tremble in our dreams.
There's a gaunt crowd on the highway—are you come
      to pray to man,
With hollow eyes that cannot weep, and for words
      your faces wan?

No; the blood is dead within our veins—we care not
      now for life;
Let us die hid in the ditches, far from children and
      from wife!
We cannot stay and listen to their raving famished
      cries—
Bread! Bread! Bread! and none to still their agonies.
We left our infants playing with their dead mother's
      hand:
We left our maidens maddened by the fever's scorching
      brand:
Better, maiden, thou wert strangled in thy own dark
      twisted tresses—
Better, infant, thou wert smothered in thy mother's
      first caresses.

We are fainting in our misery, but God will hear our
      groan;
Yet, if fellowmen desert us, will He hearken from His
      throne?
Accursed are we in our own land, yet toil we still and
      toil;
But the stranger reaps our harvest—the alien owns
      our soil.
O Christ! how have we sinned, that on our native
      plains
We perish homeless, naked, starved, with branded
      brow like Cain's?

Dying, dying wearily, with a torture sure and
    slow—
Dying as a dog would die, by the wayside as
    we go.

One by one they're falling round us, their pale faces
    to the sky;
We've no strength left to dig them graves—there let
    them lie.
The wild bird, if he's stricken, is mourned by the
    others,
But we—we die in Christian land,—we die amid our
    brothers,
In a land which God has given us, like a wild beast in
    his cave,
Without a tear, a prayer, a shroud, a coffin, or a
    grave.
Ha! but think ye the contortions on each livid face
    ye see,
Will not be read on Judgement-day by eyes of
    Deity?

We are wretches, famished, scorned, human tools to
    build your pride,
But God will yet take vengeance for the souls for
    whom Christ died.
Now in your hour of pleasure—bask ye in the world's
    caress;
But our whitening bones against ye will rise as
    witnesses,
From the cabins and the ditches in their charred,
    uncoffined masses,
For the Angel of the Trumpet will know them as he
    passes.
A ghastly spectral army, before the great God we'll
    stand,
And arraign ye as our murderers, the spoilers of our
    land!

DUBLIN, 1847

DISTRESS IN IRELAND

TO THE EDITOR OF THE LONDON TIMES

S IR,—I hope you will, in justice to those who have appointed a general collection in the churches on the 17th (the day of the Thanksgiving), and still more in pity to the unhappy people in the western districts of Ireland, who will again perish by thousands this year if they are not relieved, publish the accompanying statement . . . for the purpose of explaining why another effort of this sort is necessary.

It may be satisfactory to you that I should add my testimony on three main points, having, as you are probably aware, made this subject my principal study for a long time past, and being constantly in the habit of receiving information, both written and oral, from all parts of Ireland, in reference to it. These points are—

First—That the new poor law will be enforced in Ireland to the utmost extent of the power of the government—that no assistance whatever will be given from national funds to those unions which, whether they have the will or not, undoubtedly have the *power* of maintaining their own poor—and that the collection of the rates will be enforced as far as it can be, even in those distressed western unions in which some assistance from some source or other must be given.

Secondly—That there are certain unions in the west of Ireland where the social system was so entirely based upon the potato . . . that it was impossible that the habits of the people could be so suddenly changed, and new modes of subsistence so suddenly established, as to allow of the crowded population which had grown up under the potato system supporting themselves without assistance in the second year after the failure. And,

Thirdly—That the change from an idle, barbarous, isolated potato cultivation, to corn cultivation, which enforces industry, binds together employer and employed in mutually beneficial relations, and, requiring capital and skill for its successful prosecution, supposes the existence of a class of substantial yeomanry who have an interest in preserving the good order of society, is proceeding as fast as can reasonably be expected under the circumstances; and that if the rich and highly-favoured portions of the empire give some further temporary assistance to these distressed sections of our population, to enable them to "tide over" the shoals upon which they have fallen, the harbour will, ere long, be attained.

If you consider my testimony on these points of any public value on the present occasion, you are at liberty to make any use of it you think proper...—Believe me, Sir, yours very faithfully,

C.E. TREVELYAN

Salt-hill Hotel, near Dublin, Oct. 7.

THE TIMES, LONDON, 9 OCTOBER 1847

AMELIORATION OF IRELAND

Ireland! "O sound of fear," irksome to almost every ear. Ireland is a problem to be solved in the history of man and of nations. To offer our individual experience, we would say (and literally) that thousands of books and pamphlets have racked our brain on the subject; and that several earnest journeys of some thousands of miles through the country have increased our perplexities respecting this land of contradictions. We have pondered over many nostrums, which, and we speak in no offensive sense, had the benefit of Ireland in view. And though some were remote or theoretical, others were practical, immediate, and, to a certain extent, calculated to be useful. There were, however, unhappily, cankers in most of them. Extreme Politics and Religious differences concurred to blast the most benevolent schemes, to ameliorate the condition of Ireland. They put poison in the leaven...

AN IRISH AMELIORATION SOCIETY was formed on Tuesday last, under auspices of the most favourable character, at a meeting where General Sir George Pollock presided, and was supported by Generals Macleod, Wyatt, Caulfield, and Farquharson, Colonel Innes, the Rev. Mr. Stoddart (honorary Secretary to the Irish Relief Society),

Mr. G. Macpherson (of the house of Carr, Tagore and Co., Calcutta), Hartley Kennedy, Esq., W.P. Andrews, Esq., and other persons of high station and influence. Before this assemblage Mr. Rogers laid his plans, and explained the means by which he proposed to call the labour energy of Ireland into employment with profit to all classes, and at the same time to improve the social condition of the labourer throughout the length and breadth of the land.

Some years ago, Lord Willoughby de Eresby . . . brought forward an ingenious machinery for converting peat or turf into a solid fuel, applicable to every use to which coal could be put, and when made into charcoal, superior for many purposes to that most important mineral. Under his Lordship's direction, experiments were conducted on a large scale, and the practicability, cheapness, and immeasurable value of the invention demonstrated. Out of it sprung several beneficial plans for the economic adoption of various combinations of fuel for domestic uses, manufactures, the generation of steam, and all other ends connected with the mighty motive principles of combustion and heat. Upon Lord Willoughby's original method, Mr. Rogers has patented an improved system, and now happily called into being the Association to which we have referred, by which it will be addressed to the great national object stated to the meeting, and in the publications we have noted in the foregoing remarks. The preparation of peat fuel and peat charcoal may be carried to an unlimited extent in Ireland, and directly and collaterally afford profitable employment to the whole surplus population. From year to year thousands of acres of bog will have been reclaimed, and wheat, flax, and potatoes be abundantly grown where only unwholesome marsh and sterility prevail. It is wonderful to observe the extraordinary fitness of every part to the grand consummation desired. The peat is cut: there is labour, and labour paid in money, a fair day's wages for a fair day's work,—alone a mighty blessing to Ireland. But we must proceed step by step. The peat so cut is compressed into a most valuable fuel for every household and manufacturing use; and when converted into charcoal, it will be a means of establishing and maintaining factories wherever thought expedient, furnish a productive export trade instead of the existing expensive import of coal, and for smelting and working iron and other metals be superior to any material hitherto employed. Again, an excellent manure will be supplied for the fertilization of the soil. The operation of cutting through the bogs will effect drainage, and if limited to that single benefit would be extremely serviceable. Thus we see on every hand and in every way a prodigious

LITERARY GAZETTE AND JOURNAL OF BELLES LETTRES, LONDON, 30 OCTOBER 1847

STATE OF THE COUNTRY

EJECTMENT MURDER.—As Major Mahon, a gentleman holding large estates in Roscommon was returning home about twenty minutes past six o'clock on the evening of Monday, from a meeting of the board of guardians of the Roscommon union, he was shot dead by an assassin, about four miles from Strokestown. There were two persons engaged in the murder, according to our informant. Both fired; one piece missed fire, but the other proved fatal, lodging a heavily loaded discharge in the breast. The victim exclaimed, "Oh! God," and spoke no more. Major Mahon was formerly in the 9th Dragoons, now Lancers, and succeeded to the inheritance of the late Lord Harland's estates about two years ago, the rental being about 10,000*l*. The people were said to be displeased with him for two reasons. The first was his refusal to continue the conacre system, the second was his clearing away what he deemed the surplus population. He chartered two vessels to America and freighted them with his evicted tenantry . . .

KANTURK UNION, TUESDAY.—GATHERING OF THE PEOPLE— THREATENED ATTACK ON THE TOWN.—In its report of the proceedings of this union on the above day, the *Cork Examiner* has the following:—

"A policeman entered the board-room to say that about two thousand persons from the lower parishes of Kilbolane and Shandum had arrived at the gate, and were forcing an entrance, and that the military (who were in attendance also) refused to act; the policeman's person and gun showed some signs of outrage.

"Mr. Freeman then took charge of the civil and military force; and though stones were (literally speaking) falling in showers, he showed the greatest steadiness and courage. On some of the ringleaders being arrested, an attempt was made to rescue them by the crowd, who had to be kept back at the point of the bayonet. The people were becoming very violent, and threatening to attack the workhouse gates. Stones were flying thick and fast when Mr. Freeman ordered the police and

162 military to load; the crowd threatened to attack the town, and take with them all the money they could find, if they did not get out-door relief. Mr. Freeman threatened to read the riot act if they did not disperse quietly; the greater part of them then marched off towards the town. Mr. Freeman ordered the gates to be opened, and marched the force under his command after the crowd, who halted opposite the first bread shop they met; but they were immediately dispersed. They then marched on, but had not time to do any mischief, as the military were at their heels.

"A strange fact—more powder was purchased by these out-door relief folks on that day than was sold for the previous year in the town of Kanturk.

"The Messrs. Bruce and Barry, J.P.'s from whose neighbourhood the principal number of this troublesome mob were, gave them 2*l.* to purchase bread, the greater portion of which they applied to supply themselves with powder and ball.

"We are come to an awful crisis; the present expenditure of the union exceeds 500*l.* per week. Whence are the means to sustain this to be supplied? Surely, not from the rack-rented, overburthened ratepayers, who are daily adding to the number of the pauper lists."

THE NATION, DUBLIN, 6 NOVEMBER 1847

PROCLAMATION UNDER THE ACT
FOR THE PREVENTION OF CRIME
AND OUTRAGE IN IRELAND

PRIVY COUNCIL—His Excellency the Lord Lieutenant and the following members of the Privy Council sat on Thursday, by whom a proclamation was agreed to and issued:—Sir William Somerville, Bart. Sir Edward Blakeney, the Chief Justice of the Queen's Bench, Mr. Justice Moore, Baron Richards, Baron Lefroy, Judge Ball, Mr. Keatinge, Judge of the Prerogative Court, the Recorder, the Attorney-General (Mr. Monahan), the Marquis of Headford, the Marquis of Clanricarde, Lord Cloncurry, Sir Thomas Esmonde, Bart. Earl Fingal, and Bishop of Meath. The proclamation declares the act to be in force from and after the 29th December, in the following districts:—

The County of Limerick.

The County of Tipperary.

The Baronies of Bunratty, Tulla, Islands, Inchiquin, and Clonderlaw, in County Clare.

The Baronies of Orrery and Kilmore, County Cork.

The Baronies of Glenahiry and Upperthird, in the County Waterford.

The Baronies of Clonlish, Ballybrit, Eglish, and Garrycastle, in King's County.

The Baronies of Athlone, Ballintobber, Roscommon, Ballymoe, Boyle, and the Parishes of Crieve, Kilcoursey, Kilnemanagh, and Kilcola, in the Barony of Frenchpark, Co. Roscommon.

The Baronies of Leitrim, Mohill, and Carrigallen, County Leitrim.

The Baronies of Clonmahon, Tullyhunco, and Upper Loughtee, County Cavan; and

The Baronies of Longford, Granard, and Ardagh, County Longford.

The principal effect of this measure will be to prevent persons in those districts carrying arms without license after the 29th December. We have no doubt that in those districts where the possession of arms indiscriminately, even in dwellings, is considered dangerous to the public peace, the powers of the act for calling in arms will be made use of— and then no person will be allowed to have arms even in his dwelling-house, without license. We understand the stipendiary magistrates will be the parties empowered to give licenses.

BELFAST COMMERCIAL CHRONICLE, 25 DECEMBER 1847

THE EPIDEMIC OF 1847 IN BELFAST

A.G. MALCOLM

The beginning of 1847 was marked by the prevalence of small-pox and dysentery among the poor, and several hundred cases of these diseases were transferred from the Workhouse to the General Hospital. Both maladies assumed a grave type; and the subjects of dysentery, in particular, were specimens of the worst form we ever witnessed. Whether there was any connexion between this event and the fearful times that were about to follow, it is difficult to say; but we rather incline to the opinion, that the same atmospheric condition was evinced thus early, more especially when we remember the calamitous effect upon the vegetable creation, in the instance of Ireland's staple article of diet. However this may be, it is not a little remarkable that the very first indications of the devastating plague, in comparison with which all previous epidemics were trivial and insignificant, should make its appearance in the hold of an emigrant vessel, bound for America.

"*The Swatara*" had sailed from Liverpool, with several hundred passengers, and was many days out on her passage before the disease commenced to appear. At this very time, the winds were so contrary, that the vessel could not make further way, and the captain was obliged to return without delay. He put into this port in a very shattered condition, with several sick, and the passengers generally in a sad plight, in consequence of the scarcity of provisions. The sick passengers were landed, and after having recruited, the captain again put to sea, but had not proceeded far when she was obliged to run into Derry, in consequence this time, however, of the spread of the fever amongst the passengers. After some delay, she was once more under way, but was obliged to retrace her course for the third time. On this occasion she returned to Belfast, with a large proportion of her passengers attacked. They were removed to the General Hospital at once. The fever in the town now began to increase, and in a very short period, the Hospital was so full that the Board of Guardians were urged to give more extended relief. The numbers increased, however, so rapidly that even this could have been of little avail. Much greater accommodation was wanting to contend with an epidemic which was beginning to exhibit unprecedented strength.

Accordingly, the inhabitants were called together, on April 27th, to petition for a Board of Health, which was immediately granted. The Board was in operation on the 6th of May, and proceeded, with the greatest energy, to provide sufficient accommodation, and to carry out, upon the most extensive scale, those sanitary operations which produced such good results on former occasions. The Union infirmary was enlarged by nearly 90 beds, and a shed was erected on the grounds of the General Hospital. The old Cholera buildings, and, in short, every available spot, were filled with patients. Still it was not enough. The plague was striking down its victims, at the rate of 50 per day, and, with the addition of the College Hospital, which was now opened, the total number of cases on the 29th of May was 1,149—a number very nearly twice the annual average of previous ordinary years.

It was not, however, till the middle of July, that the epidemic reached

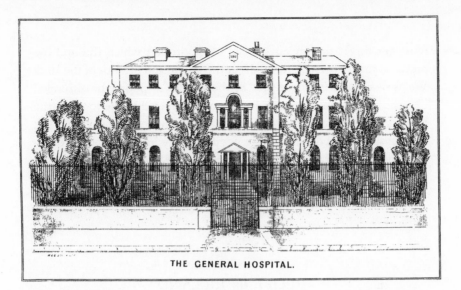

THE GENERAL HOSPITAL.

its height—the weekly admissions having risen to 660, and the number in Hospital, at one time, above 2000.

Fortunately, the weather was most favourable, which permitted the erection of canvass tents, on the workhouse grounds, capable of holding 700 patients. These were appropriated to convalescents, and very much relieved the Hospitals. Indeed, had it not been for this provision, it is questionable whether the epidemic could have been mastered, without the occurrence of those appalling scenes which disgraced, for a time, the Dublin relief authorities. Even, as it was, with all this immense accommodation, many patients had to remain for hours awaiting admission, at the gates of the Hospital.

From the date last mentioned, a gradual subsidence of the epidemic ensued. Each successive month showed diminishing numbers; and, on the 13th of November, the General Hospital ceased to receive patients. The Barrack-Street Hospital was closed in December, the Workhouse accommodation having been then sufficient. Taking the aggregate of the three Hospitals, the total number of admissions from the beginning of the epidemic till the end of December, 1847, was 13,676! to which, if we add a fair proportion for private cases, we shall have some idea of the enormous extent of this memorable pestilence. It may be safely affirmed, that one out of every five persons in Belfast was attacked during this year.

It will be readily concluded, that such a vast amount of disease must have had a corresponding influential cause. We have already alluded to the probable atmospheric condition, which, no doubt, existed; but we must not forget the prevalent state of destitution which this and the previous year witnessed, throughout the length and breadth of the land. We well remember the aspect of the hordes of poor who thronged into the town, from all parts. Famine was depicted in the look, in the hue, in the voice, and the gait. The food of a nation had been cut off; the physical strength of a whole people was reduced; and this condition, highly favourable to the impression of the plague-breath, resulted in the most terrible epidemic that this Island ever experienced.

HISTORY OF THE GENERAL HOSPITAL, BELFAST,
AND THE OTHER MEDICAL INSTITUTIONS OF THE TOWN

BELFAST, 1851

RELIEF IN IRELAND

It would be improper to close our Report for the year 1847 without some notice of the operations for "relief" which it has devolved upon this Board to execute.

Their policy, and their results, it is not for us to dwell upon, and in our successive monthly reports we have detailed the part which it was our duty to bear in the executive operations. But we may remark, that the experiment of public employment for the purpose of relief has been subsequently tried in another country, where, though confined to much smaller numbers, within the limits of a single town, and directed by the ablest men, it was attended with far more calamitous results.

In former years, seasons of partial distress have occurred in Ireland, and the local calamity by which large numbers of persons were suddenly deprived of employment and food, was met by local works of a public nature. But the measure which was good and sufficient when applied to limited districts, where such works could easily be found, necessarily fell far short of its object when applied to the whole country, because works such as roads, which were applicable to one district in which roads were wanted, were not of necessity applicable to another—still less to every other—district, in the greater part of which roads were already superabundant. Yet to roads, and works of a similar and local character, the Public Works were confined; works so purely local that grand juries were by law the parties entrusted with their execution, comprised all which the Act 9 and 10 Vic., c. 107, entrusted to this Board to execute.

But while it is admitted that merely local works, of the single class to which the relief operations were confined, were unable to meet a distress so general and so long continued, and by which artizans as well as labourers were affected, by which the relations of every class of the community were disturbed, and which involved, and were complicated by, social questions of every description, we have never ceased to express our conviction that this objection of inutility has been greatly overstated, and that the greater part of the works in the remote districts are only such as it would have been desirable at any time to have undertaken, while even in the central and better conditioned counties, the objections which have been made will cease when they are completed.

Nor is it necessary we should repeat that it is not on the ground of positive utility these works are to be judged. They should be considered solely as an effort to obtain a certain amount of labour in return for subsistence, through the medium of money wages, which effort was not abandoned till the numbers had become so great as to defy control, and to render it indispensable that the subsistence should be given by direct distribution of food, without other condition than that already required—the condition of real destitution.

It is not intended to deny the abuses which crept into every part of the system, but we think they have been greatly exaggerated, and the exception taken for the rule.

When the host had risen to 734,000, it contained large numbers unable to work, and the expenditure for their distress was most judiciously made in food relief. But it should in justice be remembered that the expenditure was still the same.

In October, 1846, 100,000 men were employed; nearly the same number remained in the month of June, 1847, and were not wholly discontinued for some months afterwards. The relief by labour, therefore, extended over nine months, the direct relief continued but for three, though the systems were in concurrent operation for a considerable time.

The average number relieved daily by labour, from October to June, was 356,314, and the expenditure chargeable to the counties was 4,462,154*l.* 6*s.* 11*d.*, of which one-half has been subsequently remitted. The total sum gives, on an average, 1*s.* per diem to each person, which, assuming him to have contributed to the relief of a family of five, places the cost of the labour relief at 2½*d.* per head, for which the repayment of half only is claimed . . .

On this subject of expense it may also be desirable here to dispel finally the erroneous impressions which have been entertained as to the cost of staff and plant; and as the accounts have now been closed, the figures are conclusive. The expense under the head of staff and plant amounted to the following per centage on the expenditure:—

For pay-clerks and others making payments	1½ per cent.
For tools and implements	1½ per cent.
Check-clerks, overseers, foremen, and gangers	5 per cent.

The whole of the superior staff, including the extra establishment in Dublin, having been borne by the Government.

Nor should the liberal arrangement which was sanctioned by your Lordships in regard to the tools and implements be unknown to the public.

In our early Reports we dwelt strongly on the difficulty we experienced in providing a sufficient quantity of tools for the daily increasing throng of labourers, and every accessible source, public and private, was put in requisition for the purpose. But we were also desirous of rendering the manufacture itself a source of relief, and with this view we incurred the inconvenience of taking numerous small contracts in the remote towns and villages of Ireland, rather than procure a more prompt and ready supply by employing the large contractors in England and Scotland.

This has been, and still is, the cause of great inconvenience and trouble, from their defective construction, and the endless claims to which it has given rise; but it answered the benevolent purpose sought by it. And when by this means a full equipment was provided for 800,000 labourers of all the various implements likely to be required, the works were ordered to close, and this gigantic mass of stores was left on the hands of the Government.

It would not have been unreasonable to have charged this whole expense to the counties, it having been incurred on their account; instead of which a valuation was made of the then remaining tools, and the counties were charged only with half the difference between that sum and the original cost; in other words, with half the wear and tear only. The total expense for tools was no less than 127,275*l.*, and their value on the close of the works being 75,000*l.*, left a sum to be charged to the counties of little more than 1 per cent. on the expenditure for labour. There is still, therefore, a large stock remaining, which we are endeavouring to dispose of as rapidly as possible, either to the several executive departments of the Government for Public Works, or to individuals by auction and by private sale.

SIXTEENTH ANNUAL REPORT OF THE COMMISSIONERS OF PUBLIC WORKS

DUBLIN, 1848

1848

"RINT" *v.* POTATOES.—THE IRISH JEREMY DIDDLER.

"You haven't got such a thing as Twelve-pence about you?—A Farthing a week—a Penny a month—a Shilling a year?"

THE OLD YEAR AND THE NEW

We enter to-day upon a new year, and as with individuals, so with nations, the first duty that suggests itself is the "taking stock," the examining our resources as compared with our exigencies, and calmly calculating not only what things ought to be done during the twelve months on which we are entering, but what means are at our disposal—what *can* be done, and what, in all human probability, *will* be done. In doing this we must, however, look not only to the present and to the future, but to the past, from which, as from a mirror, a light will be reflected whereby we may truly read the others.

The year 1847 opened on us dark and lowering. Famine stalked through the land at noon, and pestilence brooded over it in the night season. As the year advanced the darkness thickened—famine and pestilence became more exacting—our people fell before them by thousands and tens of thousands, and their emaciated corpses fed the beasts that perish, or were committed coffinless to their mother earth. The nations of the world heard the cry of our distress. America, generous America, the land of the brave and free—the home for our outcast people—hastened to our relief, and while the ships of England were lumbering her dock yards the national ships of the Great Republic ploughed the Atlantic laden with food for the famishing and clothes for the naked of this land. We were, to use the words of a distinguished Prelate, "beggars at the gates of every nation in Christendom" during the year that has just closed. But why recount here the heart-rending details—or seek to number the hundreds of thousands who fell victims to English misrule. We must leave details to the historian of this the saddest year of our history, and pass on to another topic.

The pressure of famine in '46, and the certainty that '47 would prove still more disastrous, seemed for a time to excite in the minds of the Irish gentry a feeling that they *had* a country. They knew, from the experience of the past that when danger, threatening alike *rich* and *poor*, lowered on this nation, *they* might expect as little favour at the hands of England, as those whom they helped her to keep enchained, and with a seeming earnestness of resolve that gave hope and courage to all, the Peers, and Commoners, and Gentry of Ireland met in the Rotundo on the 15th of January, and under the title of the "Irish Party" pledged themselves to stand by Ireland, and unite for her protection and advancement. Nineteen peers, thirty-five members of parliament, and some six or eight hundred of the leading gentry of this kingdom were present at that meeting. George Alexander Hamilton, as the leader of the Conservative Irish, and DANIEL O'CONNELL, as the leader of Ireland, administered the pledge of union and co-operation for *all* Ireland, and that pledge was accepted by all present at the imposing ceremony, and approved by the loud acclaims of all without. We do not propose to enumerate all the resolutions adopted, or half the things promised by the legislators who were present, and took part in what proved to be a huge mockery of a national union. Food for the starving—employment for the idle—*compensation and security for the tenant*—were prominent in the list of results which were to flow from the legislative efforts of the "Irish party." We all know how nothing but disaster and contempt came to Ireland. When Parliament met, the "*United* Irish Party" dissolved. The amended poor law which superadded out-door relief to the prison-house system was the rock on which the landlord class took occasion to split; and when ministers found it inconvenient to approve of Lord George Bentinck's great scheme for reproductive labour on Irish Railways, a large section of the so called Liberal portion of the "Irish party" allowed Ireland and her interests to float down the stream of ruin rather than run the risk of discommoding a patronage-distributing ministry by recording their votes for the measure against which they had pronounced their "*sic volo sic jubeo.*" The seeds of discord once sown, the tree grew, and the fruit ripened apace. "Reproductive employment," "Food for the famishing," "Piers and harbours," "National railways," and all the other great "permanent," as well as "immediate" measures blocked out by the National Convention, were heard of no more; and as for tenant compensation—the moment the landlord legislators crossed the channel they either forgot that there existed tenant wrongs to be righted, or remembering them, remembered them only to obstruct all efforts for their redress.

Discord had done its work—corruption had done its work. The Irish party split into sections, some sought class advantage, others preferred English party to the cause of the country to which they had so recently pledged themselves, while the few who remained true, disgusted with the conduct of the many, seceded, and the "Irish Party," from which so much was expected, ceased to exist save as a bye-word and a jest.

WEEKLY FREEMAN'S JOURNAL, DUBLIN, 1 JANUARY 1848

The condition of this portion of the county is truly lamentable. The misery of the people here is unparalleled—plague, pestilence, and famine, meet the eye in every direction, and the once happy and apparently comfortable village and neighbourhood of Cloughjordan, have now almost become a second Skibbereen! The evidence adduced at the inquest upon the miserable youth who sank beneath the bitter pangs of famine, shows the wretched state into which the unfortunate people are plunged. The sworn testimony of the mother—oh! unhappy, famine stricken mother—is enough to draw tears of pity and commiseration, even from bosoms of brass and hearts of flint! A turnip, she says, supplied her, by perhaps as needy neighbours, has been their chief, in fact their only sustenance for the last month. She further states that for the four days previous to the death of her son, the entire family were without any food whatever, when the most youthful of her children, unable longer to endure the biting gripe of hunger, and when nature had been completely exhausted, yielded his spirit to his God, and ceased to breathe the air of a land that had refused to him the common necessaries of life!

On Sunday, an inquest was held on the body in a filthy hut, which is situate on the road side, and within a mile of Cloughjordan. The interior of this awful abode of misery presented a most heartrendering spectacle. In a corner lay stretched on a litter of straw, in a state of nudity and utter helplessness. Timothy Quirke, aged 19 years, while his brother Thomas, who was about nine years old, was lying on his back close to the fire, which was composed of a sod of turf and a few sticks, which were given by the neighbours. The poor creature, whose skin was quite yellow, his limbs fleshless, and who was a wretched picture of extreme destitution, was unable to sit up or stand, such being the state of exhaustion to which he was reduced. On the floor stood trembling, and in an emaciated state, two other children, holding their unfortunate mother, Bridget Quirke, by the remnant of an old gown, and crying for food, which alas! she had not to give them, and on a table was placed the body of the deceased, which was frightful to behold! In several places in the same vicinity similar scenes of misery exist... The jury returned a verdict that the deceased died from extreme want.—*Nenagh Guardian*

THE NATION, DUBLIN, 22 JANUARY 1848

SPECIAL NOTICE TO EMIGRANTS.

FOR NEW YORK,

TO SAIL ON THEIR APPOINTED DAYS,

The following splendid ships :—
MEMNON, 1,600 tons, 26th January.
WITCH, 1,900 tons, 30th January.
SULTANA, 1,600 tons,
To sail early in February.

THE above are First-Class Vessels, coppered, and copper-fastened ; built of the best materials, and of unrivalled beauty. The 'tween-decks are seven feet in height, airy, and well lighted, fitted up with good berths for the accommodation of Steerage and Second Cabin Passengers ; and on the whole the arrangements on board these favorite Packets are such as cannot fail to afford every comfort to those embarking.

A few respectable Persons (finding their own Provisions) can be handsomely accommodated with State Rooms, in which are single and double Berths, each State Room having ventilating side-lights ; and as the number in these Apartments will be limited, every comfort may be expected.

The usual allowance of Fuel, Water, Medicines, and 1lb. of good American Navy Bread or Flour will be supplied daily to each Adult Passenger during the voyage, free of charge; also convenient apparatus for cooking.

First-class ships regularly dispatched every week to the following ports :—New York, Philadelphia, Boston, Baltimore, New Orleans, &c. ; also to Quebec, Montreal, and St. John's ; and all ports in British North America.

Persons about to emigrate to any of the above ports can obtain every information respecting rate of passage, days of sailing, &c., by application at this office, or by letter, post-paid, addressed to

WILLIAM JAMES HENEY,
5, EDEN-QUAY, DUBLIN;

Sole Agent in Ireland for the firm of Roche Brothers and Company, of 35, Fulton-street, New York ; and No. 1, Spring-lane, Boston ;

OR TO,

MR. JAMES ROCHE, SEN.,
114, WATERLOO ROAD, LIVERPOOL;

Sole Agent in England for the firm of Roche Brothers and Company, of 35, Fulton-street, New York ; and No. 1, Spring-lane, Boston.

⁎ The public are hereby informed that the parties in Dublin using the name of Roches Company, James D. Roche, Roche Brothers, and Roche Brothers and Co., of 30, Eden-qay, are not in any manner connected with the old established house of Roche Brothers and Company, of 35, Fulton-street, New York ; and No. 1, Spring-lane, Boston, Merchants, Emigration and General Agents ; and that the sole Agency in Ireland of the house of Roche Brothers and Company, of New York and Boston, is No. 5, Eden-quay, Dublin.

WILLIAM JAMES HENEY,
SHIP AND COMMISSION AGENT,
No. 5, EDEN-QUAY,
DUBLIN.

Apply to my Agents :
Mr. JOHN DUNPHY, Mountmellick.
Mr. R. H. REEVES, Ballinasloe.

THE IRISH CRISIS

C.E. TREVELYAN

The time has not yet arrived at which any man can with confidence say, that he fully appreciates the nature and the bearings of that great event which will long be inseparably associated with the year just departed. Yet we think that we may render some service to the public by attempting thus early to review, with the calm temper of a future generation, the history of the great Irish famine of 1847. Unless we are much deceived, posterity will trace up to that famine the commencement of a salutary revolution in the habits of a nation long singularly unfortunate, and will acknowledge that on this, as on many other occasions, Supreme Wisdom has educed permanent good out of transient evil.

If, a few months ago, an enlightened man had been asked what he thought the most discouraging circumstance in the state of Ireland, we do not imagine that he would have pitched upon Absenteeism, or Protestant bigotry, or Roman Catholic bigotry, or Orangeism, or Ribbandism, or the Repeal cry, or even the system of threatening notices and midday assassinations. These things, he would have said, are evils; but some of them are curable; and others are merely symptomatic. They do not make the case desperate. But what hope is there for a nation which lives on potatoes?

The consequences of depending upon the potato as the principal article of popular food, had long been foreseen by thinking persons...

The potato disease, which had manifested itself in North America in 1844, first appeared in these islands late in the autumn of 1845. The early crop of potatoes, which is generally about one-sixth of the whole, and is dug in September and October, escaped; but the late, or what is commonly called the "people's crop," and is taken up in December and January, was tainted after it arrived at an advanced stage of maturity...

In the following year (1846) the blight in the potatoes took place earlier, and was of a much more sweeping and decisive kind. "On the 27th of last month (July), I passed," Father Mathew writes in a letter published in the Parliamentary Papers, "from Cork to Dublin, and this doomed plant bloomed in all the luxuriance of an abundant harvest. Returning on the 3rd instant (August), I beheld with sorrow one wide waste of putrefying vegetation. In many places the wretched people were seated on the fences of their decaying gardens, wringing their hands, and wailing bitterly the destruction that had left them foodless." The first symptom of the disease was a little brown spot on the leaf, and these spots gradually increased in number and size, until the foliage withered, and the stem became brittle, and snapped off immediately when touched. In less than a week the whole process was accomplished...

In the third year (1847) the disease had nearly exhausted itself. It appeared in different parts of the country, but the plants generally exerted fresh vigour and outgrew it. The result, perhaps, could not have been better. The wholesome distrust in the potato was maintained, while time was allowed for making the alterations which the new state of things required...

Among the numerous causes which enhanced the difficulty of obtaining adequate foreign supplies at moderate rates during the most exigent period of the winter of 1846-7, one of the most embarrassing, was the sudden and extraordinary advance in freights, which occurred simultaneously in the ports of the United States of America, the Mediterranean, and the Black Sea...

On the 27th January, 1846, Sir Robert Peel proposed his measure for the relaxation of the duties on the importation of foreign corn, by which the scale of duties payable on wheat was to range from 4s. to 10s. per quarter, and Indian corn, which had previously been charged with the same duty as barley, was to pay only 1s. a quarter. This was to last till February, 1849, when an uniform duty of 1s. a quarter was to be charged on every description of grain. The bill passed the House of Lords on the 29th June, 1846; and Sir R. Peel announced his resignation in the House of Commons on the same day.

Immediately on the meeting of Parliament in January, 1847, Lord J. Russell introduced bills to suspend until the 1st September, 1847, the duties on foreign corn, and the restrictions imposed by the Navigation Laws on the importation of corn in foreign vessels; and he at the same time moved a resolution permitting the use of sugar in breweries; all which measures received the sanction of the Legislature. At the close of the same session, the suspension of the Corn and Navigation Laws was extended to the 1st March, 1848.

On the first appearance of the blight in the autumn of 1845, Professors Kane, Lindley, and Playfair, were appointed by Sir Robert Peel to inquire into the nature of it, and to suggest the best means of preserving the stock of potatoes from its ravages. The result showed that the mischief lay beyond the knowledge and power of man. Every remedy which science or experience could dictate was had recourse to, but the potato equally melted away under the most opposite modes of treatment.

The next step was to order from the United States of America 100,000*l.* worth of Indian corn. It was considered that the void caused by the failure of the potato crop might be filled with the least disturbance of private trade and market prices, by the introduction of a new description of popular food. Owing to the prohibitory duty, Indian corn was unknown as an article of consumption in the United Kingdom. Private merchants, therefore, could not complain of interference with a trade which did not exist, nor could prices be raised against the home consumer on an article of which no stock was to be found in the home market. Nevertheless, with a view to avoid as long as possible, the doubts and apprehensions which must have arisen if the Government had appeared as a purchaser in a new class of operations, pains were taken to keep the transaction secret, and the first cargoes from America had been more than a fortnight in Cork harbour before it became generally known that such a measure was in progress.

In order to distribute the food so obtained, central dépôts were established in various parts of Ireland, under the direction of officers of the Commissariat, with sub-dépôts under the charge of the Constabulary and Coast Guard; and when the supplies in the local markets were deficient, meal was sold from these dépôts at reasonable prices to Relief Committees, where any existed, and where they did not, to the labourers themselves. In the time of the heaviest pressure (June and July, 1846), one sub-dépôt retailed 20 tons of meal daily, and the issues from a single main dépôt to its dependencies amounted to 233 tons in one week.

The Relief Committees were formed, under the superintendence of a Central Commission at Dublin, for the purpose of selling food in detail to those who could buy it, and giving it to those who could not; the requisite funds being derived from private subscriptions, added to, in certain proportions, by Government donations. The Relief Committees also selected the persons to be employed on the Relief Works carried on under the superintendence of the Board of Works.

If the Irish poor had been in the habit of buying their food, as is the case in England, the object would have been attained when a cheap substitute had been provided for the potato; but as the labouring class in Ireland had hitherto subsisted on potatoes grown by themselves, and money-wages were almost unknown, it was necessary to adopt some means of giving the people a command over the new description of food. This was done by establishing a system of public works, in accordance with the previous practice on similar occasions, both in Ireland and in other countries. . . .

The first symptoms of neglected tillage appeared in the spring of 1846, and they were worst in those districts in which the Relief Works were carried on to the greatest extent. The improvements in progress on the Shannon and the arterial drainages were also impeded by the preference which the labourers showed for the Relief Works.

The measures of which we have been speaking, were brought to a close on the 15th August, 1846, and they may be considered to have answered their end. The scarcity being partial and local, the deficiency of one part of the country was supplied from the superabundance of others, and the pains taken to prevent the people from suffering want, led to their being better off than in ordinary years. Above all, Ireland was prepared by the course adopted during this probationary season of distress, as it may be called, to bear better the heavy affliction of the succeeding season. No misapplication of the funds deserving of notice took place, except in the instance of the Relief Works, the cause of which was as follows:—The landed proprietors of Ireland had long been accustomed to rely upon Government loans and grants for making improvements of various kinds, and the terms on which the Relief Works were to be executed being more advantageous than any which had been open to them for many years before, a rush took place from all quarters upon this fund, and the special object of relieving the people from the consequences of the failure of their accustomed food, was to a great extent lost sight of in the general fear, which in many cases was not attempted to be concealed, of being deprived of what they called "their share of the grant." . . .

The new and more decisive failure of the potato crop called for great exertions from Lord John Russell's recently formed Government . . . The system of public works was renewed . . . In order to check the exorbit-ant demands which had been made during the preceding season, the whole of the expense was made a local charge, and the advances were directed to be repaid by a rate levied according to the Poor Law valua-tion, which makes the landlords liable for the whole rate on tenements under 4l. yearly value, and for a proportion, generally amounting to one-half, on tenements above that value, instead of according to the grand jury cess (the basis of the repayments under the preceding act), which lays the whole burden upon the occupier. It was also determined that the wages given on the Relief Works should be somewhat below the average rate of wages in the district; that the persons employed should, as far as possible, be paid by task or in proportion to the work actually done by them; and that the Relief Committees, instead of giving tickets entitling persons to employment on the public works, should furnish lists of persons requiring relief, which should be carefully revised by the officers of the Board of Works; the experience of the preceding season having shown that these precautions were necessary to confine the Relief Works to the destitute, and to enforce a reasonable quantum of work . . .

The Relief Committees of the preceding season were re-organised; the rules under which they had acted were carefully revised; and inspecting officers were appointed to superintend their proceedings, and keep the Government informed of the progress of events. A large proportion of the people of Ireland had been accustomed to grow the food they required, each for himself, on his own little plot of ground; and the social machinery by which, in other countries, the necessary supplies of food are collected, stored, and distributed, had no existence there. Suddenly, without any preparation, the people passed from a potato food, which they raised themselves, to a grain food, which they had to purchase from others, and which, in great part, had to be imported from abroad; and the country was so entirely destitute of the resources applicable to this new state of things, that often, even in large villages, neither bread nor flour was to be procured; and in country districts, the people had sometimes to walk twenty miles before they could obtain a single stone of meal. The main object for which the Relief Committees were established, therefore, was to provide a temporary substitute for the operations of the corn-factor, miller, baker, and provision-dealer, and to allow time and furnish the example for a sounder and more permanent state of things . . . Such was the plan resolved upon for the campaign of 1846-7, against the approaching famine . . .

It was hoped that a breathing-time would have been allowed at the season of harvest, to enable the Board of Works to reorganise their establishments on a scale proportioned to the magnitude of the task about to devolve on them, and to prepare, through their district officers, plans and estimates of suitable works for the assistance of the baronial sessions. This interval was not obtained. The general failure of the potato crop spread despondency and alarm from one end of Ireland to the other, and induced every class of persons to throw themselves upon the Government for aid. On the 6th of September, the Lord Lieutenant ordered all the discontinued works . . . to be recommenced, and sessions were rapidly held in all the southern and western counties of Ireland, at which

roads were presented in the mass ... the cost of which, in some cases, much exceeded the annual rental of the barony. The resident gentry and rate-payers, whose duty it was to ascertain, as far as possible, the probable amount of destitution in their neighbourhood, the sum required to relieve it, and the works upon which that sum could best be expended, and who had the necessary local knowledge, in almost every case devolved these functions upon the Board of Works, who could only act on such information as they could obtain from naval and military officers and engineers, most of whom were selected from among strangers to the district, in order to prevent undue influence being used. After that, to advance the funds; to select the labourers; to superintend the work; to pay the people weekly; to enforce proper performance of the labour; if the farm works were interrupted, to ascertain the quantity of labour required for them; to select and draft off the proper persons to perform it; to settle the wages to be paid to them by the farmers, and see that they were paid; to furnish food, not only for all the destitute out of doors, but in some measure for the paupers in the workhouse, were the duties which the Government and its officers were called upon to perform. The proprietors and associated rate-payers having presented *indefinitely*, said it was the fault of the Government and its officers if the people were not instantly employed, and these officers were blamed, even by persons of character and understanding, if they were not at once equal to execute the duties which in this country are performed in their respective districts by thousands of country gentlemen, magistrates, guardians, overseers, surveyors, &c., resident throughout the country, and trained by the experience of years to the performance of their various

functions. The Board of Works became the centre of a colossal organisa-
tion; 5000 separate works had to be reported upon; 12,000 subordinate
officers had to be superintended...

The strain on the springs of society from this monstrous system of
centralisation was fearful in the extreme. The Government, which ought
only to mediate between the different classes of society, had now to
bear the immediate pressure of the millions on the sensitive points of
wages and food. The opposition to task-work was general, and the en-
forcement of it became a trial of strength between the Government and
the multitude. The officers of the Board were in numerous instances
the objects of murderous attacks, and it became necessary, for the preservation of the whole community, to have recourse to the painful
expedient of stopping the works whenever cases of insubordination or
outrage occurred.

Meanwhile the number of persons employed on the works was rapidly
on the increase... Thousands upon thousands were pressed upon the
officers of the Board of Works in every part of Ireland, and it was impossible for those officers to test the accuracy of the urgent representations which were made to them. The attraction of money wages regularly
paid from the public purse, or the "Queen's pay," as it was popularly
called, led to a general abandonment of other descriptions of industry,
in order to participate in the advantages of the Relief Works. Landlords
competed with each other in getting the names of their tenants placed
on the lists; farmers dismissed their labourers, and sent them to the works;
the clergy insisted on the claims of the members of their respective con-
gregations; the fisheries were deserted; and it was often difficult even
to get a coat patched or a pair of shoes mended, to such an extent had
the population of the south and west of Ireland turned out upon the
roads...

The plan of the Labour Rate Act... was based on the supposition
that the great majority of the landlords and farmers would make those
exertions and submit to those sacrifices which the magnitude of the crisis
demanded, leaving only a manageable proportion of the population to
be supported by the Board of Works; and the act would probably have
answered its object, if a larger, instead of a smaller, number of persons
than usual had been employed in the cultivation and improvement of
the land, and the Relief Committees had put only those who were really destitute upon the lists. Including the families of the persons employed,
upwards of two millions of people were maintained by the Relief Works,
but there were other multitudes behind, including often the most helpless

portion of the community, for whom no work could be found . . . The fearful extent to which the rural population had been thrown for support upon the Board of Works also threatened a disastrous neglect of the ordinary tillage. If the people were retained on the works, their lands must remain uncultivated. If they were put off the works, they must starve. A change of system had become inevitable, and when Parliament met in the end of January, it was announced that the Government intended to put an end to the public works, and to substitute for them another mode of relief . . .

Meanwhile the pressure on the Relief Works was continually on the increase, and the persons daily employed who, in January, had been 570,000, became, in February, 708,000, and in March amounted to the enormous number of 734,000, representing at a moderate estimate of the average extent of each family, upwards of three millions of persons. At last, the Government, seeing that the time suited for agricultural operations was rapidly passing away, and that the utmost exertions made on the spot had failed in keeping the numbers in check, took the matter into its own hands, and directed that on the 20th March, 20 per cent. of the persons employed should be struck off the lists; after which successive reductions were ordered, proportioned to the progress made in bringing the new system of relief into operation in each district. These orders were obeyed, and the crisis passed without any disturbance of the public peace or any perceptible aggravation of the distress. The necessary labour was returned to agriculture, and the foundation was laid of the late abundant harvest in Ireland, by which the downward progress of that country has been mercifully stayed, and new strength and spirits have been given for working out her regeneration.

EDINBURGH REVIEW, JANUARY 1848

To be Sold
BY AUCTION
AT NOON

On *Saturday*, the 17th of July next,

At the Office of Mr. JOHN WARNOCK, English-street Downpatrick,

THE

DWELLING-HOUSE

AND Premises in Bridge-street, DOWNPATRICK, lately in the occupation of THOMAS CROSGROVE, and held by Lease for a term of Three Lives renewable for Ever, at the yearly rent of £   , and a Renewal fine of *7/-* on the fall of each life.

The premises are well adapted for any public business. Immediate possession can be given

For particulars and terms of sale, apply to Mr. JOHN WARNOCK, or to

Robert Taylor.

Downpatrick, 20th June, 1848.

EMIGRATION OF ORPHANS FROM WORKHOUSES IN IRELAND

FREE PASSAGE TO SOUTH AUSTRALIA

INSTRUCTIONS TO POOR LAW INSPECTORS
POOR LAW COMMISSION OFFICE, DUBLIN, MARCH 7, 1848

SIR.—The Commissioners for administering the Laws for Relief of the Poor in Ireland forward for your information several copies of a communication made to Earl Grey by the Colonial Land and Emigration Commissioners, on the subject of young persons at present inmates of Irish workhouses, who may be eligible for emigration to South Australia, together with an extract from a letter addressed by Earl Grey to Sir George Grey, and communicated for the information of His Excellency the Lord Lieutenant, explaining the manner in which the emigration of such persons is proposed to be conducted.

The Commissioners are most anxious that advantage should be taken of this proposal of the Government, and that the selection of young persons should be so conducted as to insure the complete success of the experiment.

You will have the goodness, therefore, to address yourself to his object with the least possible delay, and take such steps by communication with Boards of Guardians in your district, or otherwise, as may enable you to point out the names of young persons eligible in all respects and willing to emigrate, for examination by the agent who may be authorized to make the final selection.

Your attention is especially called to that part of the letter of the Emigration Commissioners which relates to the peculiar advantage of obtaining young females, eligible and willing to emigrate, in preference to males.

You will take care that such young persons are duly and properly apprised of the prospects which await them in the event of their availing themselves of the free passage to Australia; and you will ascertain from the Boards of Guardians, distinctly, their willingness to bear the cost of outfit, and the expense of conveyance to the place of embarkation.

By order of the Commissioners

W. STANLEY, Secretary

To each Poor Law Inspector.

HORRIBLE DESTITUTION

STEALING AND EATING A FILLY

Michael Ward and Ellen Reilly, two wretched looking creatures, were indicted for stealing at Derrygimla, near Clifden, on the 3d of February, one filly, the property of Anne Kinealy.

Anne Kinealy deposed that on the day mentioned in the indictment she missed a foal, which after a search by the police, was found killed and hid in a wall; witness knew that it was hers by the skin, which was found in the same place.

Mathias Gordon deposed that on the 3d of February, he saw Michael Ward, Laurence Reilly, and Ellen Reilly, following a mare and foal, the property of Anne Kinealy; they chased them in the field; witness did not know whether they intended to kill it or not, but believed, as they bore bad characters, that they were about to catch the mare for the purpose of taking away corn; the prisoners then caught the foal and witness saw them kill it; they nearly cut off the head, and then proceeded to skin it; witness ran away; he informed the people next day of what he had seen.

Robert Allen, police constable, deposed that in consequence of informations received he proceeded to a place where he found the skin hid in a wall; Anne Kinealy identified the skin as that of her filly; witness found in the house of one of the prisoners blood upon a stool as if meat had been cut upon it; found bones like those of a filly quite fresh under the bed; heard from a steward on a road that the two prisoners would not work, and were consequently cut out of the relief list.

To the Court—Found no meal or food of any kind.

To a Juror—Is not very fond of hearsay evidence.

The jury without leaving the box found the prisoners guilty, but strongly recommended them to the mercy of the court.

The Court said a magistrate had communicated that relief was now given in that very destitute locality, and was happy to be enabled to pass a sentence which would enable the prisoners to receive it. The sentence of the court was that the prisoners be confined for six weeks from the time of committal.

DUBLIN WEEKLY REGISTER, 1 APRIL 1848

THE IRISH AMELIORATION SOCIETY

Having had the pleasure of perusing another recent letter from "FATHER MATHEW" on the subject of this Society, we [feel] that the following sentiment which it expresses should be engraved on the minds of all who desire Ireland's welfare, and would go the right way to accomplish it—"ALL THAT OUR LABOURING POPULATION REQUIRE TO MAKE THEM CONTENTED AND HAPPY IS, REMUNERATIVE EMPLOYMENT."

This is the plain and simple truth, spoken by one who knows more of the feelings and character of the mass of the Irish population than perhaps any one else . . . He has rescued the miserable Irish from their vice of *drunkenness*—may his words aid now, in rescuing them from want, by *"remunerative employment,"*—for it cannot be doubted for a moment, by any who think of Ireland's position, that nothing else will produce her pacification and welfare.

LITERARY GAZETTE AND JOURNAL OF BELLES LETTRES, LONDON, 15 APRIL 1848

DEATHS BY STARVATION

The Rev. Mr. Henry, P.P., Bunenadden, county Sligo, in a memorial to the Lord Lieutenant, complained that the following persons met their deaths by hunger, owing to the neglect of the Guardians of the Boyle Union:—

KILSHALVEY ELECTORAL DIVISION—Mrs. Kilkenny and child—after several applications for relief in vain; Mary Connell, found dead by a rick of turf; Philip M'Gowan's wife and daughter; Bryan Flanagan, found dead by the road side; Widow Davy's daughter; Andrew Davy.

KILTURRA ELECTORAL DIVISION—John May and son; Pat Marren, Widow Corlely, John O'Hara, John Healy's two daughters. Other deaths from starvation took place previous to my first communication to your Excellency not included in this list.

The Lord Lieutenant ordered an inquiry, and the allegations of the Rev. Mr. Henry were most fully proved. The Poor Law Commissioners will, therefore, doubtless remove those personages.

DUBLIN WEEKLY REGISTER, 29 APRIL 1848

THE ENIGMA

Pale victims, where is your Fatherland?
　　Where oppression is law from age to age,
　　Where the death-plague, and hunger, and misery rage—
And tyrants a godless warfare wage
　　'Gainst the holiest rights of our ancient land.

Where the corn waves green on the fair hill side,
But each sheaf by the serfs and slavelings tied
Is taken to pamper a foreigner's pride,
　　There is our suffering Fatherland.

Where broad rivers flow 'neath a glorious sky,
And the valleys, like gems of emerald lie,
Yet the young men and strong men starve and die
　　For want of bread in their own rich land.

And we pile up their corses heap on heap,
While the pale mothers faint and the children weep,
Yet the living might envy the dead their sleep,
　　So bitter is life in that mourning land.

Oh! Heaven ne'er looked on a sadder scene;
Earth shuddered to hear that such woe had been;
Then we prayed, in despair, to a foreign Queen
　　For leave to live in our own fair land;
We have wept till our faces are pale and wan;
We have knelt to a throne till our strength is gone;

We prayed to our masters, but one by one
　　They laughed to scorn our suffering land,
And sent forth their minions, with cannon and steel,
Swearing with fierce, unholy zeal,
To trample us down with an iron heel,
　　If we dared but to murmur our just demand.
　　Know ye not now our Fatherland?

What! are there no MEN in your Fatherland
To confront the tyrant's stormy glare,
With a scorn as deep as the wrongs ye bear,
With defiance as fierce as the oaths they sware,
With vengeance as wild as the cries of despair,
    That rise from your suffering Fatherland?

Are there no SWORDS in your Fatherland,
To smite down the proud, insulting foe?
With the strength of despair give blow for blow,
Till the blood of the baffled murderers flow
    On the trampled soil of your outraged land.

Are your right arms weak in that land of slaves,
That ye stand by your murdered brothers' graves,
Yet tremble like coward and crouching knaves,
    To strike for Freedom and Fatherland?

Oh! had ye faith in your Fatherland,
    In God, your cause, and your own right hand,
Ye would go forth as saints to the holy fight,
Go in the strength of Eternal right,
Go in the conquering Godhead's might,
    And save or avenge your Fatherland.

SPERANZA

THE NATION, DUBLIN, 6 MAY 1848

TO THE RIGHT HON.
LORD JOHN RUSSELL

My Lord—it is unnecessary to tell you that Ireland is in a deplorable condition. Many very wild-goose schemes are in agitation to deliver her from these misfortunes. On the one hand, we have heard of Rotatory Parliaments, Federalism, the "*Irish* Queen, Lords, and Commons," and Republicanism. On the other, we have had concession and coercion, "heavy blows and great

discouragements" to Protestantism, and great encouragement to Popery.
As in the one case the policy of your lordship and your predecessors
has done no good and the schemes of the other parties referred to above
are likely to do as little, might it not suggest itself to your lordship, that
both parties are mistaken as to the real evils of the country. If a physician
happens to mistake his patient's disease, is it not likely that the remedies
he will apply will aggravate, not cure, the disorder. Just in the same manner, if both your lordship and the republican are mistaken in the real
root of Ireland's misfortunes, it is highly probable that the state of things
which you both wish to be brought about will produce harm rather
than advantage. There is on the pages of history an instance of misery
similar to that of Ireland. The historian, one of the best deserving of
being believed,—whether you view the probity or the information of
the writer,—of any age or any country, tells the reason why that country
was miserable.

There is the strongest possible reason to believe, that there is the same
reason for the misery of Ireland that there was for that of the country
in question . . . Let it not awaken the disregard and contempt of your
lordship when you learn that the parallel instance of misery, and the
statement regarding its origin, are to be found in that old, despised book,
called the Bible. That book, if you believe it, tells you these three things
in the 4th chapter of Hosea:

1. The people of Israel were in mourning—they ate, and had not
enough.

2. It tells the cause. They lacked the knowledge of God—they were
superstitious and idolatrous: they were in consequence wicked, and in
consequence of all this God held a controversy with them.

3. The word of God farther gives this important information. Whatever
happened the Israelite was written to be a lesson and an example to us
(Rom. xv.; I Cor. x.).

Now, we have mourning and want in Ireland, just as they were in
Israel. We have the same things that caused them there, and we have
the above declaration of God that this history was our lesson to direct
us; therefore if any credit is to be given to God, the ignorance of God,
the superstition and idolatry, and consequent wickedness of Ireland, are
the cause of its misfortunes.

My Lord, six millions of the people of Ireland are chained to a system
that excludes, and is found to exclude, them from the true knowledge
of the true God . . . Farther—the spirit of idolatry (spiritual whoredom)
was the proximate cause of the iniquities of the Israelite . . .

Then, my Lord, when you stand up in your place in parliament to propose, or aid by the great power and influence wherewith you are invested, some measure to correct the vices, quell the turbulence, and remove the miseries of Ireland, remember what God has told you will *not* do so—that the establishing a system by which the people will have a lack of the knowledge of God, by which they will be made superstitious and idolatrous, will not do so, but will make it more degraded, vicious, and miserable. Such a system you acknowledge popery to be, therefore if you wish the welfare of Ireland you cannot do any thing to countenance and foster popery amongst us. Do you wish that the land should not mourn? Then set yourself to remove its multiplied iniquities. Do you wish to remove these?—Then set yourself to remove the ignorance of God that reigns among the people . . . You must endeavour to bring the knowledge of God to every cabin in Ireland. To do this you must use your endeavours to have the word of God taught and preached in every village in Ireland; and when you thus honour God by honouring His word, you may respect redemption for Ireland.

I am, my Lord,

THE PROTESTANT WATCHMAN

PROTESTANT WATCHMAN, DUBLIN, 12 MAY 1848

EXTERMINATION IN ROSCOMMON

The *Roscommon Messenger* mentions a case of extermination in that county, accompanied by circumstances of great hardship. Mr. M.R.W. Ormsby, an absentee, had set to a middleman 33 acres of land, and this person, whose name is not mentioned, re-set to several tenants. In October last 128*l*. 7*s*. being due, an ejectment for non-payment of rent was brought, and judgment had in November. The yearly rent was 120*l*. 12*s*. 11*d*. The ejectment, the *Messenger* states, was held over until the commencement of May, this year, when the ground having been tilled and the crops promising, the landlord entered on possession, evicting not fewer than *two hundred* persons. The crops were seized, the houses levelled, and the inhabitants thrown upon the world! What makes the matter more provoking is, that the evictions have, it is said, taken place by collusion between the head and middle landlords, the latter of whom will be continued in possession. Many

of the tenants were, it is said, prepared to pay all rent due, and tendered
same; but, notwithstanding, the law has had its course.

DUBLIN WEEKLY REGISTER, 3 JUNE 1848

A HARVEST HYMN

I

God has been bountiful! Garlands of gladness
Grow by the waysides exorcising sadness,
Shedding their bloom on the pale cheek of slavery,
Holding out plumes for the helmets of bravery,
Birds in them singing this sanctified stave—
"God has been Bountiful—Man must be Brave!"

II

Look on this harvest of plenty and promise—
Shall we sleep while the enemy snatches it from us?
See where the sun on the golden grain sparkles!
Lo where behind it the Pauper's home darkles!
Hark the cry ringing out—"save us, oh save,
God has been Bountiful—Man must be Brave.

III

From the shores of the ocean, the farther and hither,
Where the victims of famine and pestilence wither,
Lustreless eyes stare the pitying Heaven,
Arms, black, unburied, appeal to the levin—
Voices unceasing shout over each wave—
God has been Bountiful—Man must be Brave.

IV

Would ye live happily, fear not nor falter—
Peace sits on the summit of Liberty's altar;
Would ye have honor—Honor was ever
The prize of the hero-like death scorning Liver,
Would ye have glory! She knows not the slave,
God has been Bountiful, you must be Brave!

V

Swear by the bright streams abundantly flowing,
Swear by the hearths where wet weeds are growing—
By the Stars and the Earth, and the four winds of Heaven,
That the Land shall be saved, and its Tyrants outdriven.
Do it! and blessings will shelter your grave,
God has been Bountiful—will ye be Brave?

AMERGIN

THE NATION, DUBLIN, 17 JUNE 1848

WHAT IF WE FAIL?

Some weeks since we showed those who pay taxes and talk of their property being at stake, what is likely to come of them and their property if our projected Irish revolution fails. We showed them that they would have to pay more taxes and receive no consideration; that confiscation in their favor was out of the question; that an army of Jews, each hungering for his bond, was marshalled under the banner of England; and that the fear of revolt once over, the most merciless creditor of all would be the Imperial Treasury.

We turn to other classes now; and of them we ask in like manner—What if we fail?

The harvest of the year promises abundance, and would certainly give temporary potatoes to the paupers of the quarter acre class, under the old administration—the corn for the rent—the cattle for the taxes—and the potatoes for the people. Such was and is the social economy with which we war.

And does any man suppose that the survivors of the famine of '47 will tamely return to the social condition in which that famine first surprised them! and that those who have devoted themselves to be voices to this people—to awake them when they sleep—to incite them when they tire—to strengthen them when they droop—to make them familiar with their rights and friends of their own cause;—do they think these voices will be silent in the face of such craven and murderous temporising with a desperate malady as that would be?

No, the Irish peasantry must not return to con-acre and turnip-tops, even for a year; neither must they be any longer left at the mercy of

man-trap Poor Laws and destructive Land Laws. Either these criminal
and unchristian institutions and edicts must be destroyed, or new ranks
of this religious, loving, long-suffering people, must be swallowed in
the vortex of a new Famine. Sooner or later it would come to this again:
and the nation that could hang content by one root to life—that volun-
tarily goes to hang upon it over the black and fearful gulf whose sides
are inlaid with whitened bones—deserves to be engulphed without sacrament or lamentation. We believe, and preach, that a revolutionary, social
change has become indispensable—has been decreed with such fearful
rites as human ordinance never came to light with since NOAH's altar
rose above the surge of the subsiding Deluge. The last gaspings of one
thousand thousand human beings, perishing with green grass, or human
flesh, or maniac cries in their mouths, have commanded it, and the survivors dare not, will not, shrink from obeying that ordinance of the Dead.

THE NATION, DUBLIN, 8 JULY 1848

LETTERS TO A NOBLEMAN
VISITING IRELAND

The potato-crop being in a perilous condition, the Revolution
adjourned; and the money to feed the people, not forthcoming, it is satisfactory to find that some Irish Repeal Members
are disposed to put off political discussions for the present; and it is pleasant
to listen to the Irish Clergy raising up an affecting chorus of loyalty and
devotion to the QUEEN, of which everybody will appreciate the
candour.

"The great point now is, to begin granting money as quickly as pos-
sible, so as to enable our friends to carry on the year comfortably. Your
Lordship is pledged to this in some manner; and certain it is, that the
Irish of all classes are in need of that sort of relief. There's TIM has not
been able to earn anything in England this harvest, being engaged in
honour to stop at home and liberate his country in the 'War.' There's
PAT has sunk all his capital in the purchase of a 'dainty rifle;' and though
THADY has got his commission as Lieutenant in the BRIAN-BOROO
Body-guard, yet pay-day hasn't come round, and it stands to reason that
he must be fed somehow. There's FATHER TOM has had no fees, what
with the bad times, and the War expenses of his congregation; there's

the landlord has got in no rents; and he with bills out, mortgages to pay on, house and hounds to keep, besides his four sons hunters, the left wing of the house to finish, and all the estate to drain. How can the country get on without a loan? and whose duty is it, but that of Government, to come down with the money for poor, suffering, bleeding, oppressed Ireland?

"Go and stay at Castle Crazy, and then say if this picture of a country's desolation is overcharged. As you look on the town through the beautiful cracked French windows of the drawing-room, you will see the Park swarming with ragged cloaks and frieze coats. You will see three or four old crones squatted in the Hall porch, for whom the Masther has a joke and, very rarely now, a sixpence; as you go out of the lodge-gate (which to be sure won't open unless they come lift it), more will start out to let you pass through; if you go with the Masther to look at the nags in the stable, a score of tattered horseboys will be there to show you the way. They will show you MASTHER MICK's grey horse that ran for the Curragh Cup, or MASTHER JACK's bee meer that ran second in the hurdle race, and MISS BIDDY's chestnut filly, &c, &c.; but all the people you see, from the Masther down to poor half-witted JOE in the chimney-corner, with his feet in the turf, are in want of money, and look to you quite naturally to supply it. Don't talk about refusal. Are not the English gorged with Irish beef and corn? Who provides your pork, who wins your victories, but the Irish? If it is their right, they take it and thank you for nothing; if you refuse, you are tyrants and oppressors. Those are to be the terms of the bargain; at least if words go for anything; if Old Ireland and Young Ireland are to be believed, and if O'CONNELL and MITCHEL represent any opinions at all.

THE IRISH REAPING-HOOK.

"And while you are arranging your plans for the relief of this fine peasantry, which is now pretty quiet, being about to ask you for money, you will remember that their beautiful pikes, scythes, and dainty rifles, (delicate instruments, with which they

proposed to reap the present harvest) are all comfortably hidden away
within call. I say it behoves an English statesman to remember that
PADDY has a weapon somewhere at hand, with which he proposes to
'rise in the might of his freedom' some day, or in other words, to cut
your throat. Where are all the lopped forests of ash-poles which the
patriots cut down before harvest, and the bushels and cartloads of pikes
which the blacksmiths flung off in such a heat and ardour of insurrection? The police, with all their vigilance, have not pounced on twenty
pounds worth of old iron, the people laugh in their ragged sleeves as
they give them up old muskets without locks, and old rusty weapons,
relics of former wars. The pikes are only thrust away into the hedge
or the bog; and so the animus to use them is merely laid aside convenient.

"I don't say this is particularly blameworthy on the part of our Irish
brethren. I don't say that they can do otherwise—miserable as they are,
and instructed as they have been—but that you are bound to take account of it—and to remember that the person whom you persist in keeping in your house has been, from some cause or other, worked up to
a state of mad ferocity against you, and that he has a knife concealed
about his person somewhere, which he will use on your's whenever
he can attack you at an advantage.

"If this is the fact: if the people hates you, and you have no means
to pacify it, why should not the Irish gentlemen try their hand to settle
their own affairs in their own city of Dublin? How would their palavers
hurt us? or how would our strength be injured by leaving them to arrange their own difficulties, and provide for their own poor?

"And what if the orderly and sensible portion of the Irish are at this
minute actually prevented by you from keeping order in their country?—if the house is on fire and we keep the keys of the engine?

"Why, Sir, I say, are we to turn out and work the pump for the Irish
conflagration, and not allow them to put out their own flames with their
own buckets? Why shouldn't the Irish have a Council House or an
Administrative Assembly of their own? You never condescend to give
reasons or entertain the question. And yet there are only phrases against
it. MR. CANNING says, 'Restore the Heptarchy!' MR. MACAULAY says,
'Let the whole Empire go down together, rather than a separation ensue;'
MR. CARLYLE says, 'The British Lion will squelch the Irish Rat, but
separation must not be.' I hope to see a great party in England before
long, which shall say, 'Why not?' At any rate, that it shall be a question
open to fair debate; and that, when our Irish friends bawl out 'Repeal,'
some people will answer 'With all our hearts!' from this country too.

" 'Gentlemen,' (that band of simple-minded patriots will exclaim) 'we get no good out of you. We pay you for your pigs and oats, that you are always bragging about. As for an army, it is not for love that you shoulder the musket, but for money; and to say that we are to keep a nation of eight millions, in order that we may get forty or fifty thousand men out of it, is as if you were to tell us to burn a house down in order to roast a pig. We are tired of your brawling, your bawling, your bullying, your bragging, your begging. You stop our kindness with your curses, our pity with your ludicrous menacing and boasting; you render our confidence impossible with your double dealing. We may part from you, and yet survive, without a restored Heptarchy. We won't go down, even though we have the pleasure of your company in the ship. As for 'squelching,' that is out of the question. The British Lion has much better occupation; the business would fatigue him. The dog *Billy* can do it infinitely better. We believe that we shall be better without you than with your company; and finally, if you want Repeal, we will do our utmost efforts not to balk you.'

"Sentiments of this nature simply put forward, and conveyed to the leaders ecclesiastical and occult of the Irish party, I believe would go farther to stop the Repeal movements on the other side, than any efforts of conciliation; and I think we should begin to show that we are in earnest, and to prepare our Irish friends for the change they look for, by stopping the subsidies which they have been in the habit of drawing from this country.

"HIBERNIS HIBERNIOR"

PUNCH, LONDON, JULY–DECEMBER 1848

THE POTATO CROP

The following letter is from our Crookhaven correspondent, whose anticipations are more gloomy with regard to this esculent:—

Crookhaven, July 20th, 1848

"DEAR SIR—I left from home this day to make inquiries respecting the potato crop in Kilmoe. I am sorry to inform you that the blight of 1846 has made its appearance; that some few acres and fields suffer greatly. The green crops look uncommonly well."

We (*Clare Journal*) regret to learn that we continue to receive very discouraging accounts from the various districts of this county, relative to the appearance of this crop. We still continue to hope, however, that the alarm may be to some extent unfounded. The following letter is from an experienced agriculturist, who has had ample opportunities of inspecting the crops around a large district of the county:—

TO THE EDITOR OF THE *CLARE JOURNAL*

Miltown Malbay, 19th July 1848

"SIR—I gave you early notice last year of the appearance of the disease upon the potato stalks, which, although it showed itself very decidedly at the time, fortunately did little harm to the crops generally. I have carefully watched the appearance of the potato crop this season; I have lately had an opportunity of inspecting the crop in various districts of the county, and am sorry to say that in almost every instance where I have examined, unmistakable symptoms of disease were to be observed upon the potato stalks. The disease shows itself in various ways upon the stalks—by black blotches, just [as] if the flame of a burning candle had played upon the part for a time—by rotting at the root, which causes the stalk to look sickly, and by the leaves appearing shrivelled. Notwithstanding all these symptoms of disease being too plainly seen upon all the potato fields that have come under my notice, it is to be hoped that the disease will be arrested in its destructive progress, as it was last year, and do but little injury to so important a crop."

Your obedient servant,

J.F. CLARKE

DUBLIN WEEKLY REGISTER, 29 JULY 1848

IRELAND

THE ATTEMPTED REBELLION

The accounts which reached town on this subject in the early part of the week were of the vaguest and most unsatisfactory kind. One thing, however, appeared to be perfectly certain; viz. that the disloyal or rebellious sentiment which the Young Ireland

THE AFFRAY AT THE WIDOW M'CORMACK'S HOUSE, ON BOULAGH COMMON.

journals—the "Felon Press," as they very appropriately designated themselves—would have led the public to believe was generally diffused throughout the masses of the population of Ireland, has been shown to have been confined to a comparatively small section of the community, and, even amongst these, it had taken such slight hold, that the very first exhortation of the Roman Catholic clergy to the violently-disposed to withdraw from the further prosecution of their crude and absurd insurrectionary schemes, and resume their daily occupations of peace and order, was attended with success; and that silly dupe of his own vanity— poor self-deluded Smith O'Brien—found himself deserted by his "forces" on the very first ground he had chosen for making a stand against the authorities. The wise and humane exertions of the Catholic priesthood in dissuading their flocks from embarking in his mad enterprise with the would-be patriot O'Brien were, no doubt, seconded considerably by the people's observance of the puerile conduct of the poor gentleman himself, who seems to have thought it sufficient to play at civil war, in order to accomplish whatever revolutionary projects he had had in contemplation.

ILLUSTRATED LONDON NEWS, 5 AUGUST 1848

PROSPECTS OF THE SEASON

A very unfavourable change has occurred in the prospects of the season, but we are far yet from despairing. Potatoes which have been attacked with disease have recovered, and in no instance that we have heard of have effects been visible, such as were witnessed in 1846. The quality of the Potatoes now in consumption is decidedly of an improved character—and this, in itself, is a good sign. Besides, the blight which has re-appeared is not equally deleterious in all quarters. Rain has been partial, and it is curious that in some districts the entire crop of Potatoes has escaped to the present time.

In the neighbourhood of Dublin more rain has fallen in three days this week than in three months last year. In these three days more than the monthly average of rainy seasons has fallen, and yet a great portion of the Potatoes in the neighbourhood of Dublin are yet sound. It would appear that mere wet is not the influence under which they most decay.

There are complaints from England and other parts of the world; but they raise no apprehensions of what may be regarded a general scarcity. An abundant harvest was expected in these countries. There are some who still entertain the hope that the produce will not be much under the average.

It is consoling in Ireland that the People *cannot* suffer the destitution which they experienced in the past years. They have been saved by the alteration in the Poor Law, *provided the Boards of Guardians do their duty*. In certain districts great embarrassments must be felt, and some funds in aid of the rates must be provided. But, generally speaking, the poor *cannot* suffer as they did formerly, if the Guardians do their duty.

DUBLIN WEEKLY REGISTER, 12 AUGUST 1848

IRISH DISTRESS

WHAT WILL THE GOVERNMENT DO?
(FROM THE PACKET)

The few words spoken by Lord John Russell on Monday evening, in reply to the question put by Mr. Sharman Crawford, induce us to look forward to the forthcoming speech of Sir Charles Wood, in the committee of ways and means, with more than ordinary anxiety. In a very few days the people of Ireland will know what they have to expect from the government in the sad hour of their trial and tribulation. The member for Rochdale distinctly adverted to the financial condition of the Irish poor law unions, and also to the distress likely to arise from the ascertained failure of the potato crop, asking whether it was the intention of her Majesty's ministers to touch upon these subjects when introducing their budget. The Premier's answer, we are happy to perceive, was in the affirmative; and upon the Chancellor of the Exchequer, therefore, it will devolve to quiet the public mind of Ireland on these important matters.

It is now exactly two years since the Whigs, in their official capacity, made their first declaration in reference to the measures to be adopted for averting the famine which was then impending over our devoted country. That declaration, it is unnecessary to remind the reader, was pregnant with hope. Without detailing any specific plan of action, the prime minister solemnly pledged himself in the face of parliament, that the resources of the empire and all the means of the treasury would be employed to save the people of Ireland from starvation. The assurance was subsequently repeated with no less solemnity by Mr. Labouchere, yet we all know what happened in a few months after. Scarcely had these pompous promises been uttered when famine set in in the most appalling form, and before the spring of the following year millions of human beings had been allowed to sink into their graves, victims of withering destitution and widespread pestilence. To the principles of a spurious political economy, which would not interfere with what was heartlessly called the legitimate operations of trade, were deliberately sacrificed the lives of these doomed creatures, while monopolists were enabled to amass hordes of wealth at the expense of suffering humanity. Nor did the evil stop at that point. While the humbler classes were undergoing a process of decimation, the labour-rate act came into play, and the consequence, as our readers need not be informed, was the slow but certain confiscation of the landed property of the island to an extent unexampled, save in times of actual rebellion against the authority of the British crown, until rich and poor at length became involved in one common ruin. Such was the result of the cruel and demoralising policy of 1846, a result which has been fearfully aggravated by subsequent events, and from which, under the most favourable circumstances, the country could not be expected to recover for a long series of years.

Why do we dwell on this melancholy retrospect, when the facts must be notorious to the whole civilised world? Our sole object is to place the present exhausted condition of Ireland fairly before the government, and induce the Queen's ministers, if possible, to deal in a spirit of mercy, if not justice, with so large a portion of her Majesty's afflicted subjects. Two years ago Lord John Russell might, perhaps, be permitted to plead the "Res dura et regni novitas" in extenuation of his shortcomings, though to a man so long conversant with public business, such a plea is hardly to be conceded; but now it must be altogether inadmissible. He has had before him the lessons of experience and cannot but be aware that, weighed down as she is by the pressure of accumulated misfortunes, Ireland is totally unable to shake off the incubus by her own unaided exertions. How often has it been said during the last two years, even, by ministers themselves, that the loss of the potato crop is an imperial calamity, and should be met with the resources of the state? Let it, then, be practically regarded in that light, and we ask no more. Heaven forbid that we should ever stand before our English neighbours in the humiliating attitude of beggars; but surely there can be no humiliation in demanding the common rights of mankind. To avert the horrors of the threatened famine two things are alone necessary, and these the British government have it in their power to afford, without any detriment to the community at large. The Irish people want merely food and employment, and these can be supplied in sufficient abundance for all purposes, if our rulers will only adopt seasonable precautions and simply do their duty. It is needless to remark that the conductors of the *Packet* have never advocated the wild doctrine that the produce of the soil of Ireland should be exclusively retained for the maintenance of her own population, irrespective of the necessity which may arise in other portions of the United Kingdom. That would indeed be to proclaim ourselves a separate, if not a hostile, nation; but such a theory we utterly repudiate, and England ought to bear in mind that in all quarters of this ill-fated island, myriads of stout hearts were ready, and are now ready to shed their blood in support of British connection in every emergency. We contend, however, that loyalty and protection are reciprocal obligations, and that where the former is unquestionable, the latter should be prompt, decisive, and unlimited. Protection, therefore, we are entitled to claim, and if the government be true to the real interests of the empire, we shall not claim it in vain. We ask that no subject of the English monarchy should be left to starve, and the means of prevention are fully as adequate as they are obvious.

It was intimated by Lord Clanricarde, about a fortnight since, that the money advanced under the labour-rate act (about four millions and a half) and repayable by the owners and occupiers of land in Ireland, would not be applied for general purposes. He went further, and said that it was intended the sum should be devoted to the substantial improvement of the country, the liability of the parties owing it remaining as before. Let this debt be at once remitted to the country on condition that the landlords should expend it in procuring remunerative employment for the labouring classes, and the danger of starvation will in a great measure be at an end. Such a boon, we are satisfied, would go further to cement the Legislative Union than a hundred acts of parliament. It would prove to the world that Ireland is really looked upon as an integral portion of the British empire. We do not say that four months ago so great a favour ought to be expected from government, with the threats of an armed insurrection suspended over their heads; but that peril has happily vanished. Now, were an Irish rebellion to have commenced, and to continue only six months on anything like a general scale, it would cost the nation much more than ten millions, besides an enormous loss of human life. The loyalty, however, of the country has saved that tremendous sacrifice of treasure, and on this ground alone we should be entitled to the boon on every principle of justice. Given as a reward for the past, it could not fail to operate as an encouragement for future good conduct; and surely the reconciliation of eight millions of people to the sway of England would be cheaply purchased at so trifling a price. We fervently hope her Majesty's ministers will give due weight to this important consideration, and act a part as prudent as it would be generous.

FREEMAN'S JOURNAL, DUBLIN, 25 AUGUST 1848

The question of questions is . . . how is Ireland to be saved from an annual potato rot, and the famine which that and a poor system of agriculture leaves her a prey to, which, being the question, leads me . . . to Lord Clarendon's practical instructors.

Let us follow [one] of them.

To the neighbourhood of Macroom, in the county of Cork, Mr. John Hinds was sent . . . The custom of farming in the Macroom district was deplorably wasteful. When I visited the district during the famine months of the spring of 1847 I found all useful farm work abandoned, and the entire population working on the roads for relief out of the ten millions which was voted for the purpose by Parliament. Not a perch of ground on the ordinary farms was broken with a spade or plough at the end of March. And, had the relief works and wages not been stopped to all who were occupiers of land, and relief in food only allowed, it is a moral certainty that not a spadeful of soil would have been turned up, a grain of seed sown, or a plant planted in that district, as in others, except by a few of the gentlemen cultivators.

Being at last forced upon their own resources in 1847, the Macroom tenantry were probably more eager, in 1848, to listen to Lord Clarendon's instructors than otherwise they might have been. Mr. Hinds says he first called upon the High Sheriff, the Hon. Mr. White, who received him favourably, and gave orders that his tenantry should be collected to listen to him, which was done. The instructor then travelled through the wild tract about the lakes which are the sources of the river Lee, which runs to Cork, and forms its harbour, a tract, though wild, thickly peopled. Everywhere he went the poor farmers crowded around him with the greatest anxiety. But, alas! it was not an instructor to teach them how to till the land that they wanted; they looked for some one coming to till it for them—to find seed, pay for labour, and give them the crops . . .

If one pound of meal per day keeps these people upon the roads to break stones, a higher rate of wages than is usually offered to them by those who hire labour in that district might draw them from the roads and the pound of meal. It will hardly be credited that the "large farmers and gentry" . . . offer labourers threepence and fourpence per day, without other allowance. The facts are simply these. The poor-law allowance is the very least which medical experience orders for the bare sustenance of life. Those who seek to hire labour offer less than the poor-law allowance, and the necessities of the wretched creatures decide in favour of the poor-law and the roads... If the half, instead of the fourth or the fifth of nine shillings per week, was offered for farm labour, the miserable men of Macroom would go to the farmer who offered it, and leave the roads and the one pound of meal a day... Mr. Hinds found that the gentry did not attend his meetings, nor give him much of their countenance at Macroom...

The weather continues wet, and every heart seems sinking at the unhappy prospect for the harvest. There have only been three entire dry days in the last fortnight; still most of the corn is safe, though it may not be so fine in quality, if the weather should brighten up. The peasantry come here early in the morning with buttermilk, potatoes, and scanty gatherings of greens, to sell, and linger in the market-place over their small sales all day; but the greater number who come seem to have nothing in hand of business kind.

ILLUSTRATED LONDON NEWS, 26 AUGUST 1848

PRESERVATION OF POTATOES

The following receipt for the preservation of potatoes is given in the *Brussels Independence*, and is of particular interest at this time:—

"Place the potatoes, whether diseased or not, in a cellar upon a bed of small coal ashes. Cover them by layers of the same coal ash. Let the layer be from one to two feet thick; the disease will at once stop, and the potatoes, as also carrots, beet root, and other vegetables, will keep good above a year by means of the antiseptic virtue of the coal, the low temperature of the cellar, and the non circulation of the air. Care must be taken that the ashes of the coal or of the charcoal are perfectly dry."

DUBLIN WEEKLY REGISTER, 16 SEPTEMBER 1848

HERE AND THERE;
Or, Emigration a Remedy.

EMIGRATION

PRACTICAL HINTS TO EMIGRANTS

As compared with the Canadas, the western portion of the United States will, for a long time, possess attractions to settlers, by reason of the land being in a cleared state by nature ... Almost all the farmers of the western states are owners of the land they cultivate. When, for 100*l.*, a man can buy, stock, and cultivate 80 acres of land, there will be found comparatively few persons to come under any obligations to pay rent to a landlord. These farmers live plainly and healthily and work with their own hands for their living ... We must, however, caution those persons who are intent on becoming rich, against proceeding to those western states. There are no rich classes there, in the sense which we regard riches in this country—there is no luxury; comfort and sufficiency are the highest conditions; but they are generally diffused amongst all classes. Labour is there the first condition of life;

and industry is the lot of all men. Wealth is not idolised; but there is
no degradation connected with labour; on the contrary, it is honourable,
and held in general estimation. In the remote parts of America, an
industrious youth may follow any occupation without being looked down
upon or sustain loss of character, and he may rationally expect to raise
himself in the world by his labour. This is a very different state of things
from what we find in this old country, of rich and poor, fashionable
and vulgar, respectable, idle, and common hard working people. In
America, a man's success must altogether rest with himself—it will depend on his industry, sobriety, diligence, and virtue; and if he do not
succeed, in nine cases out of ten, the cause of failure is to be found in
the deficiencies of his own character.

DUBLIN WEEKLY REGISTER, 11 NOVEMBER 1848

EVICTIONS OF PEASANTRY IN IRELAND

A vast social change is gradually taking place in Ireland. The
increase of emigration on the part of the bulk of the small
capitalists, and the ejectment, by wholesale, of the wretched
cottiers, will, in the course of a short time, render quite inappropriate
for its new condition the old cry of a redundant population. But this
social revolution, however necessary it may be, is accompanied by an
amount of human misery that is absolutely appalling. The *Tipperary Vindicator* thus portrays the state of the country:—

"The work of undermining the population is going on stealthily, but
steadily. Each succeeding day witnesses its devastations—more terrible
than the simoon, and more deadly than the plague. We do not say that
there exists a conspiracy to uproot the 'mere Irish;' but we do aver, that
the fearful system of wholesale ejectment, of which we daily hear, and
which we daily behold, is a mockery of the eternal laws of God—a
flagrant outrage on the principles of nature. Whole districts are cleared.
Not a roof-tree is to be seen where the happy cottage of the labourer
or the snug homestead of the farmer at no distant day cheered the landscape. The ditch side, the dripping rain, and the cold sleet are the covering
of the wretched outcast the moment the cabin is tumbled over him;
for who dare give him shelter or protection from 'the pelting of the
pitiless storm?' Who has the temerity to afford him the ordinary rites

of hospitality, when the warrant has been signed for his extinction? There are vast tracts of the most fertile land in the world in this noble county now thrown out of tillage. No spade, no plough goes near them. There are no symptoms of life within their borders, no more than if they were situated in the midst of the Great Desert—no more than if they were cursed by the Creator with the blight of barrenness. Those who laboured to bring those tracts to the condition in which they are—capable of raising produce of any description—are hunted like wolves, or they perish without a murmur. The tongue refuses to utter their most deplorable—their unheard-of sufferings. The agonies endured by the 'mere Irish' in this day of their unparalleled affliction are far more poignant than the imagination could conceive, or the pencil of a Rembrandt picture. We do not exaggerate; the state of things is absolutely fearful; a demon, with all the vindictive

THE DAY AFTER THE EJECTMENT.

passions by which alone a demon could be influenced, is let loose and menaces destruction. Additional sharpness, too, is imparted to his appetite. Christmas was accustomed to come with many healing balsams, sufficient to remove irritation, if not to stanch wounds; but its place is usurped by other and far different qualifications. The howl of misery has succeeded the merry carol which used to usher in the season; no hope is felt that an end will soon be put to this state of wretchedness. The torpor and apathy which have seized on the masses are only surpassed by the atrocities perpetrated by those who set the dictates of humanity and the decrees of the Almighty at equal defiance."

ILLUSTRATED LONDON NEWS, 16 DECEMBER 1848

THE TIME FOR IMPROVEMENT

JONATHAN PIM

Can nothing then be done? Are our peasantry to be starved down to the level of our present resources? and then again to plant potatoes and live by con-acre? to subsist on the lowest food? to live in the worst cabins? and to pay, in rent, the utmost amount that can be drained from them, and yet leave enough to support existence? Are the same vicious circles of want, ignorance, and crime,—of ill-paid labour, and ill-executed work,—of insufficient capital, want of employment, intense competition for land, outrage, and insecurity (being reciprocally cause and effect) for ever to exist, and prevent improvement? Are all our former habits to be resumed, until some other failure of the potato-crop brings with it a recurrence of the present calamity? Or are we to seize the present opportunity for improvement, and, taught by the dear-bought experience of the past year, to reconstruct society on a sounder basis? To throw away the present opportunity,—to recur to our former mode of living,—again to place our dependence on a

root so liable to injury, after such painful experience of the danger,—
would be madness in us, and most culpable neglect in those who are placed in authority over us. This is the time for improvement...

Great improvements are required. The disproportion between the number of labourers and the demand for labour must be removed. The wages of labour must be raised. The truck system, the system of paying in potatoes, must be abolished, and wages invariably paid in the current coin of the realm. The labourer must be better fed, better clothed, better housed, and then he will be able to do more and better work, and will be worth his increased wages. Education must be more extensively diffused; not merely the knowledge of letters, but that religious and moral culture which may better enable us to perform the duties of our stations, and that industrial instruction which will make every man more skilful in his particular branch of business. Especially do our farmers need instruction. Great improvements in farming are necessary, if we are ever to support our peasantry in comfort. The land now under cultivation must be drained, properly manured, and properly tilled; and much land that is now waste, must, by careful and persevering industry, be brought into cultivation, or otherwise made subservient to the support of man. The cultivator of the ground must be placed in that position, in which he will have full security for the value of his labour and the outlay of his capital; and the owner of the land will then have the best security against the deterioration of his property. Above all, the supremacy of law must be upheld, not by the coercion of armed force, or the establishment of martial law, but by increasing the number of those who are interested in its maintenance, and by promoting a sound public spirit, which shall aid its execution instead of opposing it...

In the present condition of Ireland, with so large a number of labourers whose want of skill greatly lessens the value of their labour, industrial instruction seems of the greatest importance. This subject has engaged the attention of the National Board of Education. Several agricultural schools established by them are now in operation, and it is intended to establish others. From these schools much benefit may be expected. Perhaps when their usefulness is more fully proved, a trial may be made of industrial instruction in other branches...

The situation of the poor children in the workhouses, many of whom have been made orphans by the present calamity, most imperatively calls for public attention. Hitherto the education given in the majority of the workhouses has been very defective. It is evident that efforts must be made to fit the youthful inmates for earning a livelihood; or else, when they leave the workhouse, they will be fit for nothing, and will be driven to crime in order to support existence . . . Perhaps regular instruction in some handicraft trade, might very usefully form a part of the course of education required for these children. Something that may keep both mind and body actively engaged from an early age, seems essential to their proper training.

THE CONDITION AND PROSPECTS OF IRELAND, DUBLIN, 1848

LAMENT OF THE IRISH EMIGRANT

LADY DUFFERIN

I'm sittin' on the stile, Mary,
　　Where we sat side by side
　On a bright May mornin', long ago,
　　When first you were my bride:
The corn was springin' fresh and green,
　　And the lark sang loud and high—
And the red was on your lip, Mary,
　　And the love-light in your eye.

The place is little changed, Mary,
　　The day is bright as then,
The lark's loud song is in my ear,
　　And the corn is green again;
But I miss the soft clasp of your hand,
　　And your breath, warm on my cheek,
And I still keep list'nin' for the words
　　You never more will speak.

'Tis but a step down yonder lane,
　　And the little church stands near—
The church where we were wed, Mary,
　　I see the spire from here.
But the graveyard lies between, Mary,
　　And my step might break your rest—

For I've laid you, darling! down to sleep,
    With your baby on your breast.

I'm very lonely now, Mary,
    For the poor make no new friends;
But, oh! they love the better still,
    The few our Father sends!
And you were all I had, Mary,
    My blessin' and my pride!
There's nothin' left to care for now,
    Since my poor Mary died.

Yours was the good, brave heart, Mary,
    That still kept hoping on,
When the trust in God had left my soul,
    And my arm's young strength was gone;
There was comfort ever on your lip,
    And the kind look on your brow—
I bless you, Mary, for that same,
    Though you cannot hear me now.

I thank you for the patient smile
    When your heart was fit to break,
When the hunger pain was gnawin' there,
    And you hid it for my sake;
I bless you for the pleasant word,
    When your heart was sad and sore—
Oh! I'm thankful you are gone, Mary,
    Where grief can't reach you more!

I'm biddin' you a long farewell,
    My Mary—kind and true!
But I'll not forget you, darling,
    In the land I'm goin' to:
They say there's bread and work for all,
    And the sun shines always there—
But I'll not forget old Ireland,
    Were it fifty times as fair!

And often in those grand old woods
　I'll sit and shut my eyes,
And my heart will travel back again
　To the place where Mary lies;
And I'll think I see the little stile
　Where we sat side by side,
And the springin' corn, and the bright May morn,
　When first you were my bride.

BELFAST, 1848

1849–1851

W.T. GREEN

HEIGHT OF IMPUDENCE.

Irishman to John Bull. — "Spare a thrifle, yer Honour, for a poor Irish Lad to buy a bit of —— a Blunderbuss with."

EMIGRATION

A VOYAGE TO AUSTRALIA

HARK! old Ocean's tongue of thunder.
   Hoarsley calling, bids you speed
To the shores he held asunder
   Only for these times of need.
Now, upon his friendly surges.
   Ever, ever roaring, come
All the sons of hope he urges
   To a new, a richer home!
     MARTIN F. TUPPER

The tide of Emigration has unquestionably set in towards Australia, notwithstanding the gold of California may lead to a temporary diversion in favour of that country. We are persuaded, therefore, that the accompanying pictures will possess considerable interest at the present moment, over and above their artistic merit, which is of no common order. They, however, combine the actualities of experience with pictorial ability in a remarkable degree. The draughtsman of these scenes from life on board an emigrant ship bound to Australia is Mr. T. Skinner Prout, who has visited that country, and profited by some years' exploration of its natural beauties, as fit scenes for his clever pencil. Upon his voyage he drew the *arkite* episodes which an emigrant ship constantly presents, even to the common-place observer. In these Sketches, then, we have no artistic invention; they are pictures of what the draughtsman saw daily, and here presents to us with truly vivid effect. These pictures are, indeed, illustrations of the artist's own diary, which must, therefore, be the best accompaniment to them.

"Time was, when a voyage to the Antipodes was considered a very serious undertaking; when even experienced, hardy, and weatherbeaten seamen, bound to those distant regions, took their last look of dear old England, with anxious hearts and ideas of difficulties and dangers to be encountered, which were then considered to be inseparable from so long a voyage; and *long* indeed it once was, as we find by the following paragraph from 'Collins's New South Wales.' The Colonel speaking of the arrival of the first fleet at Port Jackson, New South Wales, says:—
'Thus, under the blessing of God, was happily completed, in eight months and one week, a voyage, which, before it was undertaken, the mind

216 hardly dared venture to contemplate, and on which it was impossible to reflect, without some apprehension as to its termination.' In the present day, however, a voyage to Australia is so well understood by navigators, and, generally speaking, known to be so safe, that it has become divested of its once attendant horrors; and the four months' sojourn on the ocean (the average time occupied in the voyage) to most persons passes pleasantly enough. 'Tis true there are inconveniences to be experienced; and, from the circumstance of persons of different habits and feelings being thrown and kept together, little disagreements will occasionally occur: these are amusing enough, and serve to vary the usual monotony of a sea life. I here more particularly allude to passenger-ships: in emigrant vessels there is no lack of variety; the necessary duties to be attended to for the preservation of order and cleanliness among the emigrants afford them some daily occupation, and render them more alive to those little recreations, which are frequently indulged in, and in fact encouraged by the officers of the ship. But, as a more detailed description of the manner in which the time on board is passed may be interesting, I think I cannot do better than refer to parts of a journal kept on my voyage out, and which at the same time will serve to explain the accompanying Engravings, from drawings made from sketches taken during the passage.

"Four bells. On deck. Weather thick and hazy. Wind W.N.W., and steady, ship going about seven knots. Off Madeira: distant twenty miles. Mist gradually disperses, and the beautiful island is clearly discernable, capped by the last clouds of the morning. Six Bells. A general turn out from below. Breakfast over. Emigrants on deck disperse themselves in various little groups. The schoolmaster has summoned his little class, and seated reverentially on some spars, the prescribed educational course is in full progress. A contemplative shepherd takes a solitary seat on the keel of the reversed long-boat amidships, whilst several anxious souls looking after creature comforts surround the cook's galley. Not a few are lounging over the ship's side, prying with curious eyes into the secrets of the 'deep, deep sea.' 'Portuguese men-of-war,' as Jack contemptuously calls a beautiful mollusk, common to these latitudes, pass by in hundreds, presenting to the wind their gossamer-like sails, tinted with the most beautiful pink and lilac. Flying fish have ceased to be the 'lions' they were on first acquaintance. They rise in shoals from the water in all directions, and after a short hurried flight, drop with an extended splash into their element again.

"The sun is now fast approaching the meridian, and some little bustle

is observed on the quarter-deck. The captain, two of the mates, the
doctor, and a tiny midshipman, have all adjusted their several sextants
and quadrants, and are making a steady examination of the horizon
immediately to the south. Gradually a long string of passengers ascend
from the cabin, and curious middle-class emigrants gather in the rear
of the astronomical party, who are, in fact, engaged in taking the sun's
altitude, to determine our present latitude. After some minutes, the instruments are lowered within a few seconds of each other; and the
Captain, solomnly addressing his first mate, says, 'Mr. Jones, *make* it noon.'
'Ay, ay, sir. Forrard there; strike
eight bells.' This important
business settled, conversation
then becomes general, and turns
upon what southing the ship has
made in the course of the last 24
hours. For the next hour, many
and anxious too are the enquiries
at the cook's galley; whilst the
ship's company gather round a
huge tub, with like devotion,
narrowly inspecting, in the first
place, the steward's integrity as
regards mixing the grog; and, in
the next, disposing of their
allowances, each in his own
way—some making short work
of it upon the spot; others, in
cans or bottles, carrying it away
to reserve for future enjoyment.
Two bells. Dinner is now announced, and the hatchways fore
and aft are pouring out a stream

DINNER IN THE FORECASTLE.

of hungry mortals. It is *pea-soup day*, and the cook, almost lost in the
dense and savoury atmosphere of steam which rises from the coppers,
is ministering to the creature wants of the attendant crowd, who, with
hook-pot or pannikin in hand, are patiently waiting their turn. According to the rules and arrangements of the ship, the emigrants are divided
into lots, or messes, of six or eight persons in each; and, except in the
varying nature of the provisions, the incidents of the daily dinner on
board partake very much of the same character. Sometimes, however,

the forecastle (or fox'cle, as it is called), an elevated platform in the bows of the vessel, is chosen for a select dinner-party, who, in the fresh, open air, enjoy their meal in a true pic-nic style. Tobacco is now the order of the day—the silent indulging in a pipe, the talkative enjoying a cigar—whilst all are happy. What cares, in fact, can arise upon the bosom of the wide expanse of ocean? The griefs we brought with us are forgotten, whilst all vexations have been left behind. Sleep, too, comes almost naturally to minds so situated. Thought becomes a burden where there is so little to excite it in providing for the wants of the body; therefore it is that, the pipe finished, the afternoon's nap is a retreat to which emigrants on the passage out generally retire until near tea-time, or near six bells, when the cook is again at his post—the cry of 'Tea-water!' penetrates the depths below, and soon, in noisy response, clattering hook-pans, pannikins, and pans are again rushing up the hatchways, and crowding around the galley.

"On board the good ship the *Hope*, after tea, two religious services were performed, at least, the Catholics selecting one of their party, who always read prayers; whilst to the rest of the emigrants the surgeon, as usual in such vessels, read the service of the day as set forth in the Book of Common Prayer. Eight bells struck, and another transition of thought varied the proceedings of the day. Forward are preparations being made for a dance, and a musical Jack is soon found, who, seated on a coil of rope, or perched on a spar, in a very short time is plying most vigorously the fun-inspiring fiddle. In the confined space of a ship's deck polkas and quadrilles are out of the question, though at first much affectedly fastidious disinclination is expressed against the reel and jig. But it is not long before these last reign triumphant, and delicate forms and choice spirits foot the monotonous but merry-going measure with as much enjoyment as if they moved in a minuet before hundreds of observant eyes. Now for one moment turn our eyes from the mirth-stirred bustling scene on deck, and scan the wide solitude of the surrounding ocean lit up by a splendid moon, not a sail in sight save the white swelling canvas over our head, bending bravely before a spanking breeze that is steadily urging us on in our trackless way.

"The fineness of the night tempts all from below, when the deck becomes crowded, though all appear to enjoy themselves to the full; on the poop children are gambolling, whilst those in converse sweet, or on gossip most intent, keep up a continued promenade on the deck. Descending below, there a little group surrounds some learned friend who has industriously worked the ship's course for the last day, and is

now giving a detailed report to his companions, who all busily examine 219
the amateur's well-thumbed chart, as if they knew a great deal about
it. A little beyond, perhaps, the boatswain, from his cabin door, spins
one of his long, marvellous yarns to his credulous, open-mouthed
neighbour on the opposite side. Further on again is the emigrants'
quarters, the interior of which can be seen through an opening in the
bulk-head. Good wives are now displaying their matronly qualities, but
in most cases vainly endeavouring to calm the *Baby-lonish* confusion of
tongues and screaming squall that, for at least one hour, prevails in the
family compartment of the ship. To add to the quiet enjoyment of compelled, but resigned spectators, sundry night-capped heads of disturbed
damsels, retired for the night, appear from their berths, but produce little effect by their complaining; whilst the unblanketed lower extremities
of others, more calm and philosophic, may be also seen projecting from
the narrow confines of their beds. But hark! Four bells is striking; 'Lights
out!' is heard in various quarters; and in a few minutes, save the measured
tread of the watch on deck, the rustling sails, and rippling waters on
the vessel's way, not a sound is heard."

ILLUSTRATED LONDON NEWS, 20 JANUARY 1849

NIGHT.—TRACING THE VESSEL'S PROGRESS.

TO THE LANDLORDS OF IRELAND

There can be no question that from the beginning of the year 1848 the state of this country has assumed a very disastrous aspect. A renewed and extensive failure of the potato crop has added greatly to the sufferings of the poor, and increased the perplexities which have involved all other classes of society. The burthen of poor rates has become intolerable to a people who have been themselves the principal sufferers from the loss of their crops; and the prospect of the aggravation of the pressure during the ensuing year from the continued and increasing distress and destitution in the country, has paralysed the energies even of the most sanguine and the most resolute. The peculiar evils of the present system of poor laws in Ireland, and their great inaptitude for such a country, has also naturally tended to check all exertion to prevent an increase of the rates, as the most active and well-disposed proprietor finds that all the employment he can give to his poor is of little avail without an extensive co-operation among his neighbours, which it is, from various causes, impracticable to attain, while the ill effects of a system by which such vast numbers are fed upon public doles have, it is too plain, only increased their indolence and indisposition to earn their bread by manly exertion. This system, continued in one shape or other since the Labour-rate Act was passed, while it is fast swallowing up all private property, has, at the same time, produced incalculable evils, in rendering the mass of the population listless and dead to every feeling of independence, an effect peculiarly disastrous in the case of the Irish peasantry. Altogether the prospects of the country are most gloomy, the very opposite to those which a well-ordered state should exhibit.

It is time for us to descend to the regions of common-sense: we address ourselves especially to the gentry, and to those who have any property to lose. The time is propitious for them to exert themselves. Agitation, which had ripened into rebellion, is for the present prostrate; and the influence of property will be more felt and respected by our representatives in parliament, than heretofore. While every other class is depressed and impoverished, the landed proprietors are chiefly marked out for destruction; surely, at such a time they will not lie down in indolence and apathy. If in every county they exert themselves to force their representatives into a faithful discharge of their duty, a party may yet be formed in the House of Commons, capable of protecting the landed interest of the empire. This is the great point to be looked to: unless a strong and united party of this description be formed without delay, we see nothing for the landed proprietors of Ireland but utter confiscation and ruin. Let all their energies be directed to this end, and they may be saved. They have plenty of opportunities on grand juries, and at public meetings, of causing their opinions to be heard; and if there be anything like the unanimity which the crisis demands, our Irish members will see the necessity of altering their course, or else forfeiting the confidence of their constituents for ever. But we hope our gentry will take warning; no half measures will now do; no mere petitions against the labour-rate act and poor-laws: these are mere symptoms of our malady. What is wanting is a strong agricultural party, which will deliver us from the thraldom of Manchester politicians.

DUBLIN UNIVERSITY MAGAZINE, MARCH 1849

EMIGRATION FROM DOWN

We observe, with regret, that much of the wealth and comfort of this hitherto prosperous county is being transported to the shores of America, and other parts of the Globe. It is a bad sign, indeed, of Ulster prosperity, when the Down peasantry are on the move to the far west. Yes, Down, and Antrim too, are now drooping under the pressure of burdens disproportionate to their means. What prospects, we ask, are there for the people under annually increasing taxation? Lord John Russell's rate-in-aid scheme is driving some of our farmers out of the country. Within the last few weeks, upwards of two thousand individuals, have left the districts of Newtownards, Lecale, and other parts of this county, for emigration to America, and these we can safely affirm, did not leave the country with empty purses. In one emigrant ship alone, which sailed from Belfast the other day, more than three-fourths of the passengers were from the County of Down.

DOWNPATRICK RECORDER, 14 APRIL 1849

THE QUEEN'S VISIT TO IRELAND

Her Majesty's first visit to her greatly-distressed but loyal realm of Ireland is an event of national importance. Viewed in all its aspects, present and future, it is, perhaps, the most interesting that has yet signalised her auspicious reign. The time at which it is made and the social circumstances of the people throw around it an additional importance, and invest it with a halo of hopes for the future prosperity of the country. The once loud and angry voices of political and religious factions have died away amid calamity: famine and plague have taught all classes that the real evils of Ireland are social, and not political. The landlord and the peasant, the Roman Catholic and the Protestant, the Conservative and the Repealer, the Whiteboy and the Orangeman, have been chastened by the heavy hand of affliction; and have had their eyes and their hearts opened to many things which in less unhappy times they could not or would not see. Mutual animosities, though not wholly extinct, are weakened. There is a general impression amidst all classes that the worst is over—that the culmination of evil has been reached—and that henceforward, with the sad experience of the past brought to bear upon the future, there are well-founded hopes for Ireland.

It is amidst these hopes that Queen Victoria goes to Ireland. Her presence is well calculated to increase and to brighten them. At first, there were some whisperings of dissatisfaction, and an avowed determination, on the part of a few, to take advantage of the occasion to raise the old party cries. One clown was found rude enough to hint

at mourning, and at a funeral procession as the best greeting that could 3
be given by a famine-stricken land. But these whisperings have gradually
subsided. The man of mourning was hooted and hissed into decency;
and the few malcontents have been silenced by the loud expression of
popular enthusiasm. The fervent character of the Irishman forbids any
cold or lukewarm manifestation of his feelings or his opinions. Whatever
he does, he does warmly. His gratitude, when he has any, is heart-deep;
and his welcome, when he gives it, is sincere and cordial. The world
has rung with the history of the magnificent reception which Ireland
gave to George IV. If we may judge from present appearances, the visit
of our far more beloved Sovereign will throw all the splendour and
enthusiasm of that earlier visit into the shade; and the landing of Queen
Victoria in Ireland—like a beneficent messenger of peace and good-
will—will be celebrated throughout the country with manifestations of
popular love and rejoicing, to which the previous history of Ireland can
offer no parallel. Cork, Dublin, and Belfast raise the unanimous cry of
loyalty and affection; and it is certain that the national "CEAD MILE
FAILTE," or "A hundred thousand welcomes," will be shouted on the
progress of Queen Victoria by ten times a hundred thousand tongues.
It is equally certain that every heart will do homage to one who, in
the day of Ireland's sorrow, has come to make acquaintance with her
people, and teach them by her presence how great is the interest that
she takes in their welfare, and how happy she is to do all she can to
make the Union not a barren union of parchment and of law, but a
fruitful bond of mutual confidence and affection.

The Queen, it has been alleged, will not see the dark side of Ireland.
She will not behold with her own eyes the wretchedness of the
peasantry—the fertile acres lying uncultivated for want of capital and
of skill—the roofless cabins of myriads of homeless people, and the vast
tracts of land that have never been turned by spade or plough, nor yielded
food for human kind. She will see, it has been said, the bright side only.
She will see illuminations, triumphal arches, and processions. She will
see the best, the fairest, the most enterprising, and the most wealthy
of the land congregated to do her fealty and honour. She will hear the
thunder of artillery and the shouting of the multitude, but not the wail
of distress and sickness that comes from the road-side, or from the
miserable cabins of the interior. But though, in all probability, she will
neither hear nor see, she is not ignorant of these things. It is on account
of these things that she goes to Ireland. She knows them, she deplores
them, and she will do her best to relieve them. She does not proceed

to Ireland on a holiday trip, to see new landscapes and a new people, but to perform a great and pleasing duty; and to set an example which, in future years, will make Ireland as attractive to the sight-seer and the tourist as Wales and Scotland.

In the face of calamities such as those which have afflicted Ireland, it is little that Parliaments or Monarchs can do. It is not laws that are wanted, but confidence. Hence it is that the visit of her Majesty to Ireland is calculated to produce more good than any enactments which a populace might demand or a Parliament devise. It is a proof of confidence on the part of the Sovereign which has already begotten confidence on the part of the people, and which in due season will beget confidence between England and Ireland. The English and the Irish will learn to know each other better. The example set by the Sovereign will extend to the classes of wealthy English capitalists. The more they know of Ireland, the better they will like it. From the mutual knowledge of the people will spring mutual confidence; and from confidence, all the blessing of which Ireland stands most in need. The Irishman will learn that the Englishman is not his oppressor, either in deed or thought; and the Englishman will convince himself, by the evidence of his own senses and experience, that the Irishman is not naturally turbulent, idle, vicious, or intemperate; but peaceable, hardworking, sober, grateful, and affectionate: and that he only needs fair play to develop his own energies and the resources of his country. Capital, so jealous and so sensitive, never penetrates and permeates a country where confidence is wanting; but it follows confidence, as effect follows cause. It is for these reasons, without predicting any sudden amount of benefit to be derived from her Majesty's visit to Ireland, that we anticipate the turning over of a new leaf, the dawning of a new day, the inauguration of a brighter era. English travellers will learn in time that life and property are as safe in Ireland as they are in London; that the country is fertile; and that capital, wisely expended by active and skilful men, might yield in Ireland a large return of benefit to the capitalist, and be the means of affording employment and comfort to a people whose chief desire is to avoid the poorhouse, and to live by the fruits of their honest industry. These blessings must, however, be the result of time: they are not to be snatched in a day. At all events, if the English and Irish people will but believe them possible, the greatest impediment will be removed from the way. The visit of Queen Victoria will greatly aid this consummation; and the people of England will, we are certain, look upon it with pleasure and solicitude, and be, on this occasion, "more Irish than the Irish" in the

expression of their good wishes both for the Queen and for Ireland.
They wish her most sincerely a pleasant journey and a glad reception,
and Ireland many repetitions of the Visit.

ILLUSTRATED LONDON NEWS, 4 AUGUST 1849

DANCE OF PEASANTRY ON THE LAWN AT CARTON.

DANCE OF THE PEASANTRY

At half–past eleven o'clock the Royal party quitted the Viceregal
Lodge, in an open barouche, escorted by a troop of the 8th
Royal Irish Hussars, commanded by the Hon. Mr. Sandilands.
Leaving the Phoenix Park, the Royal carriages descended the hill, and
were driven along the beautiful valley of the Liffey, passing beside the
Strawberry Beds. Travelling through the fine and diversified scenery in
this district, the Royal party took the direction of Woodlands, the splendid
seat of Colonel White, at which a handsome triumphal arch, composed
of evergreens and flowering shrubs, was erected in honour of her Majesty.
Having driven through this magnificent demesne, the Royal party

changed their escort. On arriving at Woodlands, the Hussars returned to Dublin, and were relieved by a troop of the 17th Royal Lancers, under the orders of Captain Willett, by whom the Royal equipages were escorted during the rest of the journey. On quitting Woodlands, the Royal travellers drove in the direction of Coldblow, from thence towards Leixlip, near which they were met by the students of Maynooth College, dressed in their academics, who, as the Royal equipages passed, cheered with the utmost enthusiasm—a compliment which her Majesty and her noble Consort very graciously acknowledged. The Royal party shortly afterwards arrived at Carton, and entered the demesne by the Kellystown gate.

At one o'clock, the Royal equipages entered the demesne, and soon afterwards drew up opposite the mansion. The first carriage contained her Majesty, his Royal Highness Prince Albert, and their Excellencies the Earl and Countess of Clarendon. A second carriage contained the Earl Fortescue, Viscountess Jocelyn (Lady-in-Waiting), the Hon. Miss Dawson (Maid of Honour), and Sir George Grey. The Duke and Duchess, with the members of the family already recounted, had in the meantime assembled at the grand entrance, for the purpose of receiving their Royal and distinguished guests. The noble Duke handed her Majesty out of the carriage, while the Prince gave his arm to the Duchess. The distinguished party then walked into the gardens; and, on being recognised by the crowd from without, a most hearty cheer was given. The bands of the 1st Foot and 6th Dragoon Guards, which were stationed on either side of the grounds, played "God Save the Queen," "The Coburg March," and other national airs.

After walking through the grounds for about twenty minutes, the Royal party and attendants returned to the house and partook of lunch: the general visitors being entertained in the marquees.

After the *déjeûner*, her Majesty, leaning on the arm of the Duke of Leinster, again appeared on the esplanade in front of the mansion, and made a further inspection of the rare collection of flowers, plants, vases, and statuary works, &c. The Prince Consort followed with the Duchess of Leinster; while another group comprised the Marchioness of Water-ford, the Earl and Countess of Clarendon, and his Royal Highness Prince George of Cambridge. The most amusing incident of the day soon after-wards took place. Her Majesty and party were conducted to the front of the lawn, close to the trench dividing it from the park, where the people had assembled, and there witnessed what we may term a genuine Irish jig, danced to the music of an Irish piper, by several of the Duke's

tenants and their wives and daughters. The dancing was kept up with 227
great spirit "for upwards of half an hour," to use the words of Burns,
the Royal presence having "put life and mettle into their heels." Her
Majesty laughed most heartily at the performances, particularly at the
antics of one couple, who, after concluding some most diversified
evolutions, concluded by advancing in front of their companions, and
making a very low bow, which the Sovereign acknowledged by a most
pleasing smile. All the dancers, we learned, were disciples of Father
Mathew—as, indeed, their neat and comfortable appearance would
indicate.

ILLUSTRATED LONDON NEWS, 18 AUGUST 1849

RE-APPEARANCE OF THE
POTATO DISEASE

We much regret to state, that, from the tenor of accounts from
many parts of the island, there can be no doubt of the
re-appearance of the potato disease in its characteristic
symptoms; though we are bound to add, that there is no evidence of
the malady having extended itself beyond the isolated cases which we
now proceed to enumerate:—

A letter from Saintfield, county Down, announces the spread of the
disease for several weeks past in potatoes planted about the 1st of May,
in moory land. In these the blight has not made much progress; but
among those planted in March, in clayey soil, it has latterly been making rapid progress. The blight has occurred in other parts of the same
neighbourhood.

The *Newry Telegraph*'s Armagh Correspondent, writing on Tuesday
last, says, that from the rural districts of the county Armagh, partial
accounts of the blight, but only of the stalks, have reached him. Here
and there he observed black spots and indications of decay on the stalks
and ash-leaved kidneys, but, on trying the tubers, they were perfectly
sound. In the neighbourhood of Caledon, some unsound tubers were
discovered.

The *Derry Journal* says, "Serious apprehensions are beginning to be
entertained with regard to the potato. We have been prepared for the

re-appearance of the disease, but we hope that it will be to a limited extent, as compared with former years. A letter from Westport mentions that the disease had shown itself there; and we ourselves have a letter from a gentleman of experience in the county Cavan, stating that he had observed it in a few fields. Since the evening of Sunday se'nnight, when there was very heavy rain, brown shades have come over portions of some of the fields in this neighbourhood, and the well-known black spots may be seen on their leaves; and it has happened—though, we believe, very rarely—that tubers, thoroughly tainted, have been found among those which have been cooked. On the whole, however, the produce of the crop, so far as it has been brought to the market, may be pronounced excellent."

We find the following in the *Mayo Constitution* of yesterday (Tuesday):—"Reports are quite prevalent that the blight has again appeared, and we are sorry to say such is the fact. But its spread has been very limited, and we trust little injury will result to the crop this year."

The Ballinasloe *Western Star* says—"We are deeply sorry to announce the fact of the potato crop in this neighbourhood being again diseased, though not, as yet, to a very alarming extent. The blight is particularly observable since the appearance of the lightning."

The fact of the fatal distemper having made its appearance in the West has been borne out by Mr. Edward Carroll, practical instructor at Frenchport, county Roscommon, and Mr. O'Connor, the instructor to the union of Swineford, in the adjoining county of Mayo.

Mr. Lindsay, the agriculturist for the Ennis union, has announced, in the *Clare Journal*, the appearance of the disease in that quarter. He commends the pulling up of the stalks, but we would decidedly prefer the cutting them down with a sharp scythe.

The *Freeman* states, on apparently good authority, that, on the road from Cork to Mallow, crops, which a few days previously were green, had become quite black.

Mr. John Mansergh, of Grenane, county Tipperary, states, in a letter to the *Evening Mail*, that on yesterday evening week the blight set in, and his crop is now completely withered. "I mean," he says, "to pull the stalks, and retrench with a view to save some, as the tuber has grown to its full size."

A Galway correspondent of the *Evening Mail* writes as follows:—"The potato disease has unequivocally appeared in sheltered places this week in the North of Galway, but it has not as yet appeared in the open fields, and the crop is so much more forward than usual, that I trust the greater part of it will be saved. From Connemara in the vicinity of Clifden, I have had a very melancholy report; it appears to be there in its aggravated type."

The disease has also appeared in Scotland, in numerous localities.

BELFAST NEWS-LETTER, 17 AUGUST 1849

HOW PROPERTY IS SLIPPING
FROM THE LANDLORDS

At a meeting of the magistrates and grand jurors in the county Limerick, a report, drawn up by a committee, of the financial condition of the county was read.

After referring to the wretched condition of the county, brought on by the famine of the past years, it states:—That if the events and system, which have for some years been in progress, should continue unchecked, the committee cannot but anticipate a general destruction of the ordinary bonds of society—the annihilation of property—the cessation of all profitable demand for labour, and the absorption of all classes in one common irremediable ruin, ultimately destructive to individual happiness, and fatal to the best interests of the community.

Within the last four years the grand jury taxation of the county has increased 300 per cent., while the value of property has been diminished.

The original valuation of the union of Newcastle was 109,303*l.*—it is now reduced to 75,301*l.* The reduction in Kilmallock union is from 161,698*l.* to 159,039*l.* That of Limerick, from 118,088*l.* to 106,164*l.*, and that of Rathkeale from 138,438*l.* to 120,806*l.*

The statistical tables, prepared under the directions of the Lord Lieutenant, exhibit a gradual decay of the wealth of the Limerick unions, as represented by their agricultural produce. This decay is rapidly extending, and the committee are enabled to state from their own personal knowledge and observations, that considerable and increasing tracts lie waste and uncultivated.

The number of cattle is alarmingly reduced on the pasture lands—the stacks in the homesteads have almost disappeared—many districts are left abandoned and desolate, and the doubt of reaping the harvest indisposes many from sowing; and even when agriculture is continued, the cultivator in despair at the prospect of taxation indefinitely increasing, becomes hopeless, limits all his operations, and thus diminishes the demand for labour.

Tables of the area of cultivation and produce of the Limerick unions— Limerick, Rathkeale, Newcastle, and Kilmallock:—In 1837, 52,900 acres of wheat cultivated, producing 304,000 barrels of 20 stone each; 67,500 acres of oats, producing 645,000 barrels of 14 stone; 9,000 acres of barley producing 80,000 barrels of 16 stone; 12,000 acres of potatoes, producing 820,000 barrels of 20 stone; 16,000 acres turnips. In 1848—32,000 acres wheat, producing 136,000 barrels; 52,800 acres oats, producing 260,000 barrels; 14,000 acres barley, producing 121,000 barrels, 38,900 acres potatoes, producing 772,000 barrels; 11,800 acres turnips.

It is remarkable that during 1848, whilst there was an excess of about 17,000 acres under potatoes, there was a falling off of nearly 50,000 barrels in produce. The burthens imposed by the rate-in-aid are unexampled and enormous, as the following return shows: Limerick, 5,075l. 11s.; Rathkeale, 3,020l. 3s.; Newcastle, 2,403l. 14s.; and Kilmallock, 4,448l. 7s. Total, 14,947l. 15s.

By the tabular reports received from the sub-committees, setting forth returns of annual expenditure of the amount of grand jury rate, labour rate and poor rate per pound for each union or parts of unions in the Co. of Limerick, for the years ending September 29, 1845 to 1849, both inclusive, it appears that the total taxation, 229,769l. for the year ended 29th September, 1849, amounts to a rate of 9s. 2d. per pound on the present valuation of the entire county.

Extensive tracts of land are altogether waste and uncultivated. In the electoral division of Castletown (union of Newcastle), consisting of 9,656 acres, 2,397 acres are already waste, and although this is an extreme case, it is not a solitary one, but it bespeaks the condition of other districts likewise; and too plainly foretells the fate of many more, if the present evils are left without a remedy.

The committee feel it their duty to add, that a large and increasing emigration of a new character has extended greatly, adding to the difficulties of employing labour, and of paying rates. Farmers and occupiers of land who can still command some share of unexhausted capital, are flying from the ruin they anticipate. They are thus lessening the numbers of that middle class of industrious men which Ireland so much wants, and without which no social state can be stable or prosperous; to use the words of a parliamentary witness—"Precisely those persons go whom you wish to keep, and precisely those persons stay whom you wish to go."

VILLAGE OF MOVEEN.

CONDITION OF IRELAND

Having last week introduced this important subject to our readers, and given them some of the statistics of Kilrush, we shall henceforward allow our Correspondent to speak for himself:—

I assure you (he says) that the objects of which I send you Sketches are not sought after—I do not go out of my way to find them; and other travellers who have gone in the same direction, such as Lord Adair, the Earl of Surrey, and Mr. Horsman, will vouch, I am sure, for the accuracy of my delineations. The Sketch of Moveen, to which I now call your attention, is that of another ruined village in the Union of Kilrush. It is a specimen of the dilapidation I behold all around. There is nothing but devastation, while the soil is of the finest description, capable of yielding as much as any land in the empire. Here, at Tullig, and other places, the ruthless destroyer, as if he delighted in seeing the monuments of his skill, has left the walls of the houses standing, while he has unroofed them and taken away all shelter from the people. They look like the tombs of a departed race, rather than the recent abodes of a yet living people, and I felt actually relieved at seeing one or two half-clad spectres gliding about, as an evidence that I was not in the land of the dead. You may inquire, perhaps, and I am sure your readers will wish to know, why it is that the people have of late been turned out of their houses in such great numbers, and their houses just at this time pulled down, and I will give you my explanation of this fact.

The public records, my own eyes, a piercing wail of woe throughout the land—all testify to the vast extent of the evictions at the present time. Sixteen thousand and odd persons unhoused in the Union of Kilrush before the month of June in the present year; seventy-one thousand one hundred and thirty holdings done away in Ireland, and nearly as many houses destroyed, in 1848; two hundred and fifty-four thousand holdings of more than one acre and less than five acres, put an end to between 1841 and 1848: six-tenths, in fact, of the lowest class of tenantry driven from their now roofless or annihilated cabins and houses, makes up the general description of that desolation of which Tullig and Moveen are examples. The ruin is great and complete. The blow that effected it was irresistible. It came in the guise of charity and benevolence; it assumed the character of the last and best friend of the peasantry, and it has struck them to the heart. They are prostrate and helpless. The once frolicsome people— even the saucy beggars—have disappeared, and given place to wan and haggard objects, who are so resigned to their doom, that they no longer expect relief. One beholds only shrunken frames scarcely covered with flesh—crawling skeletons, who appear to have risen from their graves, and are ready to return frightened to that abode. They have little other covering than that nature has bestowed on the human body—a poor protection against inclement weather;

BRIDGET O'DONNEL AND CHILDREN.

and, now that the only hand from which they expected help is turned against them, even hope is departed, and they are filled with despair. Than the present Earl of Carlisle there is not a more humane nor a kinder-hearted nobleman in the kingdom; he is of high honour and unsullied reputation; yet the Poor-law he was mainly the means of establishing for Ireland, with the best intentions, has been one of the chief causes of the people being at this time turned

out of their homes, and forced to burrow in holes, and share, till they
are discovered, the ditches and the bogs with otters and snipes.

The instant the Poor-law was passed, and property was made responsible for poverty, the whole of the landowners, who had before been
careless about the people, and often allowed them to plant themselves
on untenanted spots, or divide their tenancies—delighted to get the
promise of a little additional rent—immediately became deeply interested
in preventing that, and in keeping down the number of the people.
Before they had rates to pay, they cared nothing for them; but the law
and their self-interest made them care, and made them extirpators.
Nothing less than some general desire like that of cupidity falling in with
an enactment, and justified by a theory—nothing less than a passion which
works silently in all, and safely under the sanction of a law—could have
effected such wide-spread destruction. Even humanity was enlisted by
the Poor-law on the side of extirpation. As long as there was no legal
provision for the poor, a landlord had some repugnance to drive them
from every shelter; but the instant the law took them under its protection, and forced the landowner to pay a rate to provide for them,
repugnance ceased: they had a legal home, however inefficient, to go
to; and eviction began.

ILLUSTRATED LONDON NEWS, 15 DECEMBER 1849

WHAT IRISHMEN CAN DO

In the year eighteen hundred and fifty the Irish people can if they
will raise up and re-invigorate this Island. If it is still a social swamp
in 1851, the fault will lie, not with Saxon or stranger, but primarily
and in the chief degree with the people of Ireland.

How Holland grew on a sand-bank, how Portugal grew on a rib of
the Atlantic, how Venice grew on a quagmire, has been told in THE
NATION.

The people of Ireland read these marvellous narratives, and make no
doubt that in the swelter of the Rhine flood, or among the morasses
of the Adriatic, they too would have worked wonders.

But how we are to meet and put to rout our own pettier difficulties,
how Ireland will grow food for her people on a soil that teems like Sicily,
how she will find hands to rear it where an army of skilled workmen,

imprisoned in poor-houses, are impatiently clamouring for liberty and labour, how she will find fields to bear it where more than a million acres of corn land lie waste as Zahara, how she will plant her farmers in Mayo instead of transplanting them in Michigan, how she will find employment for her artizans where a whole nation have to be clothed with manufactured fabrics and lodged in houses furnished with manufactured utensils, are problems on which the Irish people have *not* fixed their minds.

The high tide of pauperism swells around the narrowing basis of social Ireland as the Rhine-flood rose against the dykes of Holland. Galway and Mayo are sinking into swamps more fathomless than the Adriatic marshes. But a Holland or a Venice might still arise above the widening morass if the people of Ireland would exhibit even now, in the last hour, Flemish industry or the lion spirit of the Venetians. It is not in our Stars good BRUTUS but in ourselves that we are underlings.

What can the people of Ireland do? What specifically can they hope to accomplish? A hard question. But reproof without counsel is insolence: and vague declamatory *unspecific* counsel is smoke where the need is for fire.

I believe if Ireland were in the hands of a wise and powerful government who would begin their task as NAPOLEON began his after the 18th Brumaire, when he attacked disorder and peculation with the same vigour he had lately attacked Austria and Italy, the reconstruction of the nation would be but one year's work.

But assuming that the Government will initiate nothing, and adopt nothing initiated elsewhere, what can the people of Ireland do for themselves? What can they do *without*, and *against*, the Government and all Governments?

The people of Ireland are more powerful in this island than Queen, Lords, and Commons, than Army, Navy, Law, and Executive. Whatsoever the people determine to do, and resolutely *hold to doing*, shall be the law of Ireland against the will of the whole world. If we are robbed and trampled upon, the chief criminals are still the people of Ireland.

THE NATION, DUBLIN, 5 JANUARY 1850

The projected meeting of farmers at Killinchy, in favour of tenant-right, reduction of rents, and financial reform, was held on Tuesday last. An important letter from Mr. Sharman Crawford was read. Mr. Crawford holds that it is for the landlord's own interest that tenant-right be legalized. If, as we believe, the interests of landlord and tenant are identical, and inseparable, what is for the interest of the tenant, must also be for the interest of the landlord. The more that improving tenants be encouraged—and a tenant-right bill will encourage none but improving tenants—the landlord will both have his rents more punctually paid, and a more respectable tenantry on his estate. Mr. Crawford gives farmers a piece of good advice—to use temperate language, and put forward nothing but just claims. This is really a dignified rebuke to some of the orators who held forth so violently at former tenant meetings. Several cases of distress suffered by tenants, and merciless treatment, "in the name of the landlord," were detailed by the leading farmers present. These cases should be contradicted, if not founded on fact; if true, they call for sympathy on the one hand, and censure on the other. These hardships, too, it is stated, were inflicted "in the name of the landlord." We have no inclination to make a general charge against agents—we know too many kind and considerate gentlemen of that class, to do so—still we are satisfied that the phrase employed was a cautious and correct one. In Ireland, many hardships have been inflicted on tenants "in the name of the landlord," by heartless, grinding agents, when the landlord himself, had he known the cases, would have been forbearing and indulgent. The agent should be a medium through which the stream of landlord benevolence should flow to the tenant; but what must be the consequence, if, on the contrary, he is rather an obstruction to prevent it. We do not see what business the Rev. Mr. Rogers had at the meeting. His speech was, to say the least, indiscreet, and calculated to do more harm than good. The Rev. Mr. Anderson, the local minister, acted in a more praiseworthy manner, and took no part in the meeting, except to propose a resolution, which was carried, with but one dissentient voice, against the late malicious burnings.

DOWNPATRICK RECORDER, 2 MARCH 1850

A NEW FOUNDATION

JAMES CAIRD

The lesson which the whole empire has got . . . has been of too sharp a nature for them silently to acquiesce in a return—even if it were possible—to such a rotten state of things. A new foundation must be laid now for building up hereafter a nation which shall be strong in the vigour of its own self-supporting power, the right arm of England, instead of its bane and its disgrace.

The only remedy therefore that can be listened to, is a total change in the agricultural management of the country. That can best be effected by the application of capital to the land, capital on the part of both landlord and tenant. The want of it at present among the landlords is sufficiently shown by the immense number of estates which are already before the new Encumbered Estates Commission, and the generally dilapidated state of the farms in the western counties; while the impossibility of giving any effectual aid to a pauper tenantry by expending capital in draining and improving their land is well illustrated . . . An influx of capital must therefore be encouraged, whether it is to come from England, or, as many believe, from the coffers of wealthy men in Ireland, who are said to be waiting for the security under which alone capital can flourish. That security may be attained by the interposition of parliament to fix a LIMIT TO THE AMOUNT OF POOR-RATES.

The effect of an unlimited rate has been already shown to discourage cultivation and increase pauperism. If carried much farther, it may end in total bankruptcy. When that period arrives, the State *must* interpose to prevent absolute starvation; so that it is but a choice of evils; for there can be little doubt that at some point assistance must be given.

It may be said,—why tax others for the faults of a particular union, so long as there is property of any description in the union? No one will buy that property with its present liabilities: the sooner you come to its relief, the easier will it be to render it effectual aid. Nor are the circumstances of the union of a common kind: its entire food has been mysteriously blighted.

And yet, again, upon what principle is the proprietor of a well-managed estate to be made responsible for the pauperism which has been occasioned by the mismanagement of his neighbours, merely because his property is locally situated within some district which has been arbitrarily assigned to it? Upon no just principle, so far as I know, except one which would include an equal burden on all who are embraced within the limits of the same civil government.

Let a limit be fixed, at whatever point the wisdom of Parliament shall decide. When the rates in any union go beyond that point, let experienced officers be sent down to take the management. Economise the cost of collection by transferring the duty to the officers of Inland Revenue: give them the power of compelling payment of the limited rate, offering inducements to prompt payment by liberal discounts, rather than by exacting penalties for arrears, and let the balance be advanced by the State.

With this should be united EMIGRATION—confining assistance to the unions in which government is obliged to aid the rate-payers. Let it be in the power of some safe authorities to send out to our colonies, as free labourers under proper precautions, such able-bodied persons as apply for relief, if they are otherwise clearly ascertained to be redundant, as compared with the requirements of the land in their union. And, until the necessary arrangements are made, let such labourers be employed *by task-work* in tilling some portions of the "deserted" land in the unions, the produce of which will contribute to the maintenance of the poor . . .

A limit being thus placed on the increase of poor-rate, the only other difficulty in the way of a capitalist is the variable amount of the valuation on which his rate is chargeable. The more he improves his property, thereby adding to the resources of the State and the employment of the labourer, and the less his neighbour follows the same course, the more unjust is the hardship when the neighbour has it in his power to demand a new valuation, by which to increase the improver's proportion of the rate, and diminish his own. The period at which such renewed valuation could be demanded, should probably be extended;—say to twenty-one years.

The way being thus opened for the influx of capital, and its secure investment in the land, and the safety of the redundant population being also provided for, measures should be taken to guard against the undue increase of population, and the possible recurrence of a second calamity. Nothing has contributed so much to the entire dependence on the potato, and the consequent increase of a miserable, half-fed, naked population, as the system of CON-ACRE LABOUR . . .

It will be for the wisdom of Parliament to determine, whether, by removing its causes, they can prevent the renewal of a system which

238 has been so fatally interwoven with the social condition of the West of Ireland.

THE PLANTATION SCHEME: OR THE WEST OF IRELAND AS A FIELD FOR IMPROVEMENT

LONDON, 1850

ADDRESS OF J.W. MAXWELL, ESQ.

TO HIS TENANTRY IN THE BARONIES OF
LECALE AND LOWER ARDS

MY FRIENDS,—I have requested your attendance here this day, that I may have an opportunity of addressing you upon the present and past relations between landlord and tenant, and our future prospects. As to the latter, I can only speak generally and indefinitely; but positively, as personally interested in the present. I entreat you will patiently and attentively hear what I think it both just to you and myself, to advance in this address.

My first object, then, is to advise you upon our present and future relations. In introducing these, I must advert to late arrangements, by which I made an abatement in the rents, upon condition of being paid at certain periods. In that arrangement, 20 per cent. abatement was given upon the rents of the current year, and 15 per cent. on the rent of the preceding year, conditional of payment within a stated time.

Having thus brought before you the past, I shall state now what I propose for the present: To make the 20 per cent. abatement to be a reduction of the rent, commencing from the 1st of November, 1848, and to allow an abatement of 15 per cent. on the rents of the previous year, *i.e.* upon rents of the year ending at Nov. 1848. I cannot allow any abatement upon rents due previous to Nov. 1847. By this arrangement, I hold to the equitable principle of advantage to the punctual tenant. Upon a careful examination and deliberation upon the matter, I think this equitable and just.

As to the future: This reduction is to *continue*; but our relative prospects are overshadowed—clouds gathering and storms threatening to revolutionize—to subvert—our relations, as landlord and tenant. The declamations of an agitating party—self-elected delegates or leaguers— assuming the advocacy of tenant interests, denouncing all landlords as unjust, extortioners, and robbers—oppressors of the poor. These gentlemen—themselves neither tenants nor landlords—assume a right to interfere in the adjustment of bargains between man and man. Property-doctors—quacks—whose sole end and aim is to destroy all property; to make confusion in the present relations between parties— killing their patient, Tenant-Right, by way of cure; advancing the most preposterous nostrums, and more than this, taking the office of legislators upon themselves—raising taxes and propounding laws. Many of these self-elected parliamentary members profess to be messengers of peace, inculcators of the doctrines of Christianity, expounders of the blessed Gospel of our Saviour. Oh! my friends, be not led astray by these professed friendships—be advised that the law of property will be upheld— that each man may do what he pleases with his own.

Pending these agitations, I cannot say what our future relations shall be. If you suffer under the law as it is, there is a means of making known your grievances by petition to the legislature, the only body who can alter and amend the law. You can address the Government and Parliament, and approach the Throne in respectful application for relief; and this at a trifling expense—the mere engrossing your petition upon a piece of parchment—no occasion to raise £10,000 for this purpose. Many of us have thus addressed the legislature. There is no bar or hindrance to this proper, decorous, and constitutional manner of seeking redress. The law, I sincerely hope, and have little doubt, will be revised during the ensuing Session of Parliament, and the relative interests of landlord and tenant defined and settled, upon the principle of compensation for prospective improvements. I would not have you to expect that an *ex post facto* law will pass, to determine the past relations between landlord and tenant, or the adjustment of property as to the past. Any such law would be productive of gross injustice. These observations lead me to treat of a matter relative to the buildings upon the farms. Although, in the leases heretofore granted, it was conditioned that during the tenancy the tenant should keep, in substantial repair, all buildings then on the lands, and all others which might be erected during the lease; to surrender, at the expiration of the lease, the same, in good tenantable condition. It was my opinion that, in many cases, the tenant had an equitable claim to compensation from the landlord, for the value of such buildings necessary and useful for farm purposes. I have, heretofore, acted upon this principle.

I must now advise you, that during the continuance of this league agitation and aggression against the rights of property, I shall fall back upon the law, and claim my rights.

There is one matter I wish to notice: The exhaustion of the soil. If I should again act upon the principle of tenement valuation to the tenant, I will deduct the value of land dilapidation.

Finally, my friends, I offer you, most sincerely, my advice to abstain from attending any of the League meetings. The violence of invective and abuse of a class—the landlords—who have not violated any present law, is unbecoming in any body of men; but most reprehensible in those professing to be ministers of the gospel of peace—abandoning their position as Christian ministers—adopting the ministry of strife and passion. It has been my anxious desire that my tenants should live in comfort. The principle of "Live and let Live" is the motto of my family. That my tenants should have the opportunity, if they have the desire, to lay by some provision for the younger members of their families, or push them forward in other avocations, since sub-letting cannot be permitted, 'tis prudent to take such forethought. However the chattel property may be available for such family provision, landlords cannot suffer their land to be security for them. Tenants cannot hold without some, now, indeed, considerable capital. I profess myself your sincere friend, as well as landlord. Hitherto, we have passed through life in the utmost harmony and affection towards each other. I sincerely hope your confidence in me will not be weakened by the machinations of agitating declaimers. I think better, and have confidence in your better judgment.

Your friend and landlord,

J.W. MAXWELL

Nov. 1850

The Commissioners were engaged on Friday, in selling encumbered estates. There was a large amount of property announced to be sold, and the attendance of purchasers, professional men, and others, was remarkably good. The following were among the estates disposed of:—

COUNTIES OF LOUTH, MEATH, AND ANTRIM

In the matter of the estate of the Hon. Chichester Thomas Skeffington, executor of the Right Hon. Thos. Henry, Lord Viscount Ferrard, owner; ex-parte Wm. Murray, petitioner.

The property in this matter comprised the following lots—the first four lots are held in fee, subject to very small outgoings. Lots 5 and 6 are held under leases for lives renewable for ever. Lot 5 subject to £147 16s head rent, and £8 5s 2d rent charge; and lot 6 to a head rent of £37 16s.

Lot 1. The town and lands of Rathlust and Annaloge, containing 255 acres, statute measure, situate in the barony of Ardee, the county of Louth.—Yearly rent, £217; quit rent and rent-charge, £15 3s 9d. Griffith's valuation, £222 18s 10d; nett profit rent, £202. Mr. St. George Smith became the purchaser for £3,400.

Lot 2. The lands of Sylogue, containing 102A 2R 29P, like measure, in the barony of Ferrard, in said county. Yearly rent, £98 14s 9d; rent charge, £3 8s 4d; Griffith's valuation, £59 4s; nett profit rent, £95. This lot was knocked down to Mr. Alexander Henry for £1,200.

Lot 3. The lands of Philipstown, containing 46A 3R 17P, like measure, situate in the barony of Ardee, in said county. Yearly rent, £56 10s; quit rent and rent charge, £3 3s 4d; Griffith's valuation, £39 11s 5d. Mr. Alexander Henry was declared the purchaser for £700.

Lot 4. The rent charge, in lieu of tithes, of the South division of the parish of Ardee, in said county; annual rent, £139 4s 3½d. Mr. Arthur Ellis was the purchaser for £1,200.

Lot 5. The lands of Ballyhoe, containing 410 acres, like measure; situate in the barony of Slane, and co. Meath; yearly rent, £307 6s 6¾d; head rent, rent charge, and renewal fine, £158 3s 2d; Griffith's valuation, £309 4s 11d; nett profit rent, £151 5s 4¾d. Mr. James Anderson became the purchaser for £1,100.

Lot 6. The lands of Massareene, called Massareene Farm, together with the Village of Massareene, containing 123A 2R 8P, like measure, situate in the barony of Massareene, and county of Antrim; annual rent, £199 4s 9d; head rent, £37 14s 11d; renewal fine, £1 5s—this lot was sold by private contract,—price not known.

COUNTY OF LOUTH

In the Matter of the Estate of William Skelton and Philip Skelton, of Villa, in the county Louth, owners and petitioners.

This property comprehended that portion of the lands of Monascreebs, situate in the barony of Lower Dundalk, parish of Ballymascanlon, and county Louth, now in the possession of the said William Skelton and Philip Skelton, and their under-tenants, held by lease of lives renewable for ever, and containing by ordnance survey 144A 2R 21P and 9½ yards statute measure.—The lands are subject to the annual payment of £10 10s, proportion of head rent, and also to an annuity of £10 10s. Nett yearly rent, £81 1s 11d.—Mr. James Gilligan was the purchaser for £500.

Mr. Tobias J. Purcel, Solicitor for the petitioner, had the carriage of sale.

Tuesday.—The first estate set up was that of Clifford Trotter, Esq., owner and petitioner, situate in Galway and King's County. Nearly the entire of it was sold, when the solicitor for the owner intimated that enough had been already realised to pay off the incumbrances. The Commissioners thereupon stopped the sale, and proceeded to set up the other estate—that of George Cripples Villiers, Esq., situate in the counties of Limerick and Kilkenny. The entire of this property was sold.

BELFAST COMMERCIAL CHRONICLE, 24 MARCH 1851

PEEL'S PANACEA FOR IRELAND

Russell. "Oh! this dreadful Irish Toothache!"
Peel. "Well, here is Something that will Cure you in an instant."

CENSUS
OF
1851

"WHERE IGNORANCE IS BLISS," &c.
(AFTER GEORGE CRUIKSHANK.)

CENSUS OF IRELAND FOR THE YEAR 1851

TO HIS EXCELLENCY GEORGE WILLIAM FREDERICK EARL OF CARLISLE, K.G. LORD LIEUTENANT GENERAL AND GENERAL GOVERNOR OF IRELAND, &C.

GENERAL REPORT

MAY IT PLEASE YOUR EXCELLENCY—We, the Commissioners appointed by the Earl of Clarendon, to take an Account of the Population of Ireland, under the provisions of the Act 13 and 14 Vic. cap. 44, beg to lay before your Excellency this, our General and concluding Report on the Irish Census of 1851—forming the Sixth Part and Tenth Volume of the series which, from time to time, we have had the honour of submitting for the consideration of the Lord Lieutenant.

Before referring to the various Tables which accompany this Report, we think it desirable to state the measures taken by us, with the sanction of the Government, in order to carry out as effectively as possible the objects contemplated by the Legislature.

The Irish Census Act, section 2, provided that the Account of the Population should be taken by "such officers and men of the Police force of Dublin metropolis, and of the Constabulary force, together with such other competent persons as the Lord Lieutenant should appoint to assist therein, according to such instructions as should be given to them by the Chief or Under Secretary to the Lord Lieutenant." The persons who were to act as enumerators having been thus defined, our attention was early given to the consideration of the proper Forms to be used in collecting the required information.

The Act directed that the enumerators should take an account in writing, "of the number of persons dwelling in Ireland, and of the sex, age, and occupation of all such persons, distinguishing the persons born in the place, or parish and county in which they were then living, and also an account of the number of inhabited houses and of uninhabited houses, and of houses then building, distinguishing those parishes and places, or parts of parishes and places, within the limits of any city or borough returning a member or members to serve in Parliament;—and also of all such further particulars as by their instructions the enumerators should be directed to inquire into—such particulars and instructions having no reference to the religion of any person or persons."

The Government being thus empowered to extend the Inquiries beyond the subjects specially named in the Act, the Commissioners, with the approval of the Lord Lieutenant, required the following additional particulars to be inserted in the returns:—The name; relation to the head of family; condition as to marriage; year in which married; state of education; if a child, whether attending school; whether the parties could speak Irish; the names, age, sex, relationship, and residence at the time of the Census, of all persons *absent from their homes*; also the names, age, sex, relationship, and occupation of the members of each family who had *died* since the Census taken on the 6th of June, 1841—together with the *disease* which caused death, and the *season* and *year* in which the death occurred.

CENSUS OF IRELAND FOR THE YEAR 1851

DUBLIN, 1856

TABLES OF DEATHS

No vegetable, perhaps, ever effected the same amount of influence upon the physical, moral, social, and political condition of a country, as the potato exercised over Ireland, when cultivated to the extent it was, immediately preceding the famine of 1845...

During the prevalence of the famine, food rose to an excessively high price; and some idea may be formed of the loss sustained by the country from the fact that *sixteen millions'* worth of produce is supposed to have been destroyed up to the autumn of 1846; while the general state of destitution may be calculated by the measures of relief afforded during the crisis of that fearful period; relief, far surpassing in amount, derived from more distant sources, and springing from the excited sympathies of a greater range of society, than any precedent can be found for in our social history upon similar occasions of national distress. Agriculture was neglected, and the land in many places remained untilled. Thousands were supported from day to day upon the bounty of out-door relief; the closest ties of kindred were dissolved; the most ancient and long-cherished usages of the people were disregarded; food the most revolting to human palates was eagerly devoured; the once proverbial gaiety and lightheartedness of the peasant people seemed to have vanished completely, and village merriment or marriage festival was no longer heard or seen throughout the regions desolated by the intensity and extent of the famine; finally, the disorganization of society became marked and memorable by the exodus of above one million of people, who deserted their homes and hearths to seek for food and shelter in foreign lands, of whom thousands perished from pestilence and the hardships endured on shipboard.

It is scarcely possible to exaggerate in imagination what people will do, and are forced to do, before they die from absolute want of food, for not only does the body become blackened and wasted by chronic starvation, but the mind likewise becomes darkened, the feelings callous, blunted, and apathetic; and a peculiar fever is generated, which became but too well known to the medical profession in Ireland at that time, and to all those engaged in administering relief.

In this state, of what may almost be called mania, before the final collapse takes place, when the victim sinks into utter prostration from inanition, some instances may have occurred at which human nature, in its ordinary healthy condition, revolts. Thus, a stipendiary magistrate stated, in the court-house of Galway, in extenuation of the crime of a poor prisoner, brought up for stealing food, that to his own knowledge, before he was driven to the theft, he and his family had actually consumed part of a human body lying dead in the cabin with them.

Generally speaking, the actually starving people lived upon the carcasses of diseased cattle, upon dogs, and dead horses, but principally on the herbs of the field, nettle tops, wild mustard, and watercresses, and even in some places dead bodies were found with grass in their mouths. The shamrock, or wood-sorrel (*oxalis acetosella*), mentioned by Spenser as forming part of the food of the famished people in his time, does not now, owing to the extirpation of woods, exist in sufficient quantity to afford any nutriment; but along the coast every description of sea-weed was greedily devoured, often with fatal consequences; even the dillisk, or "salt-leaf," though a safe occasional condiment, became the cause of disease when used as the sole support of life.

Some approximation to the amount of the immense mortality that prevailed may be gleaned from the published tables, which show that within that calamitous period between the end of 1845 and the conclusion of the first quarter of 1851, as many as 61,260 persons died in the hospitals and sanitary institutions, exclusive of those who died in the workhouses and auxiliary workhouses. Taking the recorded deaths from fever alone, between the beginning of 1846 and the end of 1849, and assuming the mortality at 1 in 10, which is the very lowest calculation, and far below what we believe really did occur, above a million and a-half, or 1,595,040 persons, being 1 in 4.11 of the population in 1851, must have suffered from fever during that period. But no pen has recorded the numbers of the forlorn and starving who perished by the wayside or in the ditches, or of the mournful groups, sometimes of whole families, who lay down and died, one after another, upon the floor of their miserable cabin, and so remained uncoffined and unburied, till chance unveiled the appalling scene. No such amount of suffering and misery has been chronicled in Irish history since the days of Edward Bruce; and yet, through all, the forbearance of the Irish peasantry, and the calm submission with which they bore the deadliest ills that can fall on man, can scarcely be paralleled in the annals of any people. Numbers, indeed, were sent to prison for petty crimes, often committed to save themselves or children from starvation, and there met their death from pestilential diseases arising from the overcrowding and contagion in those institutions; yet the slight amount of crime of a serious nature which prevailed throughout Ireland during the years of extreme destitution was remarkable; and instances occurred in which the judges, feeling that want alone drove the prisoners to its commission, directed their discharge without further punishment.

According to the Report of the Census Commissioners for 1841, the annual average emigration between 1831 and 1841 was 40,346, and from the 30th June in the latter year to the end of 1845 it averaged 61,242 per annum. Such, however, was the effect of the potato blight and the warning voice of the pestilence, that the number rose to 105,955 in 1846, after which the emigration seemed to partake of the nature of an epidemic, and in 1847 the numbers who left the country more than doubled those who departed in the previous year. Owing to a slight mitigation of the potato blight, and a consequent improvement in the harvest of 1847, there was an arrest of the exodus in the beginning of 1848, when the numbers who emigrated only amounted to 178,159; but in the following year they again rose to 214,425. In 1850 the amount of emigration was 209,054. The emigration reached its highest point in 1851, when the numbers amounted to 249,721, after which they gradually decreased to 150,222 in 1854; yet, even in 1855, long after the extreme poor, the panic-stricken, and the destitute, had passed to other countries, or had found a refuge in the workhouses, or a rest in the grave, the remarkable spectacle of whole families—usually well-dressed, intelligent-looking people—of all ages and sexes, the mere infant

as well as the extremely aged—might be observed passing through the
metropolis on the way to the emigrant vessel. Not the least peculiar
feature in the extensive emigration of this period was the amount of
money transmitted to their friends in Ireland by those who had already
gone away;—remittances which rose from the sum of £460,000, in 1848,
to £1,404,000, in 1852, and according to the reports of the Emigration
Commissioners, amounted in contributions, either in the form of prepaid
passages, or of money sent home by the Irish emigrants, from 1848 to
1854, both inclusive, to as much as £7,520,000;—remittances "which
afford so honourable a testimony of the self-denial and affectionate
disposition of the Irish."

The Society of Friends of the United Kingdom were foremost in the
field of benevolent action, and the British Association was most prompt
in its measures of charity. We learn from authority—and we quote it
because we believe in its truth—that "a painful and tender sympathy
pervaded every class of society. From the Queen on her throne to the
convicts in the hulks, expenses were curtailed and privations were
endured, in order to swell the Irish subscription." Conscious that the
arrow that flieth by day, and the pestilence that walketh in darkness,
cometh but by divine permission, a day of General Fast and Humiliation was held in behalf of those who were "in many parts of this United
Kingdom suffering extreme famine and sickness;" and, adds the author
from whom we quote, "the fast was observed with unusual solemnity,
and the London season of this year [1847] was remarkable for the absence
of gaiety and expensive entertainments." Yet, with all these efforts to
relieve famine and avert disease, hundreds died from actual starvation;
thousands wasted away in the poor-houses, and thousands also perished
from disease induced by despondency of mind and prostration of physical
strength.

At the time the pestilence commenced, the fever hospitals of Ireland
had, from several causes, decreased in number, and their funds had been
considerably reduced; but as it progressed . . . as many as 227 temporary
hospitals, either as tents or wooden sheds, or hastily-procured buildings
of more solid materials, were put in immediate requisition, and 450,807
persons were treated therein, of whom 47,302 died between the commencement of 1847 and the end of 1850.

Supposing the immigration and emigration to have been equal, and
that the increase of population by an excess of births over deaths, was
in a similar ratio to that which had taken place in England and Wales
during the last sixteen years, viz., 1.0036 per cent. per annum, the number

of people in Ireland would have been 9,018,799 on the 30th of March, 1851. But as the last Census Returns have only afforded a population of 6,552,385, it is important to account (as far as is possible in the unfortunate absence of any general registration of births and deaths) for the deficiency in the population of nearly two and a-half millions, independent of the emigration alluded to. Inevitable deficiencies must result from any retrospective inquiry derived from the remnant of a population upon a certain day subsequent to the events to which it has reference. It is manifest that the greater the amount of destitution and mortality, and the greater the disruption of the social condition of the population in any walk of life, so much the more difficult will be the attempt to acquire subsequent information, and, consequently, the less will be the amount of recorded deaths derived through any household form;—for not only were whole families swept away by disease, and large districts depopulated by emigration, or the inhabitants driven to seek a refuge in the workhouses, but whole villages were effaced from off the land. Yet, notwithstanding these difficulties, in the way of a complete enumeration of deaths, and with a great decrease of population from non-births, owing to the diminution of marriages, as shown in our Report upon Ages and Education, and other causes which, during some portion of this period, sensibly affected the question—the recorded mortality for the five last years of the decennial period upon which it is our duty to report was as great as 985,366, or very nearly one million.

Concurrent with the foregoing state of famine, and the disruption of the social condition of the people, pestilence came upon the nation in the following order:—Fever, Scurvy, Diarrhoea and Dysentery, Cholera, Influenza, and Ophthalmia . . .

The total deaths from fever during the period between 1841 and 1851, amounted to the vast number of 222,029, in the proportion of 112.51 males to 100 females. Of these deaths, about one-half occurred in the rural districts; 22,464 in the civic districts; 50,408 in the permanent and temporary hospitals, and 34,644 in workhouses and auxiliary workhouses . . .

On reviewing the history of epidemic pestilence in Ireland, we are struck by the frequency with which DYSENTERY has been an element of destruction, in lessening its population . . . We cannot, therefore, wonder that an accession of dysentery formed one of the chief causes of the increased mortality of the period, and became, next to fever, the second most fatal malady of the class of zymotic or epidemic diseases. The Census Returns have afforded a total of 93,232 deaths from dysentery, in the proportion of 75.06 females to 100 males. Of these deaths more than one half occurred in workhouses; in fact, dysentery and diarrhoea formed the great bulk of the causes of death in these institutions; the increase of these diseases dates from the year 1846. Of 283,765 persons who died in the workhouses between 1841 and 1851, as many as 70,526 were returned as having sunk under dysentery or diarrhoea, the deaths from these diseases being equal to 1 in 3.19 of the total deaths therein from all specified causes. When we remember the masses of debilitated people that were, of necessity, congregated in the parent and auxiliary workhouses during the years of famine, we cannot wonder at the great mortality from these diseases . . .

When the famine was most severely felt, and when fever and dysentery raged with the greatest violence, ASIATIC CHOLERA again invaded the Continent of Europe, and advancing with rapid and fatally marked steps, soon approached the devoted island in the West, and reached our shores at the end of 1848. For some wise and inscrutable reason, upon which man can only speculate, it seemed good to the Great Disposer of events to mitigate considerably its fatality, compared with that of its first invasion, sixteen years before; for the returns only give as many as 35,989 deaths, in which the sexes were in the proportion of 95.57 males to 100 females, showing very nearly an equality of sexes.

Although Small-pox has decreased in Ireland, both in virulence and extent, since the publication of the Census Report in 1841, there was some increase of that disease during the pestilential period of 1847, '48, and '49; yet the deaths returned to us (amounting to 38,275 in ten years,) are not, considering the present state of vaccination in this country, of sufficient amount to warrant the assertion that Small-pox influenced the great mortality of which this . . . is the analysis, although during a portion of the period it prevailed epidemically, and was also very fatal in England. Dropsies likewise prevailed as the sequel of famine, fever, and dysentery during the latter years of the pestilential period.

An epidemic of INFLUENZA pervaded Great Britain in 1847 and 1848; where, although of brief duration, it was of unusual fatality. Its advent was marked in London by very peculiar atmospheric phenomena, which have been graphically described in the Report of the Registrar-General for that year. It existed nearly contemporaneously in Dublin during the December of 1847, and the January of 1848. The number of deaths attributed to this disease, as returned to us in March, 1851, does not exhibit, however, any very manifest annual difference for the five years preceding that date. The total deaths registered from influenza were 10,753, in the proportion of 85.5 females to 100 males . . .

The foregoing array of epidemic diseases has not exhausted the catalogue of calamities affecting human life or happiness, which occurred in Ireland during the years of famine and pestilence. In every country, even in England, with all its wealth—with its workhouses and its long established public institutions—deaths from starvation are annually recorded . . . In the Irish returns made in 1841, only 117 deaths were registered from starvation for the ten years prior to that period; but from thence, according to the registration made in 1851, deaths from this cause began notably to increase, from 187 in the year 1842, to 516 in 1845. After that period deaths attributed to starvation increased rapidly so as to amount to 2,041 for the year 1846; in 1847 they reached the great height of 6,058; and in the two following years, 1848 and 1849, taken together, they amounted to 9,395. In 1850 they were even more than in 1846; and during the first quarter of 1851 as many as 652 deaths attributed to starvation were recorded. The total deaths returned to us under the head of STARVATION amounted to 21,770, the sexes being in the proportion of 70.6 females to 100 males. As many as 333 of these occurred in workhouses being persons received in a dying state, from the results of previous privation. Large, therefore, as the total deaths from this cause . . . may at first sight appear, a review of the past circumstances of the kingdom will, we think, strengthen the belief, that many more must have perished from disease remotely induced by privation during the years of famine and pestilence . . . According to provinces the proportion per cent. of deaths from starvation, to their respective populations, was, in Ulster, 1 in 1,888; in Leinster, 1 in 1,775; in Munster, 1 in 228, and in Connaught, 1 in 119.

THE CENSUS OF IRELAND FOR THE YEAR 1851

DUBLIN, 1856

THE NUMBER OF PERSONS
IN 1841 AND 1851

IN EACH PROVINCE, COUNTY, CITY,
AND LARGE TOWN IN IRELAND;
ALSO THE INCREASE OR DECREASE PER CENT. BETWEEN
THOSE PERIODS, BY RURAL AND CIVIC DISTRICTS

Unfortunately, Ireland has not been yet favoured by the legislature with a general measure for the registration of the births, marriages, and deaths of its people; and is, in this respect, an exceptional portion of the United Kingdom. We cannot, therefore, state the annual average number of births and deaths to the population; and in the absence of such a registration we conceive we can find no better data for our computations than the averages of the births and deaths which have been regularly registered in England and Wales since 1837.

In the able Reports of Mr. Graham, the Registrar-General, these averages are carried on from year to year; and in the latest of them—the Sixteenth—we find that the births and deaths registered for a period of fifteen years in all England and Wales have been at the annual rate of one birth to every thirty-one, and one death to every forty-five person living. Applying these rates to the population of this country in 1841, and assuming that the emigration was equal to the immigration, we find that the population on the 30th of March, 1851, would have probably numbered 9,018,799 instead of 6,552,385 and that, consequently, the loss of population between 1841 and 1851 may be computed at the enormous amount of 2,466,414 persons. The population removed from us by death and emigration, belonged principally to the lower classes—among whom famine and disease, in all such calamitous visitations, ever make the greatest ravages. But, notwithstanding our sudden depopulation, we have every cause for thankfulness that years of suffering have been followed by years of prosperity; for Ireland has increased in wealth and progressed in the development of her resources; as it appears that in 1851 the extent of land under cultivation, the value of agricultural stock and crops, and the proportionate number of educated among the people, were greater than at any previous period of which we have a record.

PROVINCES, COUNTIES, AND TOWNS	1841.							1851.							Difference per cent. between 1841 and 1851.	
	Rural District.		Civic District.		Total.		Total Males and Females.	Rural District.		Civic District.		Total.		Total Males and Females.	Increase.	Decrease.
	Males.	Females.	Males.	Females.	Males.	Females.		Males.	Females.	Males.	Females.	Males.	Females.			
LEINSTER.																
Carlow, .	35,847	36,325	6,581	7,475	42,428	43,800	86,228	26,533	26,853	6,483	8,204	33,016	35,062	68,078	–	21·05
Drogheda Town, .	–	–	7,646	8,615	7,646	8,615	16,261	–	–	7,947	8,900	7,947	8,900	16,847	3 60	–
Dublin City, .	–	–	104,630	128,096	104,630	128,096	232,726	–	–	119,181	139,188	119,181	139,188	258,369	11·02	–
Dublin, .	55,057	58,721	11,243	15,026	66,300	73,747	140,047	44,177	45,680	23,928	32,993	68,105	78,673	146,778	4·81	–
Kildare, .	52,888	51,202	5,142	5,256	58,030	56,458	114,488	44,583	42,736	3,945	4,459	48,528	47,195	95,723	–	16·39
Kilkenny City, .	–	–	8,765	10,306	8,765	10,306	19,071	–	–	8,919	11,056	8,919	11,056	19,975	4·74	–
Kilkenny, .	85,685	87,472	4,664	5,528	90,349	93,000	183,349	65,553	68,491	2,021	2,708	67,574	71,199	138,773	–	24·31
King's, .	65,051	65,188	7,600	9,018	72,651	74,206	146,857	49,529	49,805	5,755	6,987	55,284	56,792	112,076	–	23·68
Longford, .	54,065	54,052	3,545	3,829	57,610	57,881	115,491	38,490	38,582	2,551	2,725	41,041	41,307	82,348	–	28·70
Louth, .	47,337	49,142	7,314	8,186	54,651	57,328	111,979	38,223	39,844	6,087	6,661	44,310	46,505	90,815	–	18·90
Meath, .	86,453	85,273	6,041	6,061	92,494	91,334	183,828	67,080	66,014	3,733	3,921	70,813	69,935	140,748	–	23·43
Queen's, .	69,322	69,551	7,081	7,976	76,403	77,527	153,930	49,788	50,062	5,768	6,046	55,556	56,108	111,664	–	27·46
Westmeath, .	65,699	65,617	4,684	5,300	70,383	70,917	141,300	51,023	49,590	5,072	5,722	56,095	55,312	111,407	–	21·16
Wexford, .	84,919	88,348	12,999	15,767	97,918	104,115	202,033	72,825	75,762	14,113	17,458	86,938	93,220	180,158	–	10·83
Wicklow, .	59,552	58,340	3,937	4,314	63,489	62,654	126,143	46,042	44,364	4,188	4,385	50,230	48,749	98,979	–	21·53
Total of Leinster,	761,875	769,231	201,872	240,753	963,747	1,009,984	1,973,731	593,846	597,788	219,691	261,413	813,537	859,201	1,672,738	–	15·25
MUNSTER.																
Clare, .	135,401	132,506	8,708	9,779	144,109	142,285	286,394	95,659	99,961	8,294	8,526	103,953	108,487	212,440	–	25·82
Cork City, .	–	–	35,489	45,231	35,489	45,231	80,720	–	–	39,040	46,692	39,040	46,692	85,732	6·21	–
Cork, .	343,560	340,359	41,502	47,977	385,062	388,336	773,398	239,501	239,397	39,608	45,070	279,109	284,467	563,576	–	27·13
Kerry, .	136,014	133,392	11,293	13,181	147,307	146,573	293,880	103,522	104,631	12,989	17,112	116,511	121,743	238,254	–	18·93
Limerick City, .	–	–	21,436	26,955	21,436	26,955	48,391	–	–	24,683	29,365	24,683	29,365	53,448	10·45	–
Limerick, .	137,244	137,276	3,317	3,801	140,561	141,077	281,638	100,179	101,752	3,125	3,628	103,304	105,380	208,684	–	25·90
Tipperary, .	183,404	180,857	33,246	38,046	216,650	218,903	435,553	129,330	132,411	30,694	39,132	160,024	171,543	331,567	–	23·87
Waterford City, .	–	–	10,227	12,989	10,227	12,989	23,216	–	–	11,257	14,040	11,257	14,040	25,297	8·96	–
Waterford, .	74,302	74,905	11,047	12,717	85,349	87,622	172,971	59,365	60,391	8,333	10,649	67,698	71,040	138,738	–	19·79
Total of Munster,	1,009,925	999,295	176,265	210,676	1,186,190	1,209,971	2,396,161	727,556	738,543	177,423	214,214	904,979	952,757	1,857,736	–	22·47
ULSTER.																
Antrim, .	124,064	132,288	9,149	10,687	133,213	142,975	276,188	110,522	118,001	10,487	12,373	121,009	130,374	251,383	–	8·98
Armagh, .	104,178	107,715	9,714	10,786	113,892	118,501	232,393	86,131	89,920	9,586	10,447	95,717	100,367	196,084	–	15·62
Belfast Town, .	–	–	54,858	40,450	54,858	40,450	75,308	–	–	46,848	53,453	46,848	53,453	100,301	33·19	–
Carrickfergus, .	2,555	2,939	1,765	2,120	4,320	5,059	9,379	2,278	2,699	1,491	2,052	3,769	4,751	8,520	–	9·16
Cavan, .	116,848	118,066	3,966	4,278	120,814	122,344	243,158	83,051	83,600	3,551	3,862	86,602	87,462	174,064	–	28·42
Donegal, .	142,773	147,249	3,048	3,378	145,821	150,627	296,448	122,461	127,808	2,262	2,627	124,723	130,435	255,158	–	13·93
Down, .	156,749	167,058	16,789	20,850	173,538	187,908	361,446	134,794	145,905	17,969	22,149	152,763	168,054	320,817	–	11·24
Fermanagh, .	74,361	76,434	2,621	3,065	76,982	79,499	156,481	54,109	55,989	2,720	3,229	56,829	59,218	116,047	–	25·84
Londonderry, .	95,685	101,937	11,140	13,412	106,825	115,349	222,174	79,050	83,318	14,045	15,609	93,095	98,927	192,022	–	13·57
Monaghan, .	93,703	97,598	4,368	4,773	98,071	102,371	200,442	62,883	66,083	5,944	6,913	68,827	72,996	141,823	–	29·24
Tyrone, .	146,695	151,803	6,768	7,690	153,463	159,493	312,956	119,225	121,800	6,905	7,651	126,130	129,231	255,661	–	18·31
Total of Ulster,	1,057,611	1,103,087	104,186	121,489	1,161,797	1,224,576	2,386,373	854,504	895,203	121,808	140,365	976,312	1,035,568	2,011,880	–	15·69
CONNAUGHT.																
Galway Town, .	–	–	7,989	9,286	7,989	9,286	17,275	–	–	10,487	13,300	10,487	13,300	23,787	37·70	–
Galway, .	202,648	201,098	8,927	10,250	211,575	211,348	422,923	187,607	139,487	9,041	11,762	146,648	151,249	297,897	–	29·56
Leitrim, .	77,501	77,796	–	–	77,501	77,796	155,297	56,111	55,786	–	–	56,111	55,786	111,897	–	27·95
Mayo, .	184,964	184,174	9,234	10,515	194,198	194,689	388,887	126,007	131,926	7,257	9,309	133,264	141,235	274,499	–	29·41
Roscommon, .	122,230	121,309	4,786	5,266	127,016	126,575	253,591	81,179	81,281	5,232	5,744	86,411	87,025	173,436	–	31·61
Sligo, .	83,055	83,860	6,508	7,463	89,563	91,323	180,886	57,526	59,359	5,355	6,275	62,881	65,634	128,515	–	28·95
Total of Connaught,	670,398	668,237	37,444	42,780	707,842	711,017	1,418,859	458,430	467,839	37,372	46,390	495,802	514,229	1,010,031	–	28·81
TOTAL OF IRELAND,	3,499,809	3,539,850	519,767	615,698	4,019,576	4,155,548	8,175,124	2,634,336	2,699,373	556,294	662,382	3,190,630	3,361,755	6,552,385	–	19·85

THE CENSUS OF IRELAND FOR THE YEAR 1851

DUBLIN, 1856

POSTSCRIPT

THE ENGLISH LABOURER'S BURDEN;

Or, THE IRISH OLD MAN OF THE MOUNTAIN.

[See *Sinbad the Sailor*.

EXODUS OF THE CELTIC RACES

What has been called the "Exodus of the Celtic races" continues. The return of spring has witnessed once more the flux of the emigrational tide towards the shore of the New World. The quays of Dublin, Cork, and Liverpool are crowded with Irish emigrants, departing to other lands, and carrying with them, in too many instances we are afraid, a feeling of bitter hatred to this country. They blame England for the evils that have befallen them in their own land, instead of blaming, as they ought to do, their own landlords, their own indolence, their own religious and party feuds, and their own listless reliance upon the easily raised but miserable root, the potato. Year after year the efflux continues. Strong men that are the very life-blood of a nation, and that will become so to that great kindred nation of America, which is destined in due time to overshadow the world with its power and glory, leave our shores in countless multitudes. The greater the numbers who emigrate in any one year, the larger the amount of funds received in Ireland in the next, to enable friends and relatives to follow to the land of plenty and independence. The potato failure is thus working a mighty revolution. It has caused the property of the Irish landlords to change hands; it has converted proprietors into paupers; it has caused England to spend ten millions of money for the relief of the people with as little real benefit as if the sum had been sunk into the sea; it has consigned upwards of one million of human beings— some accounts say upwards of two millions—to a premature death by famine and fever; and it has driven the very flower of the Celtic race across the Atlantic, to subdue and to cultivate the forests and prairies of the almost illimitable regions of the Far West, and thus to open up the long-buried East, and to menace Japan and China with a European invasion. This mighty emigration pays for itself. It seeks no aid from the public purse, but it should be remembered that it establishes itself in regions that owe no fealty to the Crown of England.

ILLUSTRATED LONDON NEWS, 3 APRIL 1852

INDEX